TODAY IS TOMORROW

By Caroline Kurtz

CATALYST PRESS
Texas, USA

In North America, this book is distributed by
Consortium Book Sales & Distribution, a division of Ingram.
Phone: 612/746-2600
cbsdinfo@ingramcontent.com
www.cbsd.com

In South Africa, Namibia, and Botswana,
this book is distributed by Protea Distribution.
For information, email orders@proteadistribution.co.za.

FIRST EDITION
10 9 8 7 6 5 4 3 2 1

ISBN 9781946395672

Library of Congress Control Number: 2022934856

*Dedicated to Mark, who read a draft
and said, "Yep. That's how it was."
And to Miriam, Jesse and Kenny,
the smart, caring adults
my partnership with Mark
gave birth to.*

CHAPTER 1

My taxi driver friend hooted outside the flat, as the Kenyans say. In the gray dawn light, the trill of a nightjar had just fallen silent out in our jacaranda tree. I leaned over the bed and nuzzled my husband Mark's trim, wiry beard. He mumbled a good bye. I hoisted a duffle bag over my shoulder, peeked into the boys' rooms, and quietly let myself out.

At Nairobi's Wilson Airport, black tarmac sparkled with dew. The acrid smell of jet fuel exhaust tingled in my nose with the promise of adventure—I felt keenly alive inside a plane!

I was off to northern Kenya for the UN's aid worker orientation course, the first assignment for my new job. Mark and I had loved our previous six years working in Ethiopia. When that stint ended, we hadn't been ready to go back to the States, pound the pavement, find work. Four years in Nairobi working with the South Sudanese there—that's what our supervisors in Presbyterian Church USA (PCUSA) offered us instead. There was a top-notch international school for the boys; Mark, Jesse and Kenny would lead normal lives of office and school bus, suppers and homework in Nairobi; I would travel. *Caroline could be in South Sudan up to a third of every month.*

We signed up.

Now I climbed, with a few strangers, into the cramped UN charter. My seatbelts were so permeated with dust they felt chalky. We flew over the lush highlands around Nairobi and somewhere crossed the equator. The earth below turned brown. We landed on a huge airstrip in Lokichoggio, where development aid from around the world is staged and then air lifted in huge-bellied cargo planes to relieve the suffering of millions in South Sudan.

A white pickup covered with dings and dents, with a blue UN logo on its door, delivered us to the UN base camp. There, in the baking heat of the Turkana desert, a few miles from the Kenya-Sudan border, I joined idealists of every nation and shade.

We met in a circle of plastic chairs on a cement slab painted dark green. We scribbled notes: Operation Lifeline Sudan conventions, radio courtesy, names of warlords, implications of the ceasefire. We recorded insights on newsprint from small group discussions and taped them onto the cement block walls. We tested our emotional reactions in simulation games. The corrugated iron roof heated up like a broiler element. I brushed at a persistent fly crawling down my calf, then realized it was a slow-moving drop of sweat. I was in my late forties, pretending not to notice that I was the only one there over twenty-six.

It was 1996, and the government of Sudan had just signed a cease-fire with Commander Riek Machar, a Nuer warlord in South Sudan. John Garang, the Dinka commander of the Sudan People's Liberation Army (SPLA), was giving scornful press statements. Several other rogue commanders' reactions were completely unknown.

A man in stained khaki told us not to look captors in the eye if we were taken hostage. He showed us how to distill our urine to make drinking water in case a rogue commander came through and we had to scatter. (Keep a clean plastic bag on hand at all times for that purpose.) He said a British woman who had run to the brush in a raid survived for two weeks while they searched for her, because she had learned from the Nuers to forage. When you get to your site, make a bomb shelter, in case North Sudan Antinov's fly over. Note: any depression in the ground will do; look for snakes before diving in; keep your head down until debris, acting like shrapnel, finishes abhorring the vacuum and flies back in as fast as it shot out.

My pulse quickened in my chest, fear and excitement in an exhilarating swirl. My intrepid mom and dad had raised me for hardship in Africa in pursuit of making the world a better place. For all the racially tinged mythology of Africa as *the dark continent*, the African cultures I'd known were effusively hospitable, hopeful and kind. But I'd never lived in a war zone.

The ceasefire, I reminded myself.

A UN nurse talked about the usual—carrying extra prescription meds; waterborne diseases and their symptoms; mosquito nets. I'd lived in Africa almost half my life and never had malaria. As I scribbled my notes, I marveled. I felt hardy. Born to this.

Note: what to expect from a scorpion—not death, but eight hours of excruciating pain. *Unless you can get your hands on a Black Stone.* A Black Stone would save us from the pain, but she couldn't tell us where to get one or even what it was. Life expanded, mysterious.

Duda Suzic from Czech Republic, the UN counselor, introduced herself. She talked about self-care, about STDs, about post-traumatic stress disorder. She promised to be there for us. I would meet her again.

On the plane back to Nairobi, I studied my notebook of Nuer vocabulary words. Learning the language was a requisite for working with women in South Sudan; their education rates being low, they didn't speak English.

Back home, over supper eight-year-old Kenny said, "Guess what Dad did while you were gone."

It could be anything. Mark loved to fix, organize, and systematize the world around him. In a new house, there were endless possibilities. I looked at him and cocked my head. He didn't react.

"He drank up all the coffee liqueur!"

I laughed in surprise. We weren't a drinking family, so of course Kenny must have curiously watched him go through a bottle the previous tenant had left in our pantry. Mark might not smile at the boys' teasing, his mouth half hidden by his moustache, but his silence was something familiar to them. He always exuded a jittery energy. Now he raised his eyebrows and looked over the tops of his glasses at me as though to say, *You know how I hate it when you travel.*

He had agreed willingly enough to my new job. Now came living with the deal he'd made—cooking for himself and his sons alone, chilly sheets at night. As I laughed with the boys, I processed a packet of realizations: Mark wasn't going to like his new job; I was going to like mine; he was going to feel resentful about that; my work was going to be plenty hard without having to worry about his feelings; and my half of our income was the bigger half.

The look I gave Mark also spoke in the way that long-married people can do without saying a word, *Don't give me grief about this.* All our lives together, the energy I brought to goals was essential to our partnership. In this case, my love of travel, love of adventure, love of learning new languages had helped him reach his dream of an overseas job. "Guess what *hun gora peu* means?" I said brightly.

"I'm gonna spew?" Jesse suggested.

Kenny looked at his witty teen-aged brother with adoring eyes.

It was too late for Mark to be having second thoughts. He would manage. The boys would be fine.

Preparing for my first trip into South Sudan, I organized my language notebook with tabs for nouns, verbs, common phrases. I was well and truly oriented. I felt excited, empowered, ready for anything.

From these years later, I see how delusional I was, along with everyone else I'd been with up in Loki, all of us walking into a civil war chaos we had no capacity to truly understand. We armed ourselves with idealism. We learned how to survive. We believed that our open-hearted commitment would bring success in any small task we would try, and, if we were lucky, in some of the big ones, too.

Everyone was hopeful about the future—UN staff, Nuers, Dinkas. How do humans do that, even facing odds laid out as clearly before us as the odds of success in South Sudan? I, Women's Development

Advisor, had never organized development projects before. I was to go in, learn Nuer and Juba Arabic, sit with the women, and figure something out. No one actually knew what could be about their dire circumstances. It was all a desperate experiment. I had studied community organizing. Anything I came up with would be more than the nothing women presently had.

Our supervisors had never assigned anyone to work under Sudanese leaders before, so they were taking a risk asking Mark to be their Financial Advisor, in charge of setting up Presbyterian Church of Sudan's head office budget. Mark had taken a basic accounting course in preparation: *Accounts for the Sudanese church aren't going to be that complicated.* Any bookkeeping system Mark could help the church officers organize would be better than nothing—they had never once sent a financial report to the donors.

And we knew why PCUSA was asking us to do this. Not everyone can function deep inside another culture. "We're at the top of a very short list," I'd joked to Mark. We'd proved ourselves, thriving with Ethiopian colleagues under an Ethiopian director for six years in an Addis Ababa girls' school. I had quickly gotten fluent in Amharic and bonded with teacher friends. And we knew how to turn our goal-oriented, to-do-list-making selves on and off to flow with looser African ways of getting work done.

Mark was fluent in sign language, and that had worked well enough for his construction work. "I'm a fix-it guy. I'll help the Sudanese fix their finances," he said. And I was sure there would be something I could do to empower South Sudanese women.

Does willingness count for anything? I'm not sure anymore that it does. It's a generous attitude, but we humans are notoriously bad at predicting what we can do and how it will feel. Only in the moment do we find out. Willingness is not a skill. It was certainly a weak offering to offset the resentment, grief and fear stirred up in South Sudan by thirty-three years of war, the many millions of people gone.

I want to go back and caution my younger self. How can I say it? *Gird up your loins*, as the Old Testament stories of my childhood training would put it. Working with the traumatized South Sudanese, Mark and I were going to need wisdom and an objectivity we did not possess. Mark was more comfortable with lumber, metal and wire than the rough and tumble of human interactions, even when they weren't cross cultural and dealing with money. He was going to reach the outer limits of his resilience and almost take me down with him.

I was going to wish my willingness wasn't marbled with a need to prove my worth. I was going to wish I could react quietly, without so much heat. To stand up for myself while staying calm. Because I was setting out on my own journey, one I didn't know I needed and wouldn't have chosen.

CHAPTER 2

On the ground in South Sudan at last, I woke to the sun shining through my burgundy tent like a red spotlight. People in the village around me stirred and murmured in the Nuer language. I shifted on my camp mat, snuggled into the fuzz of my pink and blue plaid flannel sheet for a few more seconds of delicious dozing.

An hour later, I sat outside one of the huts and drank sweet breakfast tea with Elder Guy Lual, a church leader from Nairobi. The morning sunlight had already turned golden and fell hot on my face. Around me lay four huts, a latrine that looked as though it might blow over in a hot breeze, and my tent. It was a sepia scene with one splash of burgundy, the compound where I would live for two weeks, encircled by a sorghum-stalk fence. Neighbors' voices rose and fell, hens celebrated their morning successes, a dog yelped.

Three girls gathered shyly, watching every move I made. I was, in that moment, the only American for hundreds of miles around. I was probably the only white woman they'd seen up close. Or ever.

I pointed to the girls' feet and said the word in the Nuer language. When I pressed my nose and said *wuhm* in a nasal voice, they giggled. The middle sister corrected my pronunciation. I solemnly repeated after her, but my heart jolted with delight.

I spent the rest of the morning with the girls drilling me in Nuer and laughing. Nearby, Guy Lual talked intensely in Nuer with the village pastor and his assistant who were hosting us. Their wives worked quietly, doing what women do to feed the family, whoever it may come to include.

After lunch, the wife of the assistant came around the thatched eves of the kitchen hut carrying an orange plastic washbasin propped on one hip. Her nylon dress was once some American woman's nightie and had faded from pink to cream. Stretched tight across her pregnant belly, it swooped up at the hem. *"Hun gora peu,"* she said. *I need water.*

I smiled, thinking of Jesse's joke. The boys would be at school. What was Mark doing—struggling through a drawerful of receipts, or fighting Nairobi traffic to get some settling-in business done downtown? Poor guy.

The youngest sister grabbed my hand and pulled me along to the well, through the bright sunshine that felt dense with heat. On the way, we chanted the numbers together, *kel, rew, diok* and up to one hundred, which is more of a metaphor than a number. It means lost in the forest. The Nuers are cattle people, and a man's cows would scatter if he had a hundred. Besides that, a man wants to be vague about his cattle holdings. To talk about his wealth would be to invite bad luck.

Up the path ahead of us came an old woman leaning on a walking stick. Tied over one shoulder, she wore a piece of fabric that had turned the color of the dirt path. One exposed breast, long and flat against her chest, swung slightly with every step.

I stepped aside to let her pass. I bowed my head in greeting. *"Mal poindu?"* This meant, *Is your body at peace?*

Peace in South Sudan, among the Nuer people, isn't about the war with North Sudan, nor about bloody clashes with their Southern neighbors, the Dinkas. The Sudanese world is dense with spirits: malevolent spirits which people know by name, plus spirits of the dead who are still remembered and spirits of the dead who have been forgotten. All of them have to be appeased. *Mal poindu* meant, *Are the spirits leaving your body in peace?*

The old woman stopped to shake my hand. Hers was dusty, dry, wrinkled. *"Mal mi gua?"* Is it a good peace? *"Mal mi diit?"*

I dipped my head. I had a good, wide peace.

"Mal mi choom-choom?" she asked.

The girls giggled behind slender fingers, their tan fingernails rimmed in dirt. My heart lurched. *Mi choom-choom* must be an idiom, the kind I wouldn't find in a Nuer language grammar, if there was a Nuer language grammar, which there wasn't. It must be an expression that would telegraph that I had learned the language on a path to the well. It would show I knew how to *really* ask if all was well. It would show I belonged. I wrote it down in my notebook.

Then the woman reached out and pinched the fabric of my skirt between her fingers. She pulled, and the sweaty elastic band pulled away from my waist. *"Gore je."* I want this. There is no *please* in Nuer, politeness is supposed to be in the intonation.

I'd read that a 1930s anthropologist had found the Nuer's demands *imperious and incessant*. I'd thought I was ready for it, but I still bristled ever so slightly. My culture only allowed coveting other people's clothes secretly. Okay, I was there in South Sudan to help. To help women. But I wasn't going to give away the clothes I was wearing, and my language study hadn't yet gotten to the *I'm-sorry-but-no* stage. I looked at the girls for coaching. The woman waited, still rubbing the fabric of my skirt between her fingers.

"Ciagn bin nhok," Nyamal, the older sister, said. I repeated after her.

The old woman released my skirt. She nodded and shuffled away, skin loose on her bones, calloused feet bare. I was relieved. If Nuers aren't afraid to demand, at least they half expect *no*. The girls and I walked on, and I resolved to learn how to say those warm human things to the women of South Sudan that would connect me with them even when complexities meant I couldn't give them all that they might ask.

Metal shrieked on metal as we rounded the corner—a boy turning a handle made from pipes welded at angles. Hundreds of feet of rope wrapped around the bar. The sound of falling water echoed up from far below. When the bucket appeared, swinging and sloshing, the boy called the girls over and dumped it into their bright orange basin.

The handle whirled, the rope unfurled, and a dim splash echoed back. The boy stepped aside, panting. When he shook his head, drops of sweat splattered in every direction. My own sweat tickled along my backbone.

Nyamal and her sister stood shoulder to shoulder to wind up a second bucketful, laughing. Water and joy—sometimes what we need for life is so simple. The well was deep, the rope was long; the girls stopped laughing to use their breath for work, and sweat bubbled above their lips.

Done, the two younger sisters braced their feet and hoisted the orange basin onto Nyamal's head. She stilled the sloshing water with the muscles of her neck and steadied the basin with one hand. If *a pint's a pound the world around*, she had over twenty pounds of water on her twelve-year-old head.

We set off. Nyamal's heels pounded into the dust under the weight. Her spine absorbed the motions of her walking, and by the time they reached from her legs to her neck they had diminished to nothing. The water didn't slosh. The basin moved evenly forward.

This was a new well, drilled just that spring by Red Cross. With it, a few families had stayed in Waat through the dry season while the village teenagers took the cattle and followed yellowing grass back to the lush banks of the Sobat River. Tributaries that sweep down from the highlands of Ethiopia into South Sudan form the Sobat, which then joins the White Nile. The White Nile is a collection of waters flowing out of other African nations as well: the Rukara in Rwanda; the Luvironza in Tanzania; the Victoria Nile and the Albert Nile in Uganda; the Mountain Nile where it crosses into South Sudan. The waters of the White Nile join Ethiopia's Blue Nile in Khartoum and wind north, the world's longest river, through the desert to the Mediterranean Sea at Alexandria, Egypt.

The tributaries of the Nile had encircled my life since my parents first took me to Africa at age four. Psychologists might say my personality was formed by then, but my memories of being a human among other humans begin on an escarpment in Ethiopia at eight thousand feet. I'd been raised there, under the Southern Cross, which rotated from one side of the horizon to the other like a slow benediction through the night. Ethiopia's air, warmed by a tropical sun, smelled of hot pepper and ginger. It hummed with a multiplicity of languages. And I met Mark there, both of us high school juniors, both of us children of Presbyterians working in SW Ethiopia. I was raised to live in Africa, to be walking along a dusty path in Waat.

A gust blew my packable straw hat off, and the younger girls screamed. They chased it as it rolled away. Nyamal, Daughter of Peace, stopped, turned smoothly, and smiled.

"Jiom," she said and waved the fingers of her free hand past her face like wind.

I braced my language notebook at an angle against my stomach and flipped open the nouns section. The younger sisters ran back with my hat and crowded each other to watch me write. Their hair smelled of dust and smoke.

The youngest stroked my arm with fingers that dragged on my sweaty skin. Even in the shade, it had to be over one hundred degrees. She touched the freckles and moles on my arm one by one. I didn't have any way to explain flecks of melanin to a girl whose skin was all of a piece from head to toe, so dark that what glowed through the surface of her cheeks looked blue.

She took my hand and swung it happily. The quiet village and this tender attention from eager language tutors confirmed my hope: the move to Sudan was going to extend my precious claim on an African country as my home again. Who but Mark would ever have brought me back to work here? He'd shared my dreams of an adult return to Africa.

Back at the compound, Guy Lual still sat visiting with the pastor and his assistant, their Nuer language soft and breathy compared to the crackling highs of Amharic in Ethiopia.

The men all had the Nuer tribal markings, six scar lines across their foreheads. Nuer boys become men when a Man of the Cow decides it is time: when the rains are over, and there's a breeze to heal the boys' wounds; when there's grass for the cows and milk for the boys' recovery. These men had been twelve to fourteen years old when they'd lain on the ground between hollows dug into the earth on either side of their heads to catch their blood. The Man of the Cow had cut through to the bone, from ear to ear across their foreheads, and had rubbed ash into the wounds to make sure the scars would bulge up. With a sharp stick, he had also pried out their two bottom teeth. Any boy who cried out from the pain would be known as a coward for the rest of his life. And if he wasn't cut, he would be called a bull-boy forever. In cultures like the Nuers', anthropologists say men who survive coming-of-age ordeals feel entitled.

Mark had endured his own ordeal: a perfectionistic mother prone to violent anger, herself the child of a violent father. But neither Mark nor I yet understood the extent of his scarring.

Nor did we understand my own markings. My mother's father had been a violent veteran from the trenches of World War I. Mom had chuckled once, discussing a book we'd both read. The main character reminded her of her dad. "He was a badger-er," she said. "And my mom was a badger-ee."

Mom had developed a ferocious resistance to badgering. She wouldn't even give in to the badgering of leftovers in the fridge wanting to be eaten, or to dust bunnies yelling at her from under the bed. That didn't mean she hadn't picked up some skill herself in badgering.

I took advantage of a lull in the Nuer conversation, flipped through my notebook, and asked Guy Lual what I had said to the old woman on the way to the well about my skirt.

"*Ciagn bin nhok?*" he said. "That means, *It would not please me.*"

Yikes. I had hoped I was saying something gracious, like I would have in English—*I can't...I'm sorry.* Because before leaving the States, I'd collected a travel wardrobe: silk blouses from Goodwill that dried in an hour and folded flat as paper; two skirts, my cotton bandana. I'd added a Kenyan khanga cloth I could use as a skirt, a shawl, a towel or a mosquito net. My thirty pound travel-to-Sudan weight allowance had to include my tent and bedding as well as clothes. I couldn't just replace them for every trip.

I saw that I was going to have to say *no, no,* and *no* again, to dozens of requests for my things. And the bare, honest truth: it wouldn't have pleased me to give away a lightweight crinkle-skirt that never showed the dirt. Maybe frankness in the Nuer language and culture would rub off on me, teaching me how to be less accommodating, more definite. Less anxious about Mark's emotions, more aware of what would please me.

Grit crackled in the bindings of my notebook when I turned the pages, searching for my other new phrase, what the old woman said when she greeted me. I squinted through the dirt smudges to read my notes. "Here's another one, Guy Lual. What's *mi choom-choom?*"

Guy Lual laughed. "It's an expression women sometimes use. It means *sweet.*"

Mal mi choom-choom. The women of South Sudan ask if your peace is a sweet peace. Maybe in South Sudan any personal moment of peace is sweet, whether the war ends or not. A skirt, a bit of salt, tea with friends. Maybe for me back home it was the same. Any happy moment anywhere was *mal mi choom-choom.*

A boy coughed politely to get my attention; he'd been hired, with the promise of our left-over soap and our give-away t-shirts, to carry water and help the women feed Guy Lual and me. The boy pointed to a circle of sorghum stalks stuck into the ground and held together with strips of bark and lateral sticks. He pretended to scrub his chest. *"Puak,"* he said.

I grabbed my toiletry bag and towel and headed toward what must be a Nuer bathing enclosure. The UN orientation hadn't included the finer details of life in a Nuer village. I paused in the doorway, beside the open sorghum stalk door that hung crookedly on its bark hinges.

A little blue plastic basin sat on a piece of delaminating plywood, no doubt left from pallets of grain dropped out of great-bellied Hercules planes during the hunger time. A cup rocked in a few gallons of water. I stepped in and pushed the door shut. It dragged along a groove worn in the dirt. I set my sandals by the door. The plywood felt rough and gritty but it was still dry. I felt like an honored guest, called first.

Under the big Sudanese sky, now turning coral, I stripped naked. The first cupful of well water over one shoulder smelled like rain on a dusty field. A warm breeze gusted, the water on my skin cooled me, and lather dried and crackled. Goose bumps rose up on my legs.

As I rinsed and dressed, hope swelled. In Ethiopia, God's hand had painted extravagant gold and magenta sunsets evening after evening over my remote home, even though there weren't more than a few dozen people paying attention. God's hand was still painting sunsets, even over the pain and deprivation that circumscribed life in South Sudan. There had to be ways I could help women like the two who were serving us, the old woman on the path.

The girls looked up from their work as I walked in the warm evening air, back to my tent. They sat with their auntie on a mat in front of the cooking hut, feet straight out in front, picking carefully through tomorrow's sorghum, discarding tiny pebbles, dirt, and chaff. *"Shu puak?"* the woman asked. *Have you bathed?*

"Shi puak," I answered. I'd washed, and it blessed the Sudanese evening.

"Gwa elong." *Very good.* The girls looked up sideways and smiled with us, then went back to work. *Mal poindu, bodies at peace.*

CHAPTER 3

After sorghum and rice for lunch, I found a spot where I could study—a wobbly bench in a narrow, constantly shifting band of shade that curved behind the pastor's hut.

My mind wandered to home. Jesse had a soccer game today. Would Kenny remember? Would Mark miss the first half, something that always made Jesse mad?

In the sweltering afternoon heat of Waat, a man's shadow fell at my feet. He stood not much taller than me. Six ritual scars ran across his forehead, alternating with eager-to-please wrinkles. The lowest scar drooped toward his right eyebrow. I shut my notebook and offered my hand.

"My name is Nyang," he said, shaking my hand in both of his.

"Your mother named you for the crocodile," I said, pleased to recognize the word.

His face relaxed. "She wanted me to be brave."

Nyang still held my hand in his, rough and moist with sweat. "I went to university in Cairo," he said. "Waat is my home area. I have come back to be Education Director for the province. May I show you our schools?"

As we walked, dust puffed up around Nyang's splitting plastic shoes and my sandals. Anyone who would leave Cairo to return to Waat had already lived up to his mother's dreams of a son with the courage of a crocodile, I thought. Even though the drooping scar gave him a pessimistic look.

"Waat was a village of a thousand huts." Nyang said. "We had schools and a clinic."

The thousand huts, the schools, the clinic, and even the cinders and ash they had burned to had disappeared, as far as I could see. I couldn't keep myself oriented as I followed Nyang. I had no picture of how big the disappeared village of Waat had been, or how it had lain. Nuers live in compounds—a hut for the father, one for each wife and her children, one for cooking, plus cattle byres. Some hamlets might lie over a kilometer from the nearest neighbor, far enough that the man can rein undisputed, but close enough to enjoy a few benefits of neighborliness. But hot-climate trees casting lacy shade were all that was left. Their tiny leaves rustled in the breeze.

We veered between two trees to miss twisted lengths of angle iron, evidence of some warehouse where books or medicines must have been stored. A piece of metal skittered away from my toe. I stooped to pick it up—a charred brass shell.

Jesus had rhetorically asked, *Can the same spring run with both fresh and bracken water?* What we call development—medicine, literacy, vehicles—comes through science. And guns could wipe out all development. So what was science to Waat, blessing or curse? Now there was no evidence of science in Waat but twisted beams and a spent shell lying in dust that had been there for centuries. How might I bring the blessings of science to women here? The shell in my pocket dragged down the side of my skirt.

Nyang led me to a pile of rubble. "Waat once had two wells. Our soldiers came to drive the Dinkas out. Before they fled, they pounded our diesel pumps into pieces. They threw the bodies of our dead down the wells. To kill us all."

A frission of shock shot down my sweaty backbone. We stood for a moment in silence, Nyang's hand lay like a benediction on the chunks of cement that had once surrounded a well. Maybe the rustling I heard wasn't the wind, but the presence of those who had been killed when a commander had attacked Riek Machar in Waat, or of those who had died in the famine that followed their fields being burned. Maybe their spirits remained, still restless, unpeaceful in that village. In the bright sunlight, I felt them around me, the surging, moaning inhabitants of a thousand huts.

I followed Nyang's thin shoulders, in his threadbare suit jacket from Cairo days. He took me through the empty dustiness to a cement slab enclosed by a half-wall under a thatched roof.

"This was the TB clinic, but I am going to teach adult education here," Nyang said. "It is far from the school. Adults won't come if their children can hear them and laugh at their mistakes."

I imagined the generation of Sudanese who were raised after schools had been destroyed reciting out loud, pointing at black marks on pages so worn the ink was lifting off. The men would squat with their knees up to their shoulders in the thick shade of that thatch; women would sit on mats, legs straight out in front. I imagined them speaking English, no longer cut off from the rest of the world by language. Yes! I wanted to be part of his dream. I could send literacy materials. I could see to it the church funded women to teach women in this "charming" spot.

We walked on from there, through eye-scorching sunshine, to the school on the other side of the village, a stick and thatch building that listed to one side. A curl of smoke drifted up from one corner and dissipated in the blue of sky. Nyang ticked his tongue against his teeth when he saw it and walked faster.

He had blocked off the open doorway of one classroom with scraps of gray wood, but inside, a thin woman tended a small fire on the floor. Her toddler son squatted nearby, his naked body smeared with ash. Nyang spoke to her in a loud voice. She gestured and shook her head without looking up, even her body language barely above a whisper. He turned away.

"This will be the third and fourth grade classroom. But her husband died in the fighting two years ago. She has no other place to live. What can I say to her? She promises she will not burn the wood I collected to repair the school."

He showed me where he'd pounded branches into the ground and cobbled together a corner of the building. It looked like something kids would build for a fort. He was so proud. He would teach children to read, pointing with a stick to each word on a blackboard the UN would give him. And as they do all over South Sudan, the children would squat on the floor and practice writing in the dust with their fingers, so as not to waste pencil and paper before they learned their letters.

A prayer went up from my heart, *Let it be so.*

"You will help us," he said. He took me over to a sagging storage hut. "You see? Security has returned to Waat. It is safe for the NGOs to come. Tell them, at the UN. Tell them we are ready to rebuild."

I smiled at him and nodded, letting his hopefulness float away any doubts.

To impress on me how very secure Waat was, Nyang jiggled the padlock on the crooked door.

Guy Lual and I walked out the sorghum stalk gate together the next morning. The top of my head didn't reach his shoulder. He said, "I was governor of this province during the years of peace." He was referring to an eleven-year cease-fire between North and South Sudan, from 1972 to 1983. "When the truce fell apart, the CIA got me out to England. That's where my wife and children are."

I'd known Guy Lual, like Nyang, was from Waat, but I hadn't known any details. His close-cut spirals of black hair were sprinkled with white. His walk was dignified, elder-statesman personified. Oviously he had been brave during his scarring ceremony. His scars ran from one temple, across his forehead to the other. The gap from his bottom front teeth showed flashes of his pink tongue when he spoke. "Why did you come back?" I asked.

"Someday peace will come again. New Sudan will need me." He looked out at the flat horizon, so far away, broken only in a few places by scrub trees.

His family was even further away than mine. I'd seen it in Ethiopia, too: my best friend's husband went to Germany for six years to finish his PhD. The school secretary left her one-year-old with her parents for the chance to immigrate to the US. My other friend's barely-adult children took off for college in the US and never came back. If Africans could hold their families together over distances in order to improve their wellbeing, surely I could manage these separations in order to live out our dreams of living in African communities, meeting heroic people like Guy Lual, doing what I could to help women live a few of their dreams.

We ducked under the low thatch of a dark storage hut, where the air had the rancid smell of used clothing. In the back stood two big treadle sewing machines I'd brought for the women. They hulked in the shadows, still tied up in odd shaped pieces of cardboard.

Pastor Simon's hands lay dark on a yellow and orange quilt in a pile right inside the door. An old woman was bending over it. She lifted it into the square of light from the low doorway. Her grandson crowded close to her side in an adult t-shirt worn like a tunic. His skin showed black through ragged holes.

Since we were the first flight to Waat after the fighting five years before, people would have worn out their clothes and blankets, the Sudanese pastors said. Cash was useless, because there was nothing to buy that far in. It was clothes people needed. So, in addition to bringing the sewing machines to give the women, they had filled the plane with bundles big as cotton bales. They would use the clothes and blankets as pay for poles, thatch, and labor to rebuild the church.

"She is offering three bundles of thatch for that quilt," Guy Lual said.

The woman gave the quilt back to Pastor Simon and put her arm around her grandson's shoulder. As they stooped out the door, Pastor Simon put the quilt onto a second pile.

"How will he remember whose it is?" I asked Guy Lual.

His scars reflected the dim light. "He will remember. And if he doesn't, the woman will. People who can't read remember."

Pastor Simon stretched. We bent low to go out, and the fringe of thatch brushed my back. In the sunlight, Pastor Simon began to talk to me in Nuer, even though I still knew less than a hundred words, and only half a dozen of them in sentences. I knew he was talking to me because he was looking at me. I gave him eye contact as he spoke, nodding and even smiling, in our off-kilter dance, catching the non-verbal communication while I waited for the verbal to come through Guy Lual.

"When even the church is burned down, you know the village is finished," Pastor Simon told me. He gestured to the scorched mud enclosure, running unevenly in front of us, waist high. If they didn't get a roof on before the rains started, the walls would melt away altogether. "I was the only civilian who stayed in Waat. The soldiers and I lived on leaves through the rainy season. Then a few people came back. The women planted sorghum. Now the Red Cross dug a well. We will rebuild."

I hoped, oh how I hoped, they were right, that peace was coming. People couldn't fight forever in Sudan, could they? Everyone would wait for the peace to fall apart, but day would follow day and then, truly, it would be possible to rebuild Waat. The look on Pastor Simon's face told me he needed to believe Commander Riek Machar's ceasefire was already the beginning of peace. He fell silent.

"Pastor Simon can't read," Guy Lual said. "So the assistant reads to him from the Nuer Bible. He thinks about what he wants to say in his sermons. He is wise. The people love him because he stayed in Waat and did not flee. He suffered for them."

We walked back to the quiet compound for lunch. Five years since those awful Hunger Triangle days? I couldn't grasp it. How had the people of Waat not felt alone in all the earth? How had they not fallen into a pit of despair? And how could I help them? Those who'd sent me to lead women's development in South Sudan had never seen Waat. I, who'd been so hopeful, hadn't understood.

Pastor Simon and Guy Lual visited over our rice and lentil lunch (we'd also brought our own salt, and I gave thanks for that as they blessed the rest of the food in Nuer). I thought my own thoughts in English. If something broke the peace here, UN pilots would come for me, just as they had for aid workers when Commander Riek Machar mutinied against the Sudan People's Liberation Army.

It felt heavy to me, my privilege. I had not brought anything to Waat that would justify saving *my* life and no one else's. I would be saved only because my parents and my birthplace had been a lucky chance. I couldn't even call it a gift from God, because that would imply God randomly granted me a favor and withheld that favor from others. My lucky draw wouldn't transfer to anyone else. I could accept it or reject it; I could feel grateful or feel guilty, but no matter how I felt about it, the pilots would squeeze Guy Lual and me in, and not Pastor Simon. He'd be left in Waat again, with his wife and the girls, their baby brother, the assistant and his wife.

And when we came back, those who'd been left to suffer, if they survived—it would be pure grace if one day they welcomed us back.

In the dusty heat of late afternoon, I distracted myself by studying vocabulary lists in my tent. Eventually, I dozed. I woke drenched with sweat. Finally, in the slanting rays of evening, I set out to ease my thoughts with a walk to the landing strip.

As I approached, a breeze brought the shouts of a drill sergeant and the sharp blasts of his whistle. A local captain of Commander Riek Machar's militia ran recruits through their drills on the airstrip in the relative cool of morning and evening. I squinted in the still-bright sunlight. Half of the young recruits were naked. The others wore UN blankets tied under their right arms and over their left shoulders. When they finished their training, they would be given uniforms like the sergeant's, camouflage pants and shirts, more clothes than they had ever had in their lives.

They would carry automatic rifles.

They would be men.

On the path back, I passed a young soldier, taller than me but thirty pounds thinner. A Kalashnikov automatic rifle rode his back. Scars were healing on his forehead.

"*Mal-ay*," I greeted him. *Peace.*

"*Mal mi deet,*" he said. *May it be a wide peace.* His voice was high and sweet.

When the war was over, Sudan would have to build its wide peace with this generation of children raised as soldiers. The prophet Jeremiah had ranted at the false prophets: *You say peace, peace, but there is no peace.* Maybe we would also be condemned for all this talk of *mal* in South Sudan. Or maybe it would be credited to us as prayer.

The next morning, I practiced making simple sentences from my Nuer language lists, while Nyamal and her sisters took turns on grinding stones. The sorghum meal, cooked, would be our lunch. Red as the dust of Nariobi, it was full of iron and minerals and healthier than the white rice we'd brought. The girls' thin backs and sharp shoulders rose and jarred down on arms that bulged out around their elbow joints. They laughed at my stumbling efforts. Sorghum hulls crackled under the rasping of their stones.

CHAPTER 4

It was 1996 when Mark and I left our daughter Miriam in college in the US and relocated to Nairobi, Kenya with Jesse and Kenny. The wars in Bosnia, Somalia, and Congo were getting a lot of global attention, but more people had died or been displaced in South Sudan than in the other three places combined. The Sudan government had bombed rebels in the South unrelentingly. The Southern commanders had fought each other. Not only were civilians killed in crossfire, but crops were burned, cattle slaughtered, and wells destroyed. Famine was rampant. The elephants were fighting; the ants were getting trampled.

Presbyterians were donating money for South Sudan, but was it actually getting in to help suffering people? That was what Mark and I were there for. As Financial Advisor, he would track the money. I would create programs to spend some of it on behalf of women. But no expats lived in South Sudan. The Sudanese themselves were flooding out in every direction—to North Sudan, Kenya, Uganda, Ethiopia, Eritrea and across the oceans, if they could. And so we were based in Nairobi.

Other Presbyterians from the US had worked in South Sudan through other nonprofits, but no one had tried working directly for Presbyterian Church of Sudan. The experiment had started out well enough: the Sudanese pastors in Nairobi welcomed Mark. They warmed up even more when he negotiated a new office for them with subsidized rent. They promised him the bank statements he needed to set up a record-keeping system. Unfortunately, the statements were always in the hands of someone not in the office that day. Mark asked about receipts. They showed him a file drawer that resembled a rat's nest of paper scraps. He went to work organizing books, sorting through the scraps. When he finally did get the bank statements, the right person to explain how all the withdrawals matched the receipts was never in.

As for women's development work, I didn't have anything but my hopes and imagination. And for several months after we got to Nairobi, the Nuer pastors in the office had said *yes, yes, yes* to me, but didn't introduce me to any women.

I stayed busy while I waited. There was lots to do to get our family settled in. I learned to drive on the left side of the road. I figured out which groceries to buy at Uchumi Supermarket and which to buy from men on bicycles whose cross bars hung with bulging plastic bags full of vegetables. I tried to be patient. I went to the orientation course and felt even more impatient. I read up on Sudan history and—it was hard to be patient, because I was so eager for the South Sudan work to begin. Making the world a better place was bread and wine to me.

After three months, the annual donor meeting rolled around. There, a plump young woman with a new baby stood and introduced herself as Elizabeth, the Women's Department Director.

What? Why hadn't the men told me there was a Women's Department with a director?

I sat with her at tea break and tried to bond. She didn't seem all that responsive. I watched, breathing cinnamon from my milky Kenyan *chai*, as she nursed her baby. Maybe she just wasn't confident of her English? I banished my foreboding, a strategy I'd learned from an optimistic dad.

A few weeks later, Elizabeth invited me to a meeting of the Nuer women of Nairobi. I scolded myself for doubting—she was going to open the gate into my work with the women of South Sudan, after all. I picked her up at the office, and she directed me through the daily madhouse of Nairobi traffic.

Nairobi carried reminders of the British everywhere. It rankled me, the layers of absurdity left by colonial history—that day we were driving to meet Sudanese refugees in a Kenyan slum named Zimmerman.

Kenya was so unlike proud Ethiopia, where kings had used its mountains like fortress walls against European colonizers and everything had an Amharic name. How deep my allegiance to my childhood host nation went. Both Ethiopia and Kenya were fragile nation states in a world order that only recently let them in. But I doubted I would I ever love Kenya the way I loved Ethiopia.

When we got to Zimmerman, I saw no sign of the British, nor of anything prosperous: no green of nature, no blue or red of human art, only shades of cement-block gray and earth brown. I followed Elizabeth and the sound of women's voices to an open apartment door, where an older woman greeted me warmly in Nuer. Thirty or more women were crammed into the small living room behind her. Elizabeth introduced me to Nyadok, a young woman who spoke good English. She held me with her sweaty hand and I inched my way in behind her. The air was suffocating, with heat radiating off our bodies and the sun-warmed cement walls. Women exchanged shy smiles with me, mostly young women, many with babies tied on their backs in brightly colored *khanga* cloths. Nyadok guided me to low stools in a corner.

Women passed plates of rice and okra stew over each other's heads from the kitchen to us in the back. I watched Nyadok and dug in with my fingers, but unlike her, I couldn't keep the viscous green okra sauce from trailing down my chin on its way to my mouth.

As we ate, above the babble of a language I couldn't understand, I strained to hear Nyadok's voice in my ear. She explained that the meeting had been called to sort out who should be the Women's Department Director. Ah, this might explain Elizabeth's reticence with me. I wanted the backstory but had to wait and see if I could figure it out.

We passed our empty plastic plates back toward the kitchen. Next, steaming cups of *chai* came through from the kitchen. The heat in the room intensified. The smells of sweat, okra, garlic, and cinnamon made a heady mixture. I shifted on my stool so I could lean against the wall, and my heart swelled with its own warmth at being there, among the Nuer women.

When the meeting began, Nyadok murmured translations into my ear and I caught about half of what she was saying. It seemed that the church moderator's wife, the elegant older woman at the door, had been leading women's prayer and Bible study groups for years. But she didn't speak English, so the men had passed over her when it came time for the donor meeting.

I began to get a picture—Mark had said the donors complained that the Sudanese church wasn't doing anything for women. I remembered the glow on the faces of Germans, British and Americans in the donor group when Elizabeth was introduced. Would the pastors really hire her just to appease them?

Tempers in the room heated up. If Elizabeth were a good woman, someone said, she would have stepped down as soon as the donors went home. Elizabeth sat across the room, her chubby cheeks set like plums.

"She's had no experience. But there's a salary," Nyadok whispered, and raised her eyebrows meaningfully.

"Maybe she can learn," I whispered.

Nyadok looked at me and didn't comment.

Women started to shout at each other. I thought about my reading of South Sudan history, how the Nuer people hadn't ever been subdued—not by the Arabs, not by the Turks, not by the Brits.

For a while Nyadok hung in with translating. This woman supports Elizabeth; this woman insults her; she's never done anything; the older women are our true leaders. Then she petered out. But women were still yelling.

I pulled at Nyadok's skirt, "What? What?"

"The same," she said. Then she stood and shouted something.

The fracas went on and on. I staved off depression by telling myself, *When you know them...when you can understand what they're saying...maybe coming from outside the culture you can be a neutral mediator. A peacemaker.* The smell of angry sweat filled the hot room. My head ached. My eyes burned.

Elizabeth never relented.

Maybe I can mentor her, I told myself. Maybe together we could make something out of the mess the men had made among the women in Nairobi and do good work together among the women in South Sudan. Maybe my real job would be to empower Elizabeth for development work that would go on long after I was gone.

In high school I had copied a *Reader's Digest* gem of wisdom into my journal: "Love consists not in gazing at each other, but at gazing together at the world." And in our wedding ceremony, I asked my sister to sing the St. Francis song, *Make Me an Instrument of Thy Peace.* In that sweltering room, I felt a rush of gratitude to Mark. I had married a man who would play a part in bringing me to this very moment, in positioning me to change the world for women in some remote and dysfunctional spot on the globe.

But I wasn't as ready for it as I thought I was. I hadn't yet read the serenity prayer, or learned to sort between what I could control and what I couldn't. Deep in the second half of Reinhold Niebuhr's original prayer, which no one seems to remember, he asks God for another graceful perspective that I was going to need, but had never read: *Accepting hardship as a pathway to peace.*

And so, a few weeks after the big fight in Zimmerman, when the Sudanese pastors sent a message home with Mark—*We have asked an aid organization to charter a C-47 to fly supplies to Waat, would you like to go in?*—it was Elizabeth I went to, full of hope.

Elizabeth, now firmly in possession of her title, seemed excited when I told her I'd asked the aid organization to buy sewing machines for the women of Waat. I'd learned to sew on a treadle machine in Maji for such a time as this, I thought. If she would translate, we could teach the women in Waat to sew. The first of my many trips into South Sudan and already a project. I was going to be a great success as Women's Development Advisor.

The day before the flight, Elizabeth called me into the

Presbyterian Church of Sudan office. Sitting stiffly across from me in a bubble-gum pink suit, she told me she had been invited to work with women in the Kakuma refugee camp in Northern Kenya. My face brightened, another *in*.

"Tomorrow we will go to Kakuma on the bus," she said. "Will you be ready?"

I stared at her, sure there must be some two-language confusion. We went back and forth, clarifying. It was no mistake. Yes, the plane would go to Waat. But we would not be on it. *We will go to Kakuma.*

I forced a smile and said in my most reasonable voice, "Elizabeth, we can go to Kakuma any time. But this might be our only chance *ever* to go to Waat."

Elizabeth's cheeks and chin were set. I'd seen that look.

How about this, I suggested. She could go to Kakuma, I would go to Waat. Twice the work done.

"I am head of Woman's Department. You cannot go to Waat without me."

I never did resort to screaming, though I now knew it would have been culturally appropriate.

Elizabeth finally agreed I could go to Waat without her, on certain conditions: I would be there on my own, not representing the Women's Department; and I would tell the women in Waat that the sewing machines were from her.

I never found out why Elizabeth wouldn't go to Waat. Maybe she didn't want to be over-shadowed by an American who was bound to get all the attention. Maybe she didn't know how to sew and would feel shamed. Or maybe it was more complicated: might Waat be an area where women supported the moderator's wife in the women's leadership conflict, and they would scorn Elizabeth's claim to authority? Or what about this: Waat had been destroyed by other Nuers in inter-clan fighting—was Elizabeth part of the wrong clan? I finally gave up thinking about it.

There were always cultural differences no one could explain to me. Differences in ideas of privacy, for example. Differences in keeping people clued in. In Ethiopia, I'd learned to live without knowing schedules people made for me when I traveled. Future plans were held close to the chest for no reason I ever discerned. "Need-to-know basis," I would joke to other Americans who became anxious about not knowing how far we were from our destination, the plans being made for their suppers, or where they'd be spending the night.

And I would think of my mom, quoting Tennyson: *Yours is not to reason why. Yours is but to do and die.* Eventually I read the rest of the poem and was appalled: *Into the valley of death rode the six hundred.* To give her credit, Mom of all people was not someone who obeyed without question, much as she wished her daughters were easier to manage. She had been a woman of complexity and adventure—a great model for what I was off to do in Waat.

And I was committed to the women in South Sudan now, so close to the place I used to imagine being able to see from my mountaintop home as a girl. I was meant to be there, washed down from Ethiopia like the fertile silt in the waters of the Blue Nile.

I was raised to do hard things. To launch myself into a world of strangers. To feel alone. To hold my breath and trust. "You'll be fine," my folks had said, as they put me alone on the plane to fly to boarding school in Addis Ababa when I was ten. *You'll be fine*, as I joined a group of other mish-kids and boarded the plane for high school in Egypt. *You'll be fine*, as they wept and hugged me and put me on Swissair to fly alone to my passport country for college. But they forgot to give me the phone number of our friends in Switzerland. After some German-speaking young men accosted me on the sidewalk, I bought grapes and a chocolate bar and spent my chance to tour Zurich hiding in my hotel room.

Still, how could I argue with my folks? I *had* been fine, as I hid my eyes and trusted Dad to bounce the Jeep safely across the land bridge where the earth fell away thousands of feet on both sides. He *had* been fine when he unhooked the trailer and pulled it out of the mud with a rope. To get to a flat spot and hook the trailer up again, the Jeep crept around a corner, and the rope pulled taut over a ravine. We girls and Mom huddled in the dark and the rain on the side of the road, waiting for the trailer to fall over the edge and pull the Jeep down with it. But Dad was fine. We trudged up to where he idled, waiting for us, holding the parking brake tight.

How could my folks not believe we would survive, no matter the circumstance? Dad had been dropped in a glider behind German lines at twenty-one. Walking back to France, he'd stolen a bike. He found out later that it belonged to the sniper who had been picking off GIs as they drifted by. Providentially, the sniper had been taking a nap or a leak at the moment Dad stole his bike.

In Ethiopia, Dad had walked away fine from three bush-pilot crashes. He had walked through the night up the mountain to Maji followed by a leopard. He, and by extension his daughters, lived a charmed life. Hadn't I fallen on a piece of tin as a six- year-old and slit my wrist vertically? I had watched the deep slice filled slowly with blood, like a dammed-up valley. It had missed my artery by a fraction of a millimeter.

"We'll be fine," I had said to my children, as the Marxist regime in Ethiopia collapsed the year after we arrived. Two armament warehouses exploded, shaking the house, sending up mushroom-shaped clouds. We were unharmed. *You'll be fine*, as we uprooted them from Ethiopia and moved to Kenya.

Physical danger, discomfort and inconvenience couldn't touch me. It was letting people down that was torture. And Mark, like my mom, was unpredictable with love. He could go silent for days and days when he was unhappy with me, and I had no defense against the feelings of abject misery that welled up.

Setting off with Nuer men, a white woman in war-ravaged South Sudan, that was no problem. *I'll be fine*, I thought.

CHAPTER 5

The African countries where I've lived are never out of my sight, no matter how I may turn my head. Doris Lessing, raised in Rhodesia (now Zimbabwe), wrote that Africa is a low-grade fever in the blood, one that no one ever recovers from. I was infected early with the joy and pain of life in an African nation.

My Ethiopian childhood traces itself back to the Italians, who killed a whole generation of educated men during their occupation from 1935 to 1941. Desperate to rebuild his country when the war was over, Emperor Haile Selassie assigned pie-shaped sections of Ethiopia to Protestants who would build schools, open clinics, and start churches. He was careful to keep them out of Ethiopian Orthodox Church areas and Muslim regions, to avoid religious conflict. Presbyterians got a slice west and south-west from Addis Ababa. In the furthest southern corner sat the town of Maji, perched on the edge of the escarpment.

Meanwhile, Mom and Dad had met in college, gone off to seminary, and borne three daughters in four years. Then Dad got his call—a letter from Presbyterian Church headquarters, asking if he would go to Ethiopia to be a missionary.

I try to avoid that word, except in select company. "I worked in Ethiopia and South Sudan for the Presbyterian Church," I say.

People aren't fooled. "You were a missionary?"

With that, I see myself morph in their eyes from a complex human being into a stereotype. In the eyes of Christians, I turn into a saintly martyr. In the eyes of secular sceptics, I turn into a destroyer of cultures, a rabid and irrational proselytizer. They all ask, "Have you read *Poisonwood Bible*?"

Fortunately for me, Ethiopians, Kenyans, and Sudanese honor missionaries. "You left your country to come help our people!" Ethiopians said to me. "You learned our language!" In the poorest nations of the world, an American who loves them counts for a lot.

Missionaries have been excoriated in literature and blamed for many things they mostly didn't do. They are honored by Christians for other things they didn't do, either. No one sees a missionary as an ordinary jumble of human gifts and frailties.

And no one remembers that Africa figured big in the earliest history of the church, long before this age of enlightenment and European-culture missionaries. St. Augustine was a North African. The Coptic church in Egypt was started in the first century AD, the mystic Fathers and Mothers fled to the desert of North Africa, the Orthodox Church of Ethiopia was founded in the third century.

It also gets lost how mysterious faith is, and how unpredictable its transmission. In the 19th and 20th century, where Western missionaries planted seeds, Christianity swept the continent much like Islam did in the 9th and 10th, not by conquest, not by missionaries, but because ordinary Africans passed the word on to their sisters, their uncles, their cousins, and down family lines. Africans themselves found the merciful God of Islam and the Christian God of love a relief from the malevolent spirits of their world. And in Africa, people are intensely interested in God and the spiritual. Secularism—the religion in which God is irrelevant—only appeals to a few Westernized urban sophisticates.

In any case, I had never wanted to be a missionary. Some of my classmates talked about getting whatever college degree would bring them back to Ethiopia the fastest. I thought they were taking the easy way out of the hurdles before us, adjusting to US culture.

I'd had unbounded energy the year I met Mark in boarding school—competitive student; secretary in student council; Emily in the junior class play, *Our Town*; an alto in our choir; and cellist in the tiny orchestra. Then, when the last buzzer sounded I ran, books bumping on my hip bone, to the dorm. I changed from my school dress into shorts, and ran back up to the basketball court. I fell in line, usually the only girl, as the big boys chose teams. I was always chosen last, along with the middle schoolers, but I didn't mind. I couldn't dribble or shoot well, so I was humble about what I brought to a team. I could run defense. I could intercept the ball. I could pass it off. That was enough for me. I was there for the fresh mountain sunshine, for the burning of thin highland air in my lungs as I ran. For the boys.

And every day, when teams were settled, I rolled my eyes as the other team stripped off their t-shirts and made jokes about how one day I would be on the skins team.

Mark had perfected that difficult shot from out by the corner of the court, the one that could as easily be an air ball as a swish. He was several inches taller than me. Slim as I was, we probably weighed the same. Dark-rimmed glasses, dark straight hair that fell across his forehead, Mark lived up to his dramatic, dark looks on the basketball court. He was the only kid who hollered at others—the wannabe player who dribbled the ball on his foot and lost it; the eager B-team guy who broke away caught the long pass, but then fluffed the lay-up; the kid who shot when he had no chance of making it and turned over the ball. *What were you thinking? Are you an idiot?*

In the dorm, in class Mark was silent and watchful. But on the court, thunder could crash and render the rest of us silent. For someone like me, who wasn't a great player and hated to make mistakes, Mark was scary.

Right away, silently intense Mark Rasmussen decided that verbally intense Caroline was the girl for him. I watched him watching me. For a year, he was too shy to do anything more than that. And I was too ambivalent, too busy enjoying high school. But senior year, Mark let me know with his eyes that he was ready to overcome his shyness and ask me out.

I was seventeen. It was time to have a boyfriend. His devotion was hard to turn down. I gave him as much go-ahead eye-contact as I knew how to give.

For an October Friday activity ice-breaker mixer game, Mark bribed a classmate to set us up as a couple. My eyes met his in shock. It was 1967, I wasn't bold enough to ask if this was just chance. I walked ahead of him up to supper, waiting to see if he'd follow. He slipped into the seat beside me just ahead of my girlfriend.

After Mark made his bold move, I decided I wouldn't play basketball anymore. If he hollered at me on the court—imagine. Whistles. Jeers. *Oh! Oh! Lover's quarrel!* Humiliation. So after school that Monday, I walked casually up to the basketball court still in my school-day skirt. Mark ran over from a drill line.

I made some lame excuse.

He stared at me, appalled. "But it's one of the things I like best about you!"

Eventually I told him my real reason. He was even more appalled. "I would *never* holler *at you!*"

I believed that if he said so, love would forever exempt me from that stormy frown of his. I didn't yet know that marriage breaks down our independence; we become frantic for the other to protect us from all that threatens. We forget that we are each only human. We flounder. We hurt each other. We blame the other for our pain. But that doesn't happen right away.

In the safety of our relationship, painfully shy Mark did open up. He told me stories about his family and about Dembi Dollo, where his dad was a doctor in our mission. He told me his dreams and desires—evidence of an inner life I never imagined he had. I was enchanted. Love really was magic. It really would heal whatever had made Mark withdrawn and watchful.

It was in that glow of confidence and love that my years in Ethiopia came to an end. Mark and I broke up, he off to college in Ohio and me to Illinois.

There were things I knew at that age: days that began at 6:30 and ended at 6:30 no matter the season; trees that stayed green all year long; a swirl of languages and cultures; my family and my other home, in boarding school. In the US I entered a world of slang, movie stars, inscrutable fashions and dating—those things I didn't know.

I came apart completely.

I met Mark again at the end of my junior year of college. He'd been equally lost. We clung to each other as though for breath. I was emotionally intense and now deeply shaken, Mark so very shy, so very intense, so very volatile. No one in their twenties understands what it will mean to intertwine their life with another frail human being. No one told me the utter trust Mark and I felt with each other was a cocktail of Ethiopia memories and the love hormone oxytocin.

Mom and Dad had worked in Ethiopia for twenty-three years. Mark and I may have aspired to do the same when the Presbyterian Church had so unexpectedly offered us to return to the land of our youth. But it was after we had worked under the Ethiopian sister church for a mere six years, in the middle of a summer in the US, that our Presbyterian Church supervisors called and asked us to relocate to Nairobi.

Mark walked back out to his project in his Portland workshop. Dazed, he ran his thumb into the bandsaw. He reappeared out the dining room window hunched over, holding his thumb in a rag. I ran out. He loosened the rag, and sawdust floated down. His thumb looked like raw pork raggedly cut. He blanched, squatted, and closed his eyes. "I'm gonna faint," he said.

Mark got stitched up, and then, in his words, fought with God over the move for about a week. One night he got out of our bed and knelt by the side. He begged God to let him go back to Ethiopia. Suddenly he felt that he heard an answer: *Those are not your projects in Ethiopia. They are mine. Leave them to me.*

In a very real way, Mark never recovered. The joy he'd felt during our time in Ethiopia never took hold in Nairobi. For one thing, the aggressive Nuers were so different to partner with than the more gracious Ethiopians. For another, as Mark said later, *No white man should ever get between Africans and their money.* And for a third, his gifts were in the world of things—there was always a way for him to fix broken stuff. If he sometimes had to reverse-design a broken part, all the better. Mark was used to getting love for how he could help people keep their stuff working. Stuff is easy. It's people who are fraught with emotional potholes and grenades.

I had gotten excited, once we made the decision to accept the move. I had a quirky array of reasons. Development projects with South Sudanese women sounded meaningful and interesting. I couldn't believe I would get to learn Juba Arabic and Nuer. Juba Arabic, they told me, was a pidgin dialect. The Sub-Saharan Africa peoples of South Sudan had taken North Sudan's Egyptian Arabic, dropped the gutturals, and simplified the syntax.

Besides being paid to learn two new languages, working with African church leaders was how I kept a work permit to live in African nations like Ethiopia and Kenya. That made work in South Sudan great job security. No lack of needs there. People had been reduced to a Stone Age existence without Stone Age tools and clothing but punctuated by Kalashnikovs and airplanes—Antinovs from North Sudan dropped bombs, and Hercules from the UN dropped food.

My third reason for accepting the change I only admitted to Mark: the classes I was teaching at the girls' school in Ethiopia were growing every year, creeping up toward sixty students each. I was exhausted. More and more I wondered what I was really doing to make the world a better place—an existential requirement I'd always demanded of my earnest self.

Yes, I was doing a great job giving three-hundred Ethiopian girls a year their introduction to English. But how many millions of first through third graders were there in Ethiopia learning nothing but *A is for Apple, B is for Ball*? Shouldn't I be teaching teachers, if my methods were as great as my director and co-teachers said? Shouldn't I be showing the curriculum I developed to the Ethiopia

Ministry of Education, if it was so effective? I'd tried—I'd made an appointment and trotted across town with my little workbooks, but the Ministry official was out of the office. My ambitions to drive change always outpaced my opportunities.

In spite of the rough start I'd had with women in Nairobi, I was still confident about my new job. The women in South Sudan would be different. And I could give the women the sewing machines in Elizabeth's name, if that's what I had to do.

I had three goals for my time in Waat: deliver the sewing machines; get some Nuer language immersion to cement the lessons I had started in Nairobi; and figure out what women's development work might actually look like.

The one specific I'd heard from other aid workers was that women's groups all over Nile Province wanted those sewing machines. Only men had sewing machines in old Sudan. In New Sudan, women were determined it was going to be different. Sewing machines topped the list of things they wanted. The pastors in Nairobi also told me women in South Sudan wanted sugar, tea leaves, thermoses, and cups so they could run community teashops on market days. And as the new Women's Development Advisor, I was to be their source. Or rather—Elizabeth would be their source. But since I was the one with connections to donors, no one was going to be fooled about where sewing machines and tea leaves would really come from.

When we landed in Waat, men had off-loaded the sewing machines, blocky and bristling with jute tied every-which-way to hold the cardboard packing. They carried the machines with the bales of blankets and clothing, into the storage hut. When the women were ready to learn to sew, Guy Lual told me, they would build a shed out of sticks and food-aid bags, the new plastic version of gunnysacks. They would pound a couple of forked branches into the ground and lay another branch across for something to sit on. A tailor in some village hours away by foot would come to teach them.

A small group of women and I sat together in a sweaty circle on the floor one hot afternoon, with sunlight blazing between gaps in the sorghum-stalk walls of a meeting room the size of a walk-in closet. Guy Lual, the only man, sat beside me to translate. A deaconess with gray hair and wrinkles that channeled down to her lips spoke for the Waat Presbyterian Church's women's group. She was probably about forty-five, like me, but she had carried water on her head since she was a girl. She had spent decades hoeing sorghum with fire-hardened sticks, harvesting it by hand and grinding it between two rocks. Her body was worn down.

On Elizabeth's behalf, I gave her the packet of sewing supplies—scissors, brown paper for patterns, thread, pins and bobbins. She graciously bowed.

Guy Lual translated her thanks: "We want to make school uniforms, because after they are ten, girls have to stay home if they don't have clothes. The boys will go to school naked, but our girls get no education."

I loved the idea that the sewing machines could play a role in girls' education in Waat—if Nyang could get his school started again. Girls in school would certainly be development. I felt a stab of excitement.

Across from me, the pastoral assistant's pregnant wife sat, legs out, her belly stretching her nylon nightgown. Dust had left ashy gray splotches on her ankles and calloused bare feet. "We hope the UN will donate fabric for the uniforms," she said. She stroked her belly. "Then maybe the UN will buy the uniforms from us and we can use the money to help the poor women. Women whose men have been lost."

From my perspective, these women *were* the poor. They had put on their only dresses to meet with me. They weren't thinking about a typical African micro-finance scheme: sewing machines to start a personal business, thermoses and cups to start their own tea shop, a pair of goats to breed to improve their own lives. They were the church women's association, thinking about the survival of their entire community. I felt humbled. Though I had to admit, the UN donating fabric and then buying back the uniforms to give to the village children seemed like a stretch.

Now the deaconess leaned forward and rested her hand on my knee. "We hear you are a teacher," she said. "Stay here and teach us to read."

It took me a long time to answer. I had thought my job would be about taking women what they wanted—sewing machines. Tea leaves. I hadn't thought about them wanting *me*.

Beside me in the lean-to, a younger woman pulled her breast out the top of her blouse to nurse her squirming baby. This was a serious meeting with the foreign woman—toddlers had been left at home with their big sisters; babies would not be allowed to cry. We sat as we always did in chair-less Waat, on the ground with nothing to rest against. The backs of my knees burned, because we also sat like polite Sudanese women sit, with our legs straight out in front.

"Stay with us," the deaconess said. I shifted, trying to get comfortable. Dry leaves in the wall behind me rustled as I brushed against them.

Had the whole sewing machine project been an empty charade? I tried not to think doubtful thoughts. But they played through my head as I squirmed. Neither tea shops nor sewing projects made sense to me, now that I had spent a few days in Waat. All Waat had to offer was what grew out of the ground—mostly the sorghum people ate year-round if warlords didn't burn it in the fighting. The women couldn't get fabric; tea leaves and sugar would have to be flown in on charters, three thousand a shot. There wasn't even one thing about these requests that was sustainable.

The deaconess had figured it out too. "Teach us English," she said.

I didn't want to say what Nyamal had taught me: *Caing bin nhok, it wouldn't please me.* But really, as much as I hated to admit it, it would not please me to stay in Waat. There was my family in Nairobi. There was the food—after only a week, I was already forcing myself to swallow the sorghum mash, full of grit that popped and crackled between my teeth. Faith was holding my silver-packed molars together. Bread, meat, vegetables and fruit would please me.

Every day in Waat, people like the old woman on the path had demanded my pen, my notebook, my clothes, my shoes, and my tent. And just as it would not have pleased me to give away my clothes, it also would not please me to be left, as the Sudanese are, with nothing for writing. I wanted my notebook. I wanted vocabulary lists.

I had always idealized the kind of personal hero who would be pleased to settle down in one small village and do one concrete thing to make a few people suffer less. But honestly, I was not that kind of person. If I lived in Waat, every night I would lie awake and stare at the darkness gathered in the conical top of my thatched *tukel*, worrying about all the other women in all the other villages in all those vast plains. Teaching in Waat wouldn't be enough, any more than teaching in Addis Ababa had satisfied that big drive to make things better.

But trying to do enough might also be a mistake, like listening to the voices of malevolent spirits In Africa, listening to voices that lead to despair. When I was a child, missionaries had started a leprosarium in Addis Ababa. They taught handiwork skills to those who had been maimed by the disease, and they treated active cases. They built some housing. Then a young volunteer came and found that many of the lepers still slept on the streets or in the cemeteries, under the sheets of corrugated iron people laid down to shelter the graves of their dead. He ranted at the older missionaries because people were still suffering.

He worked for two years to completely end the suffering of the lepers. Then one day he killed himself.

Working in Africa meant working out ways to survive partial answers and the despair of not-enough. All I wanted at that moment in the sorghum lean-to in Waat—the best I could hope for—was some way to say *I'm sorry*. Guy Lual had taught me that in Nuer, *I'm sorry*, like *please* and *thank you*, had to come from my tone of voice.

"I have spoken to teacher Nyang," I said. I stroked the mat I was sitting on, a gray food bag. Some woman had picked through a strand of the plastic and hemmed it. "He knows a literacy teacher. I will send materials." It sounded like a lame offer. I hoped *I'm sorry* was clear in the way I said it.

The deaconess pounded on her knee. "When I was a girl, my brothers went to school," she said. "My father said, 'Why does a girl need an education?' After my husband paid the bride price, I bore him three daughters and two sons. Now I know that my father was wrong. I would give up everything for an education."

Guy Lual covered a smile with four fingers. The lean-to rustled as all the women, including me, shifted, taking in such an outburst. A Nuer woman doesn't have anything to give up. She's a beast of burden who farms and cooks and bears children—daughters to bring her husband cattle wealth and sons to bring him immortality. By age eight, Nuer boys can chant their fathers' names back fifteen generations, because a man lives on as long as someone remembers his name. So, who was she kidding?

Her voice quieted. "I would give up my husband."

Beside her, a young woman in a plaid blouse and floral skirt fell over sideways, giggling. The deaconess just looked at me; intense feelings crinkled her black eyes; gray and black twists of hair fluffed out of her loose braids. Even in the sweaty heat her hand was dry as paper on my arm. "I would give up my children. To learn English."

"When peace comes..." I said. I squeezed her hand.

We could talk about development, but really, what did it mean without peace? Only with peace would South Sudan have a currency again. Trade. Fabric. Tea leaves. Schools.

I cleared my throat, but it was closing. I could barely whisper. "When peace comes, even old women will learn English."

Guy Lual and the women clicked agreement in the backs of their throats. That was the moment South Sudan told me it was going to give me what I'd wished for, and what I'd wished for would be more than I could bear. A puff of hot air blew dust through the sorghum stalk wall.

CHAPTER 6

One morning, Nyamal asked me with sign language if she could untie my lavender and aqua bandana. She and her middle sister giggled, tugging their fingers along my scalp to part my hair in rows. I'm sure they had never touched hair like mine before, straight and fine and the color of sorghum stalks. As they braided it, I pointed and recited the colors:

Toich, all the shades of green and blue and turquoise and aqua.

Mi buoi, white, like the ceremonial sacrificial bull.

Mi sharr, black like the color of the cotton soil of Sudan, which cracks in the dry season and holds water like a cotton ball in the rains and grows the *toich* for the cattle.

Mi kuach, mottled like the crocodile and a favorite cow hide pattern. Everything in South Sudan comes back to the cattle.

The youngest sister, maybe six years old, watched us with her runny-nosed brother on her hip. They were a mismatched pair, like a cuckoo and a chickadee—his arms and legs chubby, his baby head still big for his body, and her little girl body thin.

The warm sunshine and the children's fascination with my hair lulled me. I closed my eyes.

When my young Sudanese hairdressers finished and let go of my cornrows, they immediately started to unravel. The girls laughed, surprised at hair that doesn't wrap around itself and stay where it's put. With their fingers, they combed the last of the braids back out. Nyamal's soft touch tied the scarf back around my head.

After our rice and lentils lunch, the pastoral assistant's wife recited the Lord's Prayer in Nuer for me. *"Guaara mi te nhial,"* she said. I wrote it down: *Our Father who is in the sky.* But then, *Your Kingdom come on the ground as it is in the sky* went so fast I couldn't keep up.

I played her voice back on my recorder. She laughed and turned her face to her shoulder, her hand over the blank spot where her bottom front teeth had been pried out at puberty.

Next, I labored to write the words of the Apostles' Creed. I stumbled when I tried to read them back. She laid her calloused palm on my leg. *"An Ngatha yie Kuoth,"* she said more slowly, for me. *I believe in the Maker.* The maker of the sky and the ground.

What does that Maker believe about South Sudan? I wondered. I sat with my pen still.

The assistant's wife picked up her flat basket and went back to cleaning the lentils. We sat together in the quiet afternoon heat and thought our own thoughts, in our own languages.

Five years earlier, when the Nuers mutinied against Commander John Garang, the Sudanese Peoples' Liberation Army retaliated by firing grenades and mortar shells on the UN feeding center and clinic in Waat. Over fifteen hundred people burned alive.

A crime of passion, because both the Dinka and Nuer creation stories tell how their forefathers were brothers, born of the same father. For centuries the brothers herded cattle and carried spears on the wide plains of South Sudan. Like siblings, they often fought. They raided cattle. Smaller tribes stayed out of their way. The Dinkas, like a bigger, older brother, had grown to be more in number. The Nuers, like the scrappy younger, were fiercer. That gave them a precarious balance for sharing fishing spots and grazing land all over South Sudan. But in the days of the spear, a warrior would have been ashamed to kill an elder, a woman, or a child. If he did kill another man, it was face to face, and a Man of the Cow performed a ceremony to cancel the blood debt owed to God and the earth for taking a life.

The Government of Sudan fomented the south-south fighting

by supplying both the Nuer mutineers and the mostly Dinka army with guns. As an Arab proverb says, *Use a slave to kill the slave.*

The Nuers, meanwhile, named the bullet, *To Whom it May Concern.* With a gun, a man could cause death anonymously. Blood debt piled up, and no one knew who owed it.

After the mutiny, a Nuer prophet revived (or invented) a prophecy that Sudan would be delivered by an unscarred man. All over Nuer land, the word of this prophecy spread. Commander Riek Machar Teny Dhurgon had not been scarred as a young man, so Nuers flocked to support him, the *bull-boy* with his smooth forehead. No doubt their belief in this prophecy was also spiced by dreams of looting Dinka cattle and women.

The prophet himself recruited a militia to support Riek Machar. *White is a holy color*, the prophet told the men and boys. *White will protect you from bullets.* Fresh from villages and cattle camps, they believed him. They called themselves *Jiech Mabor*, the White Army. They slathered their bodies with white ashes, dressed in white sheets tied over one shoulder, and lost their fear of *To Whom it May Concern.*

The *Jiech Mabor* joined Commander Riek Machar's militias. The Nuers, in traditional age-set units, marched south toward the Dinkas looking more like a mob than an army. They chanted war songs. When they got to the village of Bor, they attacked in waves like madmen, shouting, "You Dinkas! Drink your own blood!"

The Nuers shot men, women, children, and whatever Dinka cattle they couldn't herd away. But in evil times, evil compounds, and the Dinka cattle were infected with a bovine plague called Rinderpest, which spread in the Nuer herds until, like all plagues, it wiped out its own host and subsided. A Nilotic Wall Street disaster.

Waat, the village of a thousand huts, became Commander Riek Machar's headquarters and one corner of what the UN called the Hunger Triangle. The population swelled to fifteen thousand, as Dinka refugees flooded in. It shocked me when I learned this, that the Dinkas, under attack by the Nuers, fled to Nuer villages. But it made a certain grim sense, like a boxer who hugs his rival to stop a pounding. There was nowhere else the elderly, the women, the children could run away from the maddened Nuer militias. No Dinka village was safe, only Nuer villages would be spared. I needed superimposed transparent pages with red, green, and yellow arrows sweeping around each other to understand where the ants had scattered when the elephants fought.

Besides the cattle lost, a season's harvest was burned in the fighting. Operation Lifeline Sudan airdropped food to Waat, but it wasn't enough. The Waat of 1992, as the rainy season began, surged and moaned with suffering. Hyenas and vultures fed on corpses around the edges of the village. The air grew thick with the smell of death.

Now, five years later, the town still sat almost empty. All that destruction, still on display. But political conversations in Watt were abuzz with hope, because of Riek Machar's peace treaty. Hope for peace. Hope, like Nyang's, for rebuilding.

Commander Riek Machar was a Presbyterian. I later met him at a donor meeting. His round, unscarred face glowed, and his hope, his belief in the peace treaty, reflected off the faces of everyone around the tables: Nuer church leaders, European and US church donors, and the bodyguards flanking him. When I shook hands with him, he gave me a guileless smile and leaned in to catch my name.

"Do you think he's for real?" I asked Mark on the way home. Commander John Garang mocked Machar's peace treaty, and said only a fool would trust a treaty with the perfidious Arabs.

I couldn't read anything on Machar's face. It turns out you have to learn the body language of another culture, not just the words. When it came to politics, even church politics, Mark and I were worse than illiterate in Nuer culture.

More people had been killed by fighting between the Dinkas under John Garang and the Nuers under Riek Machar than in thirty years of attack from the armies and bombs of Khartoum. The UN called the Sudan a chronic complex humanitarian crisis. Even if the war did end, there had been so many elephants in this fight, the ants had scattered so far, trying to reach safety, most of them would never return.

And even at peace, life in Waat was infinitely fragile. That year had been a dry one, the harvest skimpy. With four months until the next harvest, families in Waat were already walking three days to other settlements to find relatives with surplus sorghum. The only net of safety a Nuer has is family. Elder Guy Lual told me this, and told me a young man whose relatives starved during a famine would have trouble finding a wife—no one would let their daughter marry into a family whose members did not care for each other in hunger times.

Supper tasted hearty. Bits of the grinding stone popped between my teeth. Anthropologists look for flat molars in craniums to know when people began growing and stone-grinding grain. I tried chewing without bringing my molars completely together. Maybe that way I could save my teeth. Maybe the bits of stone would aid my digestion like pebbles in the gizzard of a chicken.

The assistant's wife coughed all that night. It sounded like she had some kind of bronchial infection. In the morning, she patted the mat beside her, and called one of the boys over to translate. "Give me medicine." *Please* was in her eyes.

My shoulders tensed. I spread my hands. All I had was aspirin. "I am a teacher. I have no medicine." Would her natural resistance be strong enough?

She watched my face as the boy translated, then nodded and picked at a loose strand of her World Food Program mat. "You should stay here until they return from the *toich, the green,* with the cattle," she said. She smiled. "My daughter is with them."

It took me a second to make the jump from her cough to the cattle. She had asked me for something. Now, even though I had nothing to give, she was offering me what she had—community.

Sometimes Americans suggest that it's African fatalism that keeps them in poverty—they should just try harder. We want to believe in the Enlightenment myths of individualism. We don't want to look at how global policies favor us. We are uneasy if we think people accept their oppression; we want them to fight it. But maybe what we call fatalism is a gracious acceptance of fate, or luck, or something more deeply true than our myths of personal power over our circumstances. What if she had learned the secret of peace of mind? Maybe her calm acceptance of circumstances allowed her to be generous about the differences between my lucky chances and hers.

She wasn't dwelling on how unfair it was that I couldn't give her my right to fly out to Nairobi for medicine if I got sick. I was the only one doing that. I stretched to accept her offering, to be equally big-hearted in spite of wanting so much to be of use, and feeling, instead, again, utterly useless.

"How old is your daughter?" I asked.

"She is two years. She went with her cousin. They will feed her milk. When the rains start, she will come home fat and ready to accept the new one. All our young people will come. With drums and singing." She touched my knee. The boy who was translating smiled. "You should stay. We will run to meet them on the road. All our young people and our cattle. We will dance. Our village will come alive again."

I would have liked to see youth and love and dancing in this barren land. Maybe I would see the true reach of the human spirit, and how it is that people can survive on the very edge of existence. Maybe I would see beyond what people in Watt lacked, to how they found joy even in deprivation.

CHAPTER 7

Five days before the charter was due back, Guy Lual blew noisily across his glass of tea at supper and said, "Thirteen people were wounded in a cattle raid three days to the south. People are carrying them to Waat. They heard we have a charter. They hope we can take them to the hospital in Loki. Without clearance from the Red Cross, the pilots aren't supposed to bring people in. But sometimes they do. Do you want to see these people when they come?"

"They'll think I'm a doctor," I said. They'd be so hopeful when they saw my white face, so disappointed to find I'm only a teacher. A teacher who wouldn't even stay and teach. I didn't think I could bear to be revealed as that useless. But surely this gave me *something* I could do. "Let's call ahead by radio and get clearance."

Guy Lual slowly sipped the tea. "We can try," he finally said. He waved one of the teenage boys over and spoke in those tones that were beginning to feel familiar, those words I still didn't know.

The hospital sat in the UN camp in Lokichoggio, in the land of dust devils, gravel, and 105-degree weather, where the white Toyotas with rusty dents and cracked windshields drove back and forth to the tarmac past the Turkana people's low domed huts the color of the desert. Blue UN flag snapped above the compound gate. I knew that a messenger would run from the radio room to the Red Cross office with our request. He might sit there all day on a dusty bench waiting to talk to someone with the authority to decide. But I was determined. I was a master at using will-power to make things work out.

Sorghum grit snapped between my teeth like tiny electric shocks. The closer I came to leaving, the more I hated sorghum as a most-days menu.

The next evening I asked, "Have they gotten through on the radio?" I concentrated on Guy Lual's face and forced myself to swallow the daily sorghum I should have been thankful for.

He nodded but didn't meet my eyes.

We were supposed to have gotten to Waat and back out before the rainy season started, but that afternoon as we sat around in the compound—Guy Lual mentoring the young men who gathered around him, me murmuring the Apostle's Creed in Nuer—clouds piled up in the sky, heap upon heap of gray. The men watched as they talked, frown wrinkles multiplying the ridges on their foreheads. The temperature cooled.

As the sun set, the serving boys brought us our evening tea—scalding hot, dark as American coffee, sweet as syrup. Guy Lual pointed up to the gray and black sky with his chin. "Monkey told greedy Uncle Hyena that the white clouds are delicious billows of fat." The young men who'd stayed for supper sat forward, grinning. Guy Lual spoke in a storyteller sing-song. "So Uncle Hyena told Eagle to take him up. When he got close to a cloud, greedy Uncle Hyena let go of Eagle to grab the fat. He fell down to earth into a puddle. He sank so deep into the mud he couldn't move. Monkey refused to pull him out until greedy Uncle Hyena promised not to hurt him."

Everyone laughed. Then we fell silent. We thought our own thoughts about the weather and cradled our hot cups as the sky turned dark. It was those puddles of mud we were worried about.

I realized that we had been seeing the Hale-Bopp comet crossing in a flat arc over the sorghum stalk fence early every evening. "You see that?" I asked. "It's called a comet. It's a special kind of star."

The Nuers clicked in the back of their throats at the marvels of the universe and that I knew so much. One of the young men asked me about President Kennedy. He hadn't known whether to believe what he'd heard, that a president was assassinated once, even in America.

"And what is the meaning of this?" another said, holding up a water bottle. "One dot five liters."

"It's another way to say one and a half," I said.

"Such a simple thing, one and a half." His voice sounded cross but I couldn't see his face in the dark. "Why do they make it difficult?"

I opened my mouth to explain the decimal system, but thought better of it.

After lunch the next day, the clouds moved in. A wind whipped up. Dust blew into the crease of my notebook. The pages flipped shut. The hem of my skirt snapped against my legs. The girls ran to the cooking hut like chaff whirling up in the wind that comes before a storm. They bundled up their mat and carried the pots inside.

"Come in here with us," Guy Lual said.

I zipped my tent and joined the men in the pastor's dim hut, which still radiated the morning sun's heat through mud adobe walls and thatch. Lightning flashed white on the edge of my vision. I counted—thunder three miles away. Rain began. It wasn't long before it was pelting the thatch, rustling above us and splashing on the ground outside. When I stooped to look out the door, the wind was pushing at the dome of my tent, knocking it back and forth. I sat back down and listened to my woofing tent fight to stay upright, pulling against pegs I had pounded into dust on a hot, clear day.

The wind finally quieted, and the rain shifted to a steady downpour. I waded barefoot out to my tent. I had pitched it in a hollow, and now rainwater was seeping up through the bottom. I threw clothes that were not yet wet into my bag and folded the edges of my sheet up onto my camp mat, which fortunately lay on a slight rise at the back.

That evening, the bathing enclosure smelled of mud, old soap, and wet sorghum stalks. Ants, flooded out of their tunnels, swarmed up over the plywood and milled around on one end. The air was chilly and the cold water shocked my skin. I kept my eye on the ants while I soaped down. I rinsed off by cupfuls. I washed my feet, but there was nowhere to put them except back into my muddy sandals.

Just before dark, Pastor Simon came to my tent with a red and blue quilt over his arm. The young boys behind him lugged an old metal bed, made of angle iron and rusty springs, like a decrepit version of the beds I'd slept in as a child in Maji. Mud bulged up around the edges of the UN plywood the boys laid down under the legs of the bed.

In the dark, I prayed for UN clearance. Surely the Maker would agree with me and would want to make a way for the gun-shot patients to get medical help. The tent just cleared my face and my feet. The air smelled of dank mud. I started awake in the night, gasping to pull oxygen out of one hundred percent humidity.

In the next morning's bright sunlight, I draped my damp bedding on the sorghum fence to dry. *We'll be fine*, I told myself. There were still two days for the sun to dry the airstrip.

Over rice, lentils and sweet, hot tea at noon, we prayed for peace, for God's blessing on the food, and for sunshine. But as we ate, the clouds blew in again. When I felt the first drops of rain, I ran all my bedding and clothes into the still, warm air of the hut. The sky dumped sheets of water on us. The whole world turned gray. *Jiom* tried once more to flatten my tent, and now the bed's angles appeared and disappeared under rippling burgundy nylon.

The next morning, I threw my quilt over the fence again to dry. This time, the sorghum stalks fell silently, like sodden dominoes.

Guy Lual and I walked out to look at the airstrip. The cotton soil of South Sudan, dark as the skin of the Nuer people and full of deep cracks when it is dry, swells in the rain and doesn't drain. Huge puddles on the airstrip shone silver, reflecting the gray sky.

"We must pray for sunshine," Guy Lual said.

"Any word from Red Cross?" I asked. He stared at the sky and didn't answer. I prayed a litany all the way back to our compound. Or maybe I just abjectly begged.

It rained again that afternoon. Guy Lual stretched out on the hand-hewn bed with its rawhide strapping. He stared up at the red and orange cloth that was hung above the bed to catch bits of thatch and termite droppings. I sat in the square of light coming through the low doorway fringed with dripping thatch. I whispered the Lord's prayer in Nuer. Our *Guaara*, who art in *nhial*. *Stop the rain.*

Spray blew in on my ankles and with it, tiny dots of mud that stuck and dried.

The day the charter was to come for us, even the morning sky looked bruised and dark. In our breakfast tea, sugar sat half an inch thick on the bottom of our glasses.

"The sugar is now finished," Pastor Simon said. He blew loudly across the amber surface of his tea. That final, extra teaspoon of sugar would make our last sip sweeter than honey. That was the Nuer way, not to parse things out, drinking our tea slightly bitter to make the sugar last, but finishing with a flourish.

For lunch we ate sorghum with lentils. The rice was also gone.

A boy ran in from the radio office to tell us that the charter had landed in Akobo. It would arrive in Waat in an hour and a half.

As we exited through the collapsing fence, we joined a stream of people heading to the airstrip for the afternoon's event. A boy took my duffle. My wadded up clothes and sheet were stuffed in with the wet tent.

The *canoe of the* sky showed up right on time, tiny as a mosquito at first. I couldn't take my eyes off the black silhouette as it grew. The lowering clouds looked ready to dump our afternoon deluge, and puddles from the day before still stretched silver across the airstrip. Unlandable. That's the UN term for South Sudan airstrips in rainy season.

The crowd of about a hundred people, the whole dry season population left in Waat and me, smelled of sorghum-stalk smoke and sweat. I rested my right hand on Nyamal's shoulder and her sisters fought over the fingers of my left. Guy Lual tipped his head back and his eyes followed the plane descending toward the other end of the airstrip.

"Will he try?" I asked. The adventure junkie in my mind was yammering: what a story that would be, months and months in South Sudan, I'd come out fluent in Nuer. Thin as a rail. I imagined sleeping in my tent through the rains. Would I have as much resistance to infection as the pastoral assistant's wife, whose cough was clearing up?

I was instantly ashamed of my thoughts. The definition of adventure was that it be finite, that it all work out. For these girls, for Pastor Simon's family, Waat was not adventure. They had another rainy season to survive.

And I had a family. A husband who would miss me. Boys who needed a mother. How ambivalent was I really about those roles? Wife. Mother. Something must be wrong with me, that I would even have that thought about staying in Waat.

Worst of all, two more mouths to feed would decimate the pastor's skimpy food stores. We really needed to not get stuck in Waat.

The C-47 continued to drop. Surely the pilot could see the water by now. Surely he would pull up and leave us there.

The plane touched land. It bounced and hit a puddle. Sheets of water flew over the wings, over the propellers, over the windows. The plane shimmied to the left. It straightened out and slowed, as it came to us, sinking deeper, pushing up a wave of solid black mud.

The plane oozed to a stop and loomed above us. Everyone shouted in one voice. We ran to it: women with babies on their backs; naked children; people wearing new used clothes; people wearing UN blankets tied over their left shoulders; and me, girls skipping barefoot in the mud on either side, my dirty hair covered by the turquoise and purple bandana.

The pilot climbed down and walked off the airstrip. He stood, hands on his hips, watching the crowd. South Sudan bush pilots were cowboy kings. They liked danger and hardship pay. Some of them might have come to Sudan because they cared about human suffering, but soon enough, they all got hardened by flying in and back out again day after day, leaving suffering people behind. Watching him, my emotions knotted up: appreciation that he had taken the risk and landed, envy at his dispassionate calm.

My first glimpse of the mechanic was of tan hairy legs in brown work boots. As he came around the plane I saw the rest of his legs, bare up to the edge of his khaki shirt.

"Get shovels," he said, and five tall, blue-black young men looked at each other, as if to ask, *He doesn't know Waat was burned to the ground five years ago?* Then they went to work with their hands, pulling chunks of mud away from around the wheels.

The mechanic shouted about the shovels again. He waved his arms, and his shirt lifted up for a view of pale upper thighs and nylon leopard-spotted briefs. I blinked quickly, hoping he didn't see me looking. But he came over. "I don't usually dress this way. It was wet in Akobo. I took off my jeans to dry. Do you have a cigarette?"

I almost laughed at his embarrassment, but annoyance followed too quickly. What was he doing, in from Kenya, asking me for anything? *Chiang bin nhok*—it would not please me! "We've been here two weeks," I said. "We don't have any more rice, we don't have sugar. Why would I have a cigarette?" I took a deep breath and scraped a splat of mud off my leg. "Some of the older men have local tobacco. They might trade you for something."

"That would do." He looked around speculatively. Nuer youth were still scrabbling with their hands in the heavy mud around the big nose wheel. Thunder rumbled. Then, nearby, the adrenaline-jolting crack of gunfire.

"Oh my god," he shouted. "Why didn't you tell me there's insecurity? We've got to push!"

"That's the only—" I started, but he was gone.

CHAPTER 8

The mechanic waved his muddy crew to one side of the plane. As I ran to join them, Guy Lual, jogging beside me said, "Don't worry. The soldiers shot a mad dog."

Mad dogs, wet tents, gritty food. My last wish for adventure in Waat dissipated. I was finished. Mud squeezed over the soles of my sandals, between my toes, and under the buckle.

The girls wiggled into spots beside me on the tail fin. We leaned our bodies into pushing. The mechanic shouted. Aluminum bit into my palms. My pulse beat in my neck and temples. My ears roared. The crowd shouted.

Slowly, slowly, the small back wheel turned. Slowly we rotated the plane. We pushed that huge beast around until it could roll back out the ramp of mud it had carved going in.

I panted from the effort. Beside me, Guy Lual stretched his back. "The pilot says he has weight allowance for nine of the patients," he said.

I shouted over the noise of the crowd. "Only nine?"

He didn't answer, just called something in Nuer to the group of patients and their caretakers, waiting in the shade of an acacia tree. People flooded over to help.

Someone needed to triage. But Guy Lual stood aside, watching as able-bodied men lurched toward the plane under the weight of the patients. The pilot was climbing the ladder to the cockpit. Was anyone in charge?

Anthropologists call Nuer culture *acephalous*, a headless culture. *The One and The Many*, the Nuers say. During peace, every man is his own king and they are The Many. But when a family or a clan or the tribe is threatened, The Many choose a leader and become The One. That's part of what makes them so fierce. But it also makes for massive chaos. They will only accept a leader they choose by consensus. With clouds threatening above and mud sucking at the airplane's wheels below, The *Many* in Waat had no time to become *One*. I wanted so badly for this one good thing to happen, but I was completely outside the culture, outside the language, outside any chain of command.

The mechanic waved his arm—all-aboard. I, the one American, was carried toward the plane in the crowd, as if riding the tide to shore.

Guy Lual pulled me up the three aluminum steps. Muddy hands at the edges of a basket lifted a wounded child onto the floor beside me. His head was wrapped with dingy gauze, his eyes were closed. I could have touched my finger to my thumb around his knee.

A woman had been lifted up onto the aluminum floor as well, her arm and chest wrapped. She slumped, breathing hard. Below me, a sea of bodies engulfed the plane. Voices ricocheted off the aluminum. My ears rang. Two men hoisted up a pole with a blanket tied to both ends to make a sling for the body they carried. A foot protruded from one end, one thin layer of skin covering bones.

The mechanic shouted. "Nine! Only nine!"

No one was listening. Behind me, Guy Lual's voice rose above the rest but no one listened to him, either. I looked once more at the chaos, the milling heads below the aluminum floor, the wounded, sprawled on the floor of the plane in blood-clotted bandages. To the Nuers, the randomness of this chaos-equals-fate must seem more fair than someone choosing who should go. They would turn on the one who chose. They would accuse him. They would fight. Not even Guy Lual wanted that responsibility. So, like the mystical Pool of Bethsaida in Jesus' time, he who moved first into the waters would be healed.

I walked up the inclined floor to half a row of seats that had been bolted near the front. The window felt cold against my forehead.

Thirteen patients and nine spaces and no one in charge was not something God had asked me to do anything about. I had wanted to learn in Waat what I could do to help. I had learned instead how much I couldn't do.

I couldn't take guns away from all those young boys and give them bicycles. I couldn't teach the women English. It hadn't come clear to me what this new job of mine could do to relieve the suffering of Sudanese women, but on this trip for sure, what I could do, I'd done. I had lived with the Sudanese. I'd eaten their sorghum and they'd eaten my lentils and rice. Together we'd enjoyed the luxuries of salt, sugar, tea. I'd laughed and talked with them. I'd learned a few words of their language.

The seat beside me shuddered under Guy Lual's weight. The air that followed him from the other end of the plane roiled my stomach—the smell of death. I pulled my sweater over my face. Guy Lual held a hand over his nose. His arm in the tan suit coat pointed back at the body in the blanket sling. I half stood to see.

"Guinea worm," he said. "Gangrene." His voice came muffled, through his hand. "Someone put him on. For the hospital."

A dying man had been sneaked on? Not one of the wounded? Anger surged up in me. I was spinning back into thinking someone should sort out who should be on the plane and how to make it happen. But what did I know, and who'd asked me to judge whether someone dying of guinea worm deserved a space less than someone wounded in a cattle raid? The complexities of South Sudan collided in my aching head with the desire to organize things for the best outcome. My stomach curdled at the smell.

I knew about guinea worm. The larvae were big enough to be filtered out of drinking water with a simple piece of fabric; all over Loki young people wore President Carter's *Eradicate Guinea Worm* campaign t-shirts. If the larvae weren't filtered out, they hatched in people's intestines and made their way into muscle tissue. Then they burrowed their way out, centimeter by centimeter.

I'd heard that the pain was excruciating, but if you got impatient and pulled, the worm would break off and rot in your flesh. That school attendance went to about thirty percent during guinea worm season. That children sat at home in pain, waiting for the worms to inch out, rolling them up carefully on sticks.

The light darkened. As I sat in a pool of anguish over the dying man, the mechanic ground the doors shut, metal on metal, behind me. Out on the muddy airstrip, people were carrying five unlucky patients back away from the plane. My little friends, in tall brown grass at the edge of the airstrip, jumped and waved when they saw my face looking out. I waved back, one hand over my nose.

The propellers revved.

Then they whined to a stop. The mechanic burst out of the cockpit and ran down the sloping floor to the back. Aluminum shrieked again as he opened the door. The light brightened. I pulled in shallow breaths through my mouth, through my sweater. I gulped down saliva. I sat firm. If I sat still enough, we'd go.

I couldn't eat one more bite of sorghum. I couldn't sleep one more night in my tent, now rolled up and sticky-damp in my duffle. I suddenly felt desperate to get back to my life, to Mark. To Jesse and Kenny. I wanted to see Miriam again, my firecracker daughter, now in college at the University of Portland. I wanted my Persian rug. My rose-and-navy quilt.

Below me on the ground, the pilot ran toward the side of the airstrip. His shoulders heaved and he rested his hands on his knees. His head hung loose from his neck. He shook it three times.

The mechanic walked by, on his way back to the cockpit. "Our friend had a birthday," he said, beside my shoulder. "We all got a little soused."

I didn't look up, just watched out the window as our hung-over cowboy vomited again. But sitting put wasn't going to get us out of Waat after all. When I stepped out the door, onto the plane's aluminum ladder, fresh air felt clean and light in my lungs. Nyamal and her sisters clustered around me before I even touched the ground, three girls pushing each other to hold two white hands.

The mechanic checked on the pilot again, then came to Guy Lual and stood with his hairy legs astride, his hands on his hips. "That smell. The pilot can't fly with it. The patients have to come off." He looked away. The slightest defensive note sounded in his voice. "We don't have clearance from Red Cross."

"Take the old man off," I said, "Let the rest go." But neither of the men said anything. Guy Lual walked heavy and slow, the translator of bad news, over to the medic.

Like a dream with the sound off, people gathered around the plane again. As if everyone knew it had been too good to be true. Men climbed up the ladder and lifted the patients out into other waiting hands. No one spoke. The child in the basket lay as still as the water in the basin on Nyamal's head at the well.

The plane sat empty. *"Insha Allah,"* Guy Lual's voice said beside me. The unsearchable will of God. Thunder rumbled closer. The pilot climbed back into the cockpit. The crowd watched.

"Load up, load up," the mechanic shouted to Guy Lual and me.

The plane had smelled of fuel and oil, and dust from a thousand trips into the bush. Now, it also smelled of rotted flesh. I'd flown to boarding school and back on C-47s like this one. They'd also reeked—of animals, sweating men, kerosene and untanned hides. I'd learned I wouldn't throw up if I lay my head on a sister's lap. I didn't care anymore that Guy Lual thought that I, as a guest and a woman, should have one of the seats I shook my head and lay down on the aluminum floor, pillowing my head on the damp duffle.

Pastor Simon had wanted me to keep the quilt he had brought me when the rain started, but at home I had sheets and blankets to spare. "Keep it here for me. When I come again, I will use it," I told him. What were the chances I would ever see Waat again? I had learned in Ethiopia that graciousness is more important than the facts. It was not a lie. It was not false hope. It was softening reality so we could bear it.

The plane roared. *Please, God.* My body rocked as the left, then the right wheel lurched out of the track. Muddy water struck the windows. The plane rattled and shook. Then it labored, and finally lifted into the air.

The plane creaked and dodged and bucked through storm clouds to Loki. My hipbone dug into cold aluminum. The hair on my arms and legs bristled up. I shivered and covered my eyes with hands crusty with dried mud. There were no airsick bags. If I vomited all I would have was the floor. Fortunately, I was good at willpower.

In the shower stall at the UN base camp, sun-warmed water poured over me. I stood enclosed by tin walls painted emerald green, under the gray disk of a shower head. The twist of a bent nail held the wooden door shut. The cement floor was slippery with soap residue. It felt shockingly, comfortingly civilized. I scrubbed soap all over my body and ran the dirt from Waat off. Brown shampoo lather slipped into the drain.

I would eat vegetables for supper in the UN mess hall. Someone would layer mangoes and slices of pineapple artistically over each other, yellow and orange, on the fruit buffet. I would have choices: meat and potatoes, maybe lasagna, maybe ratatouille.

It was going to be a tough spiritual discipline, to allow myself to enjoy it. To leave what I had seen in Waat to God. To be grateful for what I had and dodge guilt for the mystery of why I had it.

The water looked clean and pure pouring over me. I knew it wasn't, but I lifted my face and opened my mouth and let it run in, warm against my tongue.

From a nail by the door hung a broken mirror. I had been to Waat and back. I had lived for two weeks on rice and lentils and sorghum and tea. I had said *no*, and *I can't*, and *I'm sorry*, to almost everything people wanted from me. I had pushed a C-47 out of the mud and had left behind those patients who'd hoped for help. The world was so heartbreakingly unjust.

And my face looked just as I remembered it.

The pastoral assistant's wife seemed to hover behind me, *Shu puak?* she would have asked me.

Shi puak. I had bathed. And evening was coming.

I tried to pretend it was enough. But it wasn't. I hadn't done anything, really, in Waat.

CHAPTER 9

Presbyterian Church of Sudan claimed membership near one million, but in the middle of a civil war, how do you count? Sudanese had flowed into Kenya by the hundreds of thousands, fleeing the fighting. They were required by the UN to stay in refugee camps on the border. Since no one can tell Nuers what to do, people drifted back and forth from camps to the slums of Nairobi, always looking for some way to get to England, Australia, or the United States.

After the moderator of the Presbyterian Church of Sudan in the south made his way to Kenya, partner churches in the US and Europe set him up with enough money to rent a small office. They didn't foresee that soon any pastor who could get to Nairobi would be there in self-imposed exile, asking for a title, a desk, and a salary.

The pastors wrote heart-rending grant requests for the suffering in South Sudan. But did any of the money make its way out of Nairobi? There were no reports to suggest it did. And what about the Land Cruiser the Sudanese had asked for, to transport them around Nairobi? The donors had ponied up a grant, the money was gone, and there was no vehicle.

Church leaders needed Kenyan shillings to live in Nairobi. The membership in Sudan had no access to cash, and could barely feed their families. So the pastors in Nairobi depended for living expenses on the donors, who had absorbed the concept of the healthy Three-Self Church—self-led, self-supported, self-propagated—and wanted it for their sister church in South Sudan. These donors from Holland, Germany and the US now waved the three-self flag to excuse not wanting to pay ongoing, ever-expanding living expenses for other people's church leaders.

But the dynamics they'd set up undercut their own goals for the partnership. The prospect of money in Nairobi drew church leaders out of their misery in South Sudan and cut them off from their parishioners. It led them to spend all the money from grants, given for development in South Sudan, to support their families living in Nairobi. There was never any left over for travel or for interventions on the ground, a situation created by the best of intentions gone awry.

When the donors asked about results from the projects they'd given funds for, when they fussed and scolded and demanded reporting, the pastors had said, "We are only ignorant Africans. We need a financial advisor."

The donors fell for it. They brought in Mark to sort out the mess, as though reporting on earmarked grants was only a matter of setting up the books.

Mark was a careful, conservative man, with a giant sense of right and wrong. He hated to lose or waste anything. He straightened the nails he painstakingly pulled from old two-by-fours when we remodeled our house in Portland. He picked up bolts and washers from the street, where they'd tumbled off passing cars, and kept them, sorted in tin cans and baby food jars, because he knew they'd come in handy. He hung onto everything.

When we rafted the Zambezi, he fell in and a Teva was torn off one foot. He never forgave the river—one perfectly good sandal left behind, useless.

And even though Mark wanted to keep his life organized and under control, we'd been hit with chaos early in our marriage.

Mom and Dad, still in Ethiopia, wished us well. Mom sent me a dress she'd made out of fabric woven in the ornate geometric shapes Ethiopians use to border their festive shawls. But Mark's parents washed their hands of us—we'd been living in sin. What the lack of support from parents meant about our fragile emotional underpinnings was invisible to us at the time. We were young, in love, full of confidence that we could make of our lives whatever we could dream.

Hippie friends gathered with us, the women in long loose shifts, the men in wide bell-bottoms, for a wedding under a weeping willow tree.

In late August, we moved to Chicago, where I'd been hired to teach at-risk students in a Catholic girls' high school. I was pulled in to take the place of a dearly loved, Cat Stevens-singing, Siddhartha-reading teacher who had left without a word of farewell. An announcement was made; the girls' questions were evaded; we were still at the tail end of the Least said, Soonest mended era of David Copperfield's formidable aunt.

I became the teacher the girls loved to hate.

The tension built. In a student forum, they demanded I be fired. I left, shaking. My fellow teachers focused on the crisis. No one asked how I was doing. I couldn't settle my racing mind, night or day. I thought I might be having a nervous breakdown. I was afraid to tell anyone.

Mark moved us, after school let out, to southwest Minnesota, where he could pursue a farming dream. I spent six months as the hired hand's wife, alone in a farmhouse. The only bright spot in my life was a weekly visit to the Sioux Falls, South Dakota public library after I shopped for groceries. There, I discovered a new set of friends: Gloria Steinem. Kate Millet. Betty Friedan. Simone de Beauvoire. My new friends gave me stunning news: my world was stacked against me.

My life passed before my eyes: yes, I had been valedictorian of my boarding school class; yes, I'd scored the highest of high SAT scores; and yes, only the boys in my class were called in for college and career conversations. I was told, *Get a teaching certificate. A woman never knows.*

In the middle of a Minnesota farm summer, propped up against a huge floor pillow we'd gotten as a wedding gift, the power differential between men and women was revealed to me in a flash one day—all policemen are men. It was no doubt literally true in 1973.

Mark had been my ally in all my other forays against injustice. Now he thought I was attacking him. He was working from sun-up to dusk and his thin body had become tan and rock-muscled. He always washed up to his elbows for lunch, but the dust of the fields and the tractors clung to him, his shirt and jeans shed chaff around him at the table at lunch. All I had to do was feed him; in exchange he would work his guts out for us. And I wanted to talk about how unfair life was for women?

He had no idea how bored and unhappy we farm wives were in that rural corner of the state, tasked with nothing but cooking, laundry, and sweeping up around the table after a meal. Wiping our babies' noses, if we had babies.

On the farm is when it started, the times that Mark later described as our not being on the same side any more.

He's defending the indefensible, I thought.

In December, our one hundred-year-old farmhouse burned to the ground with everything we owned. I marvel that this was our story. A young couple, trying so hard, hit with so much, so early.

We limped back to Chicago in our 1964 Bug and bought an eight-bedroom Edwardian mansion with two other families, planning to make that poor Chicago neighborhood a better place.

I had marched in the Vietnam War protests. I had studied community organizing. The Old Testament prophet in me came out, longing for justice, railing against the rich and powerful as I emerged from the loneliness of the farm.

I insisted Mark take responsibility for his share of our meals, and he gave cooking a try. I knew what he was doing when he asked me again and again where we kept the garlic powder—this man who could always find a screw the right size when he needed it. His grown kids later laughed at their dad, who could refuse to accommodate someone else and still avoid conflict. They called him *passive-resistant*.

Evenings in Chicago, Mark and I played gin rummy and fought over the cards. There is no more telling sign of distress in a marriage than rage in a card game.

When it came to what we were demanding from the other—the unconditional love we'd never had—neither Mark nor I had a flicker of self-knowledge. It had only taken us two years to come apart. Not forever. And not as long as we both should live. None of us know, when we marry young, how many ways there are for two people, full of hope, to let each other down.

Mark's mother's anger had been hot and ferocious. It had incinerated Mark's attempts to stay safe. I understood that later. But in Chicago, as I flooded Mark with words, I would see the pain in his eyes, his helplessness to answer or defend himself, and I still couldn't stop. Mark protected himself the only way he knew how— by going silent, withdrawing love, attention, connection. I, who was famous in our family for what my sisters called an overdeveloped conscience, who followed after Dad in my passion about making the world a better place, who wanted to be an instrument of peace, instead found ways to make my husband feel deeply rejected.

Mark retreated to the alley behind our commune and spent his after-work time hanging out with the guy neighbors, working on our VW van. He swept the glass up after nights when gang flare-ups in the alley led to Molotov cocktail exchanges. Everyone who drove in and out of that alley knew his name. I had the social change rhetoric, but he had the simple relationships that could have led to organizing our neighborhood against gentrification. We should have been a great team. But we couldn't help Chicago make peace when we were at war with each other.

Feminist insights made me want to talk about power. The lessons I needed, such as how to love a good man like Mark and still stand on my own solid piece of earth, would come later, gradually, partially, over the decades.

That summer, I talked about organizing demonstrations to stop torture in Chile. I read and slept instead. I read and reread *The Golden Notebook* by my idol, Doris Lessing, as though her character could be my guide through the chaos. A woman whose life is falling apart keeps a notebook she calls *Signs of the Times*, where she collects dire headlines and news clippings.

My own best friend in Chicago was a divorcee who married her sister's ex-husband. The two other couples we lived with eventually split up. One of the men committed suicide. Everyone's life was messy. I admonished myself—*There is no reason you will be exempt from the marriage-crushing signs of the times*. I was ready to give up.

For my birthday, Mark framed two posters from the Ethiopian Tourism Organization to hang in our bedroom. He was conjuring Ethiopia, maybe, to hold back the flood of disappointment, disillusionment, despair.

Meanwhile, Ethiopia itself was veering leftward. Dad was turning mission compounds, schools and clinics over to Ethiopian church leaders, preparing to close the mission and leave his career. Mark and I made one last visit.

When we returned to Chicago, we both felt that all-too-familiar reverse culture shock in what should have been home. We turned to each other again, the only ones who understood how it felt to be so torn. Inexplicitly, Ethiopia had done the magic Mark had hoped for.

Dad turned off the last lights of the mission when all but a few Presbyterians had been expelled by the new Socialist Republic of Ethiopia. Mark and I caravanned to Portland, Oregon with my parents, our baby girl, and my two youngest siblings in a school bus and Volkswagen van.

We've left all that mess in Chicago, I thought. *We've made it through.* At our best, Mark and I were well-matched in so many ways: born and raised Presbyterian, with shared years in Ethiopia; responsible oldest children; hard workers, as though by Calvinistic DNA; frugal and careful with money; unshakably dedicated to the best for our children. We were also friends.

Mark listened and laughed at the stories of my adventures. He was a slow reader; I read novels aloud so we could discuss them. One summer, I retold *Watership Down*, evening by evening as I read it.

He told me about his fix-it adventures of the day over supper, asked my advice for remodeling projects, and took me to see the work of his hands. Our skills were different, but when we were at our best, we loved to peek into the life of a person so different from us.

A colleague of his once told me, "Mark has a daily quota of words. We can tell when you're traveling, because then he spends his words on us. When you're home, he saves them for you."

After we moved to Portland, Mark ventured again out of his shell. I committed myself to a new vow, to be the world's best model of a wife. Invisible to me at the time was the cultural wind I was responding to, especially strong in the church. Unsurprisingly, the patriarchal church and patriarchal organizations such as Focus on the Family loudly proclaimed that the Bible supported patriarchy. Anita Bryant had emerged as the spokeswoman for true womanhood. Male theologians began to write dire reports that American culture was unraveling because feminism was destroying appropriate male and female roles.

Feminism had felt like a fresh breeze of reality in my face until the personal and cultural backlash blew up like a grenade. I didn't have enough confidence to withstand the reproaches—*hostile, shrill, man-hating*—even as I resisted them in my mind. I told myself I had to make reasonable compromises for the sake of personal peace. For the sake of my daughter.

And did I know I was truly and unconditionally worthy of love? That was a question buried too deeply to ask. I retreated into malaise as I stopped teaching to raise Miriam and then Jesse. I babysat other children whose mothers were working for wages. I started doing all the cooking—but look, Mark cleaned up after supper! I thought I was still counter-cultural, shopping at a food co-op and second-hand stores, resisting consumerism and oppression. But when it came to my role as a woman, I had been cowed by the badgering of the church teaching "complementarianism"—what pleases God is men and women in their complimentary roles.

It is only now, almost fifty years later, that Beth Allison Barr, a church historian, the wife of a Baptist pastor, has studied the wave I was so resignedly carried along on. Her book, *The Making of Biblical Womanhood*, has become a best seller in the Christian publishing world. Even in that conservative milieu, it has a 4.76 rating out of 5 on Goodreads, and 94% five stars Amazon reviews. Its popularity suggests I wasn't the only woman who submitted but chaffed.

Mark started a remodeling business in Portland. I bit my tongue and said nothing when he spent day after day in his garage, unable to face going out to look for work. He wanted work to come to him, and it did, by word of mouth, but very slowly. Miriam qualified for free breakfast and lunch at school. Our healthcare cost was subsidized until President Reagan's punitive war on poverty cut us off. I qualified for WIC when I was pregnant with Kenny.

Later, we sometimes mused, looking back together over those sad, hard, early years. Mark said we wouldn't have had such a rough time if we had defied our parents and gone to the same college. We could have supported each other through the wrenching away of Ethiopia. That's how he wanted to rewrite our story.

I didn't want to rewrite anything. By the time I went to Waat, we had been married for twenty-three years, and though I could be a sucker for regret, I had none on this subject. If we rewrote even the smallest thing from the past, who knows—we might not even have stayed together. I found that thought unbearable. We'd been together so long that I didn't want to change anything. And what about our precious children? For me, musing over the phases of our relationship was comforting, like stroking the soft old pieces of favorite childhood dresses my grandmother worked into my patchwork quilt.

After the Chicago years, we never again fought about the

trip-wire issues of marriage—money, sex, children. We only fought about love. We asked each other only, *Can I trust you to love and respect me?* We'd hurt and betrayed each other in ways that would, when we felt enough stress, come whistling back like ghosts.

Home from Waat, for a couple of weeks my stomach hurt. If it was bacterial, why would it hit only after I got home? "I'm re-adjusting to oils and spices after weeks of sorghum," I told Mark. But I knew it was more emotional indigestion than physical.

The nagging questions I'd struggled with since childhood had come back full force; I'd done nothing to deserve this comfortable life. Why was I the one born in Allegheny General Hospital in Pittsburg, not in a hut in Waat? What did I owe the world for my privileges? With what currency could I pay? All around me, Ethiopians and Sudanese were ready to cheat, lie, or forge someone else's name just to get immigration papers *to* the States. Was it enough that I had left the promised land of the US to try to make things better here?

Not that anything looked like it was going to get better. Waat, as I got some distance on what I'd seen, was like cold water in the face. And while I was away, Mark had not only been lonely, but his frustration with the Nuer pastors had also built up. Frustration, nothing. He was feeling increasingly humiliated. The air in our house got heavier and heavier. Mark hardly ever smiled.

We should have found a coach right then and there. Someone to sit everyone down and warn us—the Sudanese pastors, Mark, and me. *All of you are volatile,* this wise mentor would have said. *The next few years are not going to go well unless you slow down. Be patient with each other! Show respect at every turn!*

But there was no one to warn us. We were all the wisdom we had.

And there was a particular grant that Mark was guarding with his life, his reputation. Balking at the Sudanese church's rising expense in Nairobi, donors had proposed the pastors move their offices and families to a smaller town to the north—less expensive;

still good schools; closer to Loki, where they had to go anyway to do their development work across the Sudan border. The donors had put together a grant to pay for their moving expenses. But the pastors hadn't moved.

On the Friday before the next donor meeting, Rev. X, the Presbyterian moderator, gave Mark a bank statement and told him to verify to the donors that the money was still safely in the bank, waiting for the move.

In the meeting, Rev. X reported: the pastors were organizing their families to move.

The donors turned to Mark, who nodded and held up the bank statement showing the moving grant still there in full.

The next week, Mark learned that when he left the office, statement in hand, Rev. X had run to the bank, withdrawn the money, and handed it out. The pastors rushed home and made one more overdue rent payment in Nairobi.

Mark's face looked gray and pinched as he told me. I couldn't remember the slightest hint of the moderator's lie on his round face and scarred forehead. For once I was so shocked, I had no hopeful, encouraging words for Mark. Surely it wasn't possible for our four-year assignment to crumble completely.

CHAPTER 10

Soon after the incident of the disappeared moving funds, I was working on a donor update when our laptop screen blinked and went blue. I had no patience for fidgeting, and digital fidgeting was the worst kind.

Mark was happy for an excuse not to go to the office. He got out all the manuals that we Boomers remember from those early PC days and spent the rest of the day doing his special fix-it voodoo. At supper he reported success. I was delighted. I thanked him. The day off seemed to have refreshed his mood. Looking back, studying us from these many years later, I see that his moods had become my atmosphere, because of course, I had already been that basket-ball teammate who'd fluffed plenty of of lay-ups that should have been easy. Shots I should not have taken.

When I went to my desk the next day, eager to wrap up the report, I found the many thick manuals open, piled on each other. Scraps of paper with Mark's penciled scribblings lay scattered all around, and neither the surface of the desk nor my report draft was anywhere to be seen.

"Mark, did you think the office fairies were going to clean up after you?" I said.

He'd often said, *You should have been a lawyer—you have a quick wit and a sharp tongue.*

In defense of my annoyed self that day, if it had been the car Mark had been fixing, he would have cleaned up his tools. In his world, the house was up to me and the fairies. Still, with Mark as unhappy as he was, it was a blurt I should have swallowed. And if I claim that I was sensitive to his moods, why *didn't* I bite my tongue? Anyone who's gotten caught in a relationship that requires tongue-biting knows how the best intentions to keep the peace can fall apart in a split second.

Mark was furious.

I backpedaled and apologized quickly. I appreciated the working computer. I said I was sorry. I said yes, I was wrong to criticize instead of thanking him. Neither of us thought of the fact that I had thanked him the night before. These are the hair-splittingly sensitive moments of justice or injustice that happen in a marriage, when pain and panic flood us and we can't sort them out.

Mark didn't speak. He didn't look at me. He left for the office shooting angry sparks out every pore. He came home from work in the same storm of anger. Supper was a grim affair for me. The boys, thankfully, filled the silence with chatter about school, then ran off to do homework and build Legos.

Mark was not one to see that both of us made our contribution to a tense moment. His mom had been a blame-machine, and he had learned well. He never, ever made the first attempt to reconcile. I always did, and usually before he was ready.

He, who usually fell asleep when his head hit the pillow, lay cold and stiff as rebar beside me that night, as I suffered in anxious loneliness until I was finally tired enough to sleep.

In high school, after the most furious fight I ever had with a sister, I'd sadly told Mark the story. I was carrying a huge load of guilt for my rage, with no perspective on the appropriate level of remorse I should be feeling. What I needed was someone to remind me that no one is their best self all the time, and that families are where we most easily become that worser self. But I didn't have that perspective. I had decided I was just be too hard to live with.

It was one of those events when a crack in the crust of my earth opened up and, if I had known what I was looking at, I could have seen how deeply I believed I had to behave myself into deserving love.

"Maybe I should never marry," I confessed to Mark.

He was not the person to turn to, never having seen unconditional love himself. He said, "Yeah, maybe you shouldn't."

I suppose when he married me anyway we both believed—as we all do until we learn better—that love would exempt us from the messy parts of the other's human self. In Kenya, all those years later, we had already learned how fallible we both were. We had survived that awakening. This rift would also pass.

But Mark wouldn't look at me the next morning. We each spoke only to Jesse and Kenny over breakfast. Mark drove them to meet the Rosslyn school bus. When he came home, he poured himself another cup of coffee and sat down at the end of the table.

"I'm done," he said. "In Chicago, I gave up ever making you happy. Now I see it's true."

Self-blame rose up from that crevasse like an icy blast. Adrenalin ran up from my ankles and across my shoulders. Maybe I really was too hard to live with. Maybe I shouldn't have married.

Mark went on: I had always been critical; I had never really loved him; I'd only ever liked him for what he could do for me. And worst of all, *You don't respect me any more than the Nuers do.* Given how harsh his mother had been, given that she targeted him and excused his brothers, respect was life itself to Mark.

Like South Sudan—after years of conflict, years of so-called peace—our marriage now lurched along. Mark silently ate the meals I cooked. He trudged to the office, the hopeless drawer full of receipts, the run-arounds. We each related to the boys, keeping their raft afloat. Mark was so often silent anyway, they may not have realized anything was wrong. And Mark and I suffered through nights in parallel exile on the far edges of our bed, not touching.

My heart ached for us—would we have to bail and go back to the States? My heart ached for our boys. How could we rip them up for a third move in two years? We couldn't. Kenny had struggled in school in Ethiopia with a classroom that weirdly had thirteen girls and three boys. Now he had a best friend. He loved his teacher.

Jesse had made it onto the varsity soccer team as a freshman. We had to stay and see this four-year assignment through.

I felt too guilty to ache for myself. I only thought, *How could you have made the problem worse?*

But I still hoped the storm would pass. How could it not? It was 1996, almost twenty years from the time of despair in Chicago. Doesn't grace hold, once it kicks in? Peace would taste so sweet when it broke out again.

Several weeks later, Mark packed up for a trip to Ethiopia for three weeks. I think we both hoped his time away would take the pressure off, warm the personal ice age we'd dropped into.

We'd agreed he would take a taxi to the airport, because it made me so nervous to leave the boys alone; anything could happen, and there'd be no way to let them know why I wasn't home when they woke up. But it had been raining. After Mark's alarm buzzed that morning, guilt had kept me awake under the quilt my grandma made me, and the navy flannel sheets that smelled of our sleepy bodies. "Maybe I should just take you."

"Umm. That would be sweet. You sure?"

I hadn't been sure. But I'd welcomed a chance to do something he'd call sweet.

Our guard pulled the gate open for us in pre-dawn darkness. In an hour the equatorial sun would leap over the horizon and the thin highland air of Nairobi would warm. Nairobi sits higher than Denver, our famous mile-high city. It sits the same distance south of the equator as Addis Ababa sits north, but Nairobi is half a mile lower in altitude and positively tropical, compared to Addis Ababa's mountain-top feel.

In the light of a street lamp, golden sunrise blossoms bobbed gray against the black mass of vines on our gate. Fire finches were waking up in the bougainvillea hedge. The sweet trill of the nightjar had only just stopped. I would never escape the pull of moments like this. They soothed every pain. They reassured me that everything would work out. I wanted to call this my home. Forever. The achingly beautiful mountain-high world of East Africa.

At the Westlands Roundabout, the streets were empty, silent and shiny with overnight rain. This was where street children sniffed glue and accosted or picked the pockets of passersby. They were sleeping now, somewhere in the slums, in a place where I didn't have to see them for a few minutes, didn't have to tell myself, *Surely you could do something for them. Absolutely, you should.*

I drove without speaking. Mark was never one to chat, even in our easiest of times. We passed Nyayo Stadium, Uchumi Supermarket, and Nairobi Game Park, off to the right in the dark, where flat-topped acacias stood guard over animals no one saw from the highway.

I nosed our white Nissan up to the curb at Jumo Kenyata Airport. Excited energy emanated off Mark, already halfway back to our beloved Ethiopia. He patted his pocket, checking once more for the passport stretching it wide and the ticket sticking out the top. His speckled green eyes shone behind black-rimmed glasses as I turned to say good-bye. He was better at leaving than at being left.

Two policemen strolled in our direction. Mark pointed at them with his chin, the Ethiopian way. "Uh-oh."

Ethiopia had been in our faces with its curiosity toward for-eigners—little boys, who ran behind the Jeep through the town of Maji when I was young screaming *Firenj, firenj, foreigner*--but that was just anoying. Kenya was another story, a culture with violence woven through it. In the slums of Nairobi, if criminals were caught by neighbors, they might get *the necklace*, an old tire doused with kerosene and lit.

Driving in Nairobi required not only that we stay on the left side of the street, not only that we watch for the craziness of other drivers from any direction, but also that we watch for the teem-ing pedestrians, who might dash across the street without looking, or who walked along the edge of the tarmac to avoid the dust or mud where sidewalks should be. Besides the trauma and pain of an accident, a mob could form within seconds and mete out vigilante punishment.

I felt particularly vulnerable as a woman in a country where the weapon of choice for domestic violence was a machete. Recently, I'd read a newspaper report on some girls who had been trampled to death in their dorm when boys came through, raiding. "The boys didn't mean any harm," the headmaster said to reporters. "They only wanted to rape a few girls."

The approaching policemen's uniforms looked black in the pre-dawn light. They both had round heads, round cheeks, and the round stomachs of Kenyans who can eat well. Eating well for ordinary people in Nairobi meant plenty of goat stew. It meant fried meat and fried potatoes and fried bananas. It meant lots of *ugali*, maize meal cooked dry enough to use for scooping up the stew or *sukuma-wiki*, the push-me-through-the-week greens fried in onions and lard. Eating well for ordinary people in Nairobi meant *chapatis*, borrowed from Indian and Pakistani immigrants, now a national food, with lard kneaded into the dough until it couldn't absorb any more and the flattened patties sizzled on the grill.

I squeezed Mark's knee and ignored the policemen. "Have a good trip."

Mark sat still, watching them. "Fishing," he said.

Sunday afternoons on the highways out of Nairobi, policemen fished by putting out roadblocks, vicious spikes on twisted metal plates that looked as though tanks had rolled over them. The police shook down Sunday drivers and *matatus*, public transport vans. The airport was a great place for fishing. Fish pulled right up to the curb.

When a policeman had stopped me two months earlier, on my first venture out on the left side of the road, he'd found I was not carrying my driver's license. But he hadn't asked for money. Friends hardly believed me when I told the story. For one thing, they said they wouldn't have stopped—he didn't have a car or radar, after all. But I had been new to Kenya, and I always did hope for the best.

I gave the policeman a ride to the station. He booked me, and

I gave him a ride back to his beat. By the time I dropped him off, I knew all about his home area and his five children. That's how the system worked in Kenya and Ethiopia. Everyone is connected in the end.

But Kenyans and foreigners both debated what to do about the rampant corruption that had taken over Kenya. President Moi was from one of the smaller tribes, and he stayed in power by leading the corruption parade, keeping everyone in his debt. Being on the take had become a national pastime.

Idealists argued that if none of us paid bribes to police, they would eventually give it up. Realists said a lot of the bribes were more like the original meaning of tip—To Insure Promptness. We usually weren't paying for something illegal, just helping service people feed their families. Police, nurses, teachers—what should have been the middle class—weren't paid enough to meet Nairobi costs of living. Kenyan parents had to tip teachers to teach their children; people had to tip nurses to care for their relatives in the hospital. There were fifty and sixty students in classrooms, nurses had almost as many patients—priorities had to be set somehow, so in the Kenyan system, a tip made that difference.

The taller Kenyan policeman squinted at our Nissan Sunny. He tapped his Bic pen on his hand. Only wrongdoers have to fear the authorities, St. Paul had said, so I turned my face away and popped the trunk as Mark got out. The rear-view mirror reflected white. When he slammed the lid down, Mark's thin shoulders in the mirror turned and dipped for the suitcases.

Then he and the policemen came together, right in my blind spot. I could feel them there; I could hear their voices. When I pressed back into the seat, I saw the policeman in the side mirror, his head jutting forward.

Mark came to my window. I rolled it down and frowned. His fist on the windowsill held a rolled up Kenyan shilling note.

"I let the car registration expire," he said. He held up his fist. "I offered them five hundred shillings, but they want a thousand."

Mark loved to find solutions. When he was twelve, he had put wheels and a propeller on an old electric shaver and made a vehicle that buzzed across the floor until it flicked the plug out of the socket and drifted to a stop. He had unscrambled more than one miswired three-way switch that had baffled electricians. He once took a spring from a ballpoint pen and used it to fix the switch on my desk lamp. He could always find a way to make stuff work. He took the same approach to ethics.

But he knew he'd better check with his wife, the woman with the over-developed conscience, the one who hated injustice so deeply. He knew she wouldn't want to be part of the problem, paying bribes in Africa's second most corrupt country.

I groaned. "Why do they want so much?" That was an odd question for a purist. There's a practical streak in me, too; frugal Scots blood.

The fine for not carrying my driver's license had only been two hundred and fifty. A thousand shillings was about twenty dollars, but the amount was immaterial, it was a rhetorical question, and Mark knew that. He went back to his negotiations.

If only I'd stayed in bed.

Through a wall of glass flecked with raindrops, fluorescent lights inside the terminal flickered above chipped Formica counters. A cleaner in a royal blue jumpsuit pushed his almost bristle-less broom.

Mark came back to the window. "They won't budge."

He pulled away, and the policeman leaned in. His lips separated for a smile, his cheeks bunched, his good-guy white teeth shone two feet from my face. "Madam, you have broken the laws of Kenya," he said in a jovial voice. "You will go to court."

I held tight to the steering wheel, my arms stiff. The universe paused a moment, waiting for me. I kept hoping it was fair to call Africa home as long as I was putting in the work to make it a better place. Paying to get out of going to court didn't have much of a role in world improvement—this bribe couldn't be considered a tip. I tilted my head and looked up at the policeman. "If I've broken the laws of Kenya, I shouldn't cheat the courts of Kenya, should I?"

The policeman was not amused. He straightened up. Lips tight, he opened the ticket book.

I let out the breath I'd been holding and climbed out of the car. What I really wanted next was for Mark to give me a big reassuring hug. A kiss that would tell me he still loved me. That all was forgiven. What I said was, "I can't believe you got me into this."

"Me?" Mark said. He paused, to give me time to get it straight exactly who was at fault. Everything we said those days had overtones. Then his voice softened. "Listen, don't fight downtown traffic. It'll be stressful enough. Call Peter Kimani." His look told me he was sorry I'd chosen the high road on this one, but he'd long ago given up trying to save me from myself.

He had unloaded the two suitcases full of gifts for our Ethiopian friends. Now he turned and braced his back under the weight of the suitcases, his tight, compact body so familiar. So dear. Over his shoulder to the policemen, he said, "You could have had five hundred, now you have nothing. See what happens when you get greedy?" He was in great form, looking forward to Ethiopia and playing the Kenyan national game with the policemen so early in the morning.

The taller policeman hid his chuckle by leaning over the pad. His partner smiled. They had bonded with Mark over the bargain-ing, which is always about relationship. Now they watched him go through the glass door with bemused expressions, reluctantly saying good-bye to the big one that got away.

The policeman turned to me, pulled his mouth back in line and pointed to my ticket with the cap end of the Bic. "Do you know where the court is?" The pertinent facts were circled. Friday. Nine o'clock.

I folded my arms across my sweater. "Last time I went to traffic court at eight-thirty like my ticket said, but only the cleaning lady was there. The judge didn't even come until ten-thirty."

His dark eyes widened. "You must be there at nine o'clock," he said. "Nine o'clock sharp."

CHAPTER 11

When I called Peter Kimani over our crackling Nairobi phone line, I could tell he smiled at hearing from me. He would be teetering on stones in the El Niño puddle that surrounded the chipped red post for a public phone. When he wasn't out on a job, he parked his taxi there and waited for calls. Taxis were cheap in Nairobi and saved fighting traffic and parking, if you knew an honest driver.

"Yes, Madam," Peter said. "I am available. Where do you need to go?"

I told him the name of the court. There was a moment of silence.

"Oh Madam. That is the criminal court."

It was my turn to fall silent.

"Don't worry, Petah will take care of you," he said. And that was so classic. All my life, when African people had come to consider me as one of their own, someone was always available to help out.

The morning of my court date, Peter pulled up to our gate and hooted his horn. Shreds of duct tape hung from the visor of his taxi. Muddy water sluiced along the side and seeped in under the door as we drove. I moved my feet closer to the gearbox, took shallow breaths of air filthy with the smell of mud and musty carpet.

El Niño had been dumping rain on Kenya for nine months straight. Peter eased the car into a pothole the size of a small pond and as wide as the road. When he revved the engine to climb out the other side, the glove compartment popped open. He looked sideways at me in apology and banged it shut three times, but it wouldn't catch.

I tried to smile. I was hoping to pass through court with calm and serenity. To do that, I needed to remember the bigger point behind my not paying the bribe. I had thought as a teen-ager that if I was going to pray *on earth as it is in heaven*, I needed to put heavenly things into action—in other words, to live an ethically pure life. I grew out of teen age absolutism, so now *ethically responsible* was the goal.

Peter pulled into a bare courtyard with leaning acacia trees and a cement and wrought iron fence. The low, colonial era building's cement plaster had been stained by the Kenyan earth and chipped through to gray on the corners. The color faded from rust red down by the bare mud to rusty beige near the top. Peter came around to let me out of the taxi, since the passenger handle was broken on the inside.

From an overflowing dumpster on the other side of the wall came the smell of sour garbage—moldy orange rinds, mango seeds, and banana peels composting in the everlasting rain. The mess had a few spots of yellow, blue, and red from Supa-loaf wrappers and tri-pack cartons of Lala, sweetened clabbered milk.

We walked toward the wide, double door. Peter's face looked like a poster announcing, *Leave hope behind all ye who enter here.* On a stool by the door, a man in khaki sat looking down. I held out my ticket.

His eyes passed over it and back to the floor. "Traffic cases at eleven."

Oh brother. "The police told me to be here at nine o'clock sharp." I pointed to the blue circle on my ticket.

The man on the stool looked out at the acacia trees to show just how interested he was in me and my scheduling problem. I showed Peter the dark blue circle. He shrugged, hands wide, and gave his most sympathetic smile. *Don't hate Kenya.*

And I didn't hate Kenya. Really, how would the policemen know just when traffic cases were tried? I'd been in East Africa long enough to know, if I'd remembered, that numbers are metaphors. I ran the translation in my head. The policeman had been saying,

Your case will come up sooner or later. Get to court in good time so you don't miss your call.

"You sit, Madam, I will wait," Peter said, and ducked his head, polite. He joined the other drivers leaning against their rusting taxis. Gray light filtered through the acacia lace and camouflaged the rusted *mbati* roofs of slums behind them. The men were chewing on toothbrush twigs, spitting fibers, laughing at each other's Swahili jokes, passing the time pleasantly together the way Kenyans do when they wait. Patient. The way I aspired to be while I waited.

The courtroom looked like a Kenyan church or classroom, benches in crookedy rows and dried mud in tread-shaped chunks on the floor, the smell of damp cement. One fluorescent light worked. Up front, the judge's podium, gavel and all, loomed over mahogany tables. Benches behind a rail on a platform faced it sideways.

I couldn't shake the thought of home—writing, resting, thinking, looking out my back window at the Jacaranda tree blooming lavender in the back yard. Instead, the muscles in my back were going to burn along my spine after hours on a backless bench. My knees were going to ache.

Step into foreign bureaucracies with a blank mind, I recited to myself. This was my method for waiting: *don't imagine what will happen next. Don't hope for the best. Always take a book.* I chose a seat under the light, at the end of the bench so I could lean sideways against the smeared stucco wall. I took *Middlemarch* out of my bag.

Of course, that could backfire too. An Ethiopian petty bureaucrat in 1990 had said it was my fault I sat all afternoon under the hot Ethiopian highland sun outside the driver's license renewal office. "We called you," he said. He said I was reading and had missed my turn.

He must have said, "Mrs. Kooorrr-tis." That's how Ethiopians always said our last name. His assistant, whose job it was to be his microphone, had shouted, "Mrs. Pooorr-sis." I had looked up and frowned into the afternoon sun. *Poorsis?* I had gone back to my book.

Even now I thought the official might have done something to get my attention, something like giving me a nod when I looked up. After all, mine was the only American name and I was the only white person in the group sitting not fifteen feet away from his open office door. But the license renewal office of Socialist Ethiopia was not a service industry, so there they had let me sit, reading, smelling dust and feeling the mountain-high intensity of the sun on my face. It was a reminder of that tough truth many people had learned before me—Ethiopian bureaucracy chews up idealists.

I must have soaked up idealism across the placenta, Dad just back from World War II and in seminary. He told us girls, when we were grown, that his own childhood, on a farm on the dry high desert of Eastern Oregon, was rough only because of the depression. He said with the depression and World War II over, he thought it would be possible to raise a perfect family. His voice betrayed his grief that the dream hadn't worked out.

My sisters and I each dealt with his impossible expectations in our own way. I wasn't high-minded because I was a Christian, I was a high-minded little soul from my earliest memories of trying to supervise my toddler sister and keep the baby from falling off the bed. Once I got tagged as the good girl, the pressure never let up. By eighth grade, in boarding school in Addis Ababa, our dorm mother called me in for personal devotions and gave me a special verse: *Be ye therefore perfect, even as your Father in Heaven is perfect. Matthew 5:48.*

Years later I researched that verse—some translations said *be holy*, and the word in Greek meant *dedicated*, or *set aside for a purpose.* That, I could relate to: set aside to be the good girl. But perfect? I knew even as a child I wasn't going to reach those heights. What I needed, then and still, was help in figuring out how to be responsible without demanding the impossible from myself. This day in court might turn out to give me some data, if I could just remember and apply it in the next unexpected challenge.

Kenyans drifted into court. Mostly their clothes didn't have the whitest whites or the brightest brights. I'd chosen my own clothes carefully, nice enough to look respectful of the court, but not to stand out. I still felt so, so foreign in my floral rayon skirt, my Clark's sandals, my pale *muzungu* feet, with toes permanently stained by the rust colored dirt.

Clothing rustled. No one even whispered. A preschooler in shorts and muddy Bata Bulas with no laces stood by his mother's knee. He half-wrapped himself in her pleated nylon skirt and stared at me. Probably everyone else did too, when I wasn't looking. A *muzungu*. In criminal court. Their minds were clicking over the possibilities of what she might have done. Other than secretly looking each other over, we waited silently.

A perfect family. What was Dad thinking? That's not just idealism. That borders on idiocy. Of course, Dad was barely over twenty when he set himself that goal, and there I was, drifting toward fifty, and maybe just as much a fool for thinking I could do anything to help in South Sudan.

I'd thought there couldn't be a better place to practice my twin passions: living in Africa and helping make the world a better place. But my experience in Waat, and Mark's experience so far advising the pastors in the office, did not make helping the Sudanese look hopeful.

Mark advised them not to pay their children's school fees with a grant for educating pastors in South Sudan. He advised them that the grant for buying sewing machines couldn't be used to pay Elizabeth's salary. He advised them not to pay their rent with money donors sent for their children's school fees; what would happen when school started again?

"God will send us a Good Samaritan," they said. They were getting more and more annoyed with his advice. They said they were a sovereign church and reporting back to the donors about how they used project grants was economic colonialism.

The Sudanese church leaders and their money didn't want to be fixed. Mark was in despair. More and more, he came home silent and resentful. I listened. I empathized. But it didn't matter how reasonable I stayed for how long, sooner or later his anger turned against me, and when I finally snapped at him, he said, "See."

Mark didn't want to be fixed, either.

A sister had emailed me a story: *Day after day before dawn a woman dragged her husband's drunken body into the house from the lawn where he'd collapsed.*

One morning her neighbor came out on the stoop. "Honey, just leave him where Jesus flang him."

The story made me laugh, but as the oldest sister of seven, when something was flang, somebody had to pick it up. That somebody had always been me. I didn't know how to leave things. I didn't dare. Being super-responsible was the currency I traded in—hard work in exchange for love. I wasn't any more capable of stopping my efforts to listen Mark out of his anger than he was of letting it go, or than the pastors were of using their grants for development, not for living expenses.

Up front, a side door scraped and popped open. We all stood. Behind the mahogany, the Kenyan judge looked small. His thin, faint mustache might have been drawn on with charcoal. He glanced down, flipped his robe out behind him, and sat. We sat too, with a rustle of clothes and a clunking of benches on the chipped cement floor. Other men in black regalia had come in with the judge. They sat without even a glance at who might be in criminal court that day.

A man at the front table began sorting and stamping files. Others busied themselves with briefcases, papers, and pens. They spoke softly to each other. They nodded and passed things. The rest of us sat watching, not making a sound: unseen witnesses.

After a few minutes, the bailiff came through a back door, smart and upright, with a Billy club in his right hand. He bowed to the judge. When he stepped back, a line of young men walked in and sat. I could only see the first boy, with his fraying khaki pants and dirty blue t-shirt, and a row of knees facing the judge.

"James Oduro."

James stood, a boy of sixteen, maybe twenty.

I didn't expect what happened next, because Ethiopia was never colonized. Amhara speakers are proud of their language, proud of their *fidel*, the only indigenous alphabet in all of sub-Saharan Africa. Courts in Ethiopia are held in Amharic.

But poor James—the judge lit into him in Kenyan British English. James stood, head down, and waited for the man in the middle to translate into Swahili. Which he did loudly, without looking up. He never paused with the file stamping, wood echoing under layers of paper. He shouted, as though James might be deaf as well as ignorant. He didn't bother translating James's answer back from Swahili to English for the judge, because everyone in Kenya spoke Swahili. Just not in court.

I was a foreigner, with options galore, but I would be the only person that day judged in my own language. It seemed so unfair to James, the little guy. He sat down. The gavel banged. The witnesses never rustled, never whispered.

Boy after boy stood. *Middlemarch* couldn't compete with what was happening in court. The boys were given court dates. They were ordered back to their rural villages. They were charged fines, twenty- and thirty-dollar fines, impossible sums for penniless boys who'd come to Nairobi to seek their fortunes and found only the police. I watched the judge and officials for any sign of compassion for those boys on the bench. The files were taking up all the men's attention. Always on the side of the underdog, my outrage grew.

At ten thirty the judge got up without warning. I clutched at my book and notebook and stood with the crowd. Without a glance our way, the black-dressed men filed out through their door. None of the folks around me had been called up. They must be the families of the boys from behind the back door. They sighed a hundred huge, sad sighs and wandered out.

Peter appeared dark in the doorway, back lit in gray. I gave him what I thought George Eliot would have called a rueful smile, and sidestepped out to the aisle. The man in khaki still sat by the door. I held my ticket out to him again, hoping to find out what to expect, now that it was time for traffic cases.

He didn't look up. His voice was flat. "Go to Kĩnyanjui."

My mouth formed to ask one of the W questions but I couldn't think which one.

He waved left, the way you would shoo a chicken. "Kĩnyanjui."

To the left, stairs went up, red, gray and black speckled cement. My sandal caught and I stubbed my toe on the requisite uneven riser of a Kenyan stairway. On the landing, behind glass and bars, a policewoman was stamping more files.

I leaned down to the circle in the glass and opened my mouth. *Kin*—what was it? She stamped with one hand, waved left with the other. Everyone seemed to know where I should go and why, but no one was telling.

I wandered through the breezeway to the balcony. Closed doors lined up, blank, every five feet in each direction. Would a rainbow appear over the place I was supposed to go? Or a great light? My shoulders rounded forward with every step. The British had introduced prisons and courts to Kenya. Part of the colonial system. I was upset for Kenya that courts would still be so patronizing, even with Kenyans in charge. No trace of traditional dignity, village-elders dispensing justice under spreading trees. For starters, it would help if somebody looked us criminals in the eye.

I'd put my hand to the plow and refused to cheat this court. Now that it came to stumbling along in rough furrows behind my oxen, I was confused—what was the point? Doing the right thing wouldn't change the wrongs. The policemen weren't going to give up fishing. The court wasn't going to ask for my feedback and become a gentler, kinder place. It was no longer so clear what I was accomplishing.

At the end of the balcony, one door was open. I looked in. A policeman and two policewomen, round under their stiff uniform shirts, sat stamping those never-ending files.

The final point in my system for surviving African bureaucracy was, *Try irony.* "I am looking for somebody," I said. "It starts with K."

They laughed. That sound, so human, so real, popped my cynical moment. The policeman tipped back on the legs of his chair. "I am Kĩnyanjui." He looked at one of the women. "Go downstairs and see if her file has been sent to the courtroom."

Ah. My file.

The policewoman leaned her elbow on a stack of files, her smiling cheek against her hand. "Yes, it has," she said.

We all laughed then. She'd stamped my file and imagined me, the *muzungu* criminal, caught in the nets, forgot to register the car, too naïve to pay tea money. She'd wondered when I'd show up to check on it—and here I was.

Kĩnyanjui's snug shirt jiggled. "You should have come to see me sooner."

I opened my mouth, indignant. How could I do that when no one would so much as look at me?

"Anyway, don't be angry," he said. He spread thick fingers on the layers of paper on his desk and pushed himself up to stand. His black and white eyes looked right at me and his smile sparkled. "To be angry won't help you, will it? What is there to be angry about? You have found Kĩnyanjui, your file is there. Now your case will be heard and soon you will be finished."

Calm acceptance, that talent I coveted. He was offering his wisdom as a gift, so I inclined my head in thanks, but above my smile, my nostrils flared and I opened my eyes extra wide to show my great gratitude.

The policewomen giggled over their paperwork, and Kĩnyanjui rubbed his stomach. We laughed together one more time.

When the man at the front table called my name, adrenalin jolted through me. I had hoped to walk to the front as smooth as fluid, but I felt terribly self-conscious. Usually, I loved being the only white person in an African adventure, creeping under the edges of another culture. But criminal court had become a little too sad and grim for me. Other than Peter, out with his friends, I was alone. It's not the way, to let someone suffer alone. My little Ethiopian first graders had even taken a friend with them to go from class to the bathroom. I walked to the front, my elbows and knees moving as though they were peg jointed.

The first boy in the next group out the back door met me at the top of the criminal box. We all instinctively sat the same way, our hands folded in our laps. Our arms made polite V's, and rested on our thighs in shades of brown and beige.

"Caroline Kurtz."

I stood.

The crowd of witnesses disappeared. The judge's small tidy ear was even with me, the backs of the others' heads below me. The air went thin, and I had to breathe fast.

"You are accused of driving an unregistered car. Is that true or not true?"

"I have registered the car," I said, in the don't-be-mad-at-me voice I'd learned so well as a child. I cleared my throat and braced my shoulders. "Here are the papers."

"Were you or were you not driving an unregistered car? Answer yes or no."

Shame stung on my cheeks. "Yes."

"One thousand shilling fine."

Well. That explained the stubborn policemen—the bribe commensurate with the crime. They must have figured they were providing a service, saving time and humiliation in court for the same low price.

I sat again. The air at bench level was thick with the smell of damp clothing, dirty socks, hair, skin, and sweat. Slowly the heat drained from my body.

The elderly court cashier hobbled over to me. I took out a blue thousand-shilling note, so worn and dirty it draped across my hand. President Moi smiled up from it with his candidate smile from thirty years before. My sandal bumped my neighbor's cracked plastic shoe. He pulled it away and tucked it under the bench. I handed the bill over the bar to the cashier. He waved his fingers toward the door.

"Now?" I mouthed.

He smiled and nodded. I could have hugged him for that smile. Human kindness could survive in a Kenyan criminal court after all. I brushed away the thought that the Jameses needed it more than the foreigner. I'd felt all the outrage I could handle for one day. I hitched my bag over my shoulder. My aching knees crackled as I stepped down the big drop from the bottom step of the criminal box to the cement floor.

Every eye but the judges' and councils' must have watched me. Every step I took was stiff. My relief left me queasy. Behind me, the sounds of thumping, and the dance in two languages continued. Ahead, the light beyond the door hurt my eyes. Faces and dark eyes to either side blurred past.

On that long walk to the door, I pried my fingers off the demand that my choices change even the smallest of the world's injustices. I had done what I thought was right, I had played my part in a Kenyan justice system, and I was walking out forever, leaving it where Jesus flang it. And if I could find bemused acceptance for the dysfunctions of Kenya, maybe there was still hope I could do the same for Mark and his displaced anger.

Peter and I rattled back through traffic. A *matatu* turned right from the left-hand lane inches in front of our headlight. Peter slammed on the brakes. The other driver leaned out his window and waved. Peter laughed and shook his head. I sat back smiling, trusting him to get me safely home.

CHAPTER 12

As Mark and I struggled to make something of our attempts to work with the Sudanese, our mentor Bill Lowrey proposed that all the Presbyterian Church of Sudan pastors come together for a General Assembly. Some, from their self-imposed exile in Nairobi. The others stuck in South Sudan, trying to survive. How else could the church hold together?

The pastors chose the village of Ayod, another town from the hunger triangle, when the Southern People's Liberation Army splintered in 1991. Mark chartered a *canoe of the sky* to transport those of us in Nairobi.

We met in Ayod's rebuilt church hall. Roofs in round thatch *tukuls* are held up by rafters that radiate out from a strong center pole to the perimeter. In rectangular buildings, something has to hold up the ridge line. In this church, throughout the inner space, forked poles sat at angles, bracing the rafters. It gave me the feeling of sitting in a forest, with tree trunks leaning and stretching all around.

Elizabeth had not been included in the church group from Nairobi, and no local women had been invited. I sat in a corner, on a bench made from a long, split log about eight inches wide. It rested on stubby forked branches. I sat in the corner because I was the only woman, and so that I could lean sideways, when my back got tired, against the brush that filled the spaces between the thin poles of the structure. Dust tickled my nose whenever I disturbed the bristly wall. I had brought a knitting project with me. Keeping my hands busy helped me listen to languages I couldn't understand.

I listened, tried to ignore my aching back, my aching knees. In the heat of the day, my fingers grew sweaty and pulled against my knitting yarn, making my stitches too tight.

Meanwhile, Mark had decided he would make the financial situation come alive to the less educated pastors of South Sudan. He asked a few questions and made calculations in a small notebook. When he was called up to the podium, which had been made by hand with an adze, he looked thin, pale and short next to his Sudanese translator. He also looked nervous—he hated public speaking.

Mark gave that year's financial report not in dollars. Not in Sudanese or Kenyan shillings. He gave the report in cows, the medium of exchange in South Sudan. *This many cows had been given to the church*, he said. *This many cows had been sent to the church in South Sudan. This many cows had been eaten in Nairobi.*

Educated Nuers from Nairobi were furious that Mark would patronize them, as though they couldn't understand finance. But the uneducated pastors did understand. For once.

Rev. X, the moderator, was replaced. Mark fell asleep in our stuffy grass *tukel*, on a mat next to me, feeling satisfied. Justified. Rev. X had used Mark to lie to the donors. Now Mark had found a way to work around him to do what he was hired by the donors to do: render accountability.

But the officers of the church were absolutely not going to change and actually send grant money into South Sudan, when they needed it so badly in their expensive but slummy Nairobi apartments. Each of the many big families' many children needed uniforms, notebooks, pens. Bouts of malaria and other tropical diseases regularly sickened members of the tight-knit Sudanese community in Nairobi—someone was always being taken to the hospital.

Of course they didn't want to stay in South Sudan to be bombed by North Sudanese Antinovs or slaughtered by rogue South Sudanese commanders. Of course they didn't want to live under a tarp in a hot, dry Kakuma refugee camp. Of course they would find some way to live, even under stress, in Nairobi. They were educated men, not cattle herders! And if there was money in the bank, how could they *not* choose to use it for the needs at hand? One of the church officers had told Mark, *Those people have their gardens. We are the ones starving in Nairobi.*

Mark had reacted with outrage. "If it's so easy to survive in South Sudan with a garden, what's he doing in Nairobi?" Shades of gray were not a strong point for either of us.

The needs were real. They just weren't what the donors were giving the money for. Was using stories of the desperate circumstances in South Sudanese to fund their lives in Nairobi okay? The Nuers thought so. The donors didn't. Mark was in the middle.

And what did the donors actually expect from him, hired by them but working under the Sudanese?

After the financial report in cows, the new moderator understood that if he had any hope of serving more than one term, Mark had to go. The pastors went to Bill Lowrey and said things that he never passed along to Mark and me.

Bill told Mark to take a break from his assignment, stop going to the office. Bill would work on it.

Mark was shocked. His ability to fix anything, from cars to toilets to light switches, had always made him a hero. Especially during our six years in Ethiopia. Now he was, for the first time in his life, a failure. As the charter flew us back to Nairobi, Mark descended deeper into his dark, dark place.

I had no idea what had just happened. Not really. I thought the South Sudanese pastors' anger would settle down. I thought Bill Lowrey would figure out how Mark and the Nuers could get back to working together.

But now, without work to anchor him, Mark spent an hour or more every day, after the boys left for school, raging. He didn't bother to be mad at the Sudanese. He raged at me. I too had disrespected him, the one person in all the world he had chosen to open his heart to. Neither of us figured out that his anger was actually free-floating, looking for a target. The vortex of love and resentment is so powerful, it overrides rational thought.

A sister sent me the book, *I Don't Want to Talk About It*, about how depression in men can show up as anger. *Boy Howdy*, my dad would have said.

But Jesus said to turn the other cheek. That model Christian wife I both resented and was shaped by was supposed to support her man, the head of her household. I thought that listening patiently, undefensively would be healing. Mark would come to the end of his anger. He'd see that I truly loved him.

Mark was a good man, but he had fallen off the cliff of his emotions. And I do know this: a man drowning in shame and self-doubt has centuries of law, has cultural approval, has examples in life and literature for where to turn for relief. He can always take it out on a woman he loves. This affects millions and millions of women all over the world. I had expected my enlightened self and my enlightened husband to be above that. But we weren't.

The boys knew that Mark was home from the office every day, on probation or in exile or something. They could see how miserable he was. When he didn't come down for supper one evening, it was tender-hearted Jesse, a sophomore in high school, who went up and crawled in bed beside Mark.

Jesse smooshed his face up against Mark's bare, freckled arm. Tears ran in the seam between them. "I love you, Dad, just the way you are."

The next morning Jesse made Mark promise not to give up. Before bed, he made Mark promise again. Morning and evening, promise by promise, Jesse walked Mark back from the edge. I was grateful Jesse's love could get through to Mark. It seemed that mine just made him mad. For someone who thought love was transactional, it was a frightening place to be.

I called headquarters in Louisville. They authorized counseling for Mark. They asked me to hang in with the Sudanese. We were all they had for this mess of a partnership.

After I got back from Waat I had written a grant for sewing machines and sewing lessons for South Sudan women. *Let them have their sewing machines, if it would give them hope*, I thought. After the grant came, Mark had told me the pastors were using the money to pay Elizabeth's salary. There were no funds for me to travel into South Sudan, or for anything to do with women's development. So I was also stranded at home.

Eventually, after Mark was banned from the office, Education Director Kuong learned that I was a teacher and proposed shifting me from women's development to teaching. Since the education money came from the UN, which kept tight reins on it, Kuong was the only officer in Presbyterian Church of Sudan actually doing work in South Sudan.

First, he sent me to teach English refresher courses to young Nuer men for weeks at a time in the dry, hot, god-forsaken Kakuma refugee camp. Next Kuong asked me to teach teachers in Nyal, South Sudan.

"Dad's big issue was abandonment," Miriam screamed at me after he died. "Why did you keep traveling, when you knew how much he hated it?"

"What he really hated was looking for a job back in the States," I yelled back. "I was working for us both."

The UN had stopped shuttling people up to Loki by plane, so I took Kenyan public vans up to catch the UN charter into Nyal—a grueling eighteen-hour adventure I never needed to repeat.

In the heat of Loki that night, fatigue drilled recurring fears deeper and deeper. Was my leaving the boys at home with a depressed father dangerous? Was I taking the cheap and easy path to get away from the grim tension at home, using work as an excuse? I weakly told myself that maybe my being away would help Mark rebalance.

I had commented once that blamers and blame-ees seem to find each other, marry and live "happily" ever after. But that insight didn't show me a way out of feeling responsible—because whatever Mark accused me of, there was some truth. I was never, had never been good enough to him.

Only now do I see how harsh I was with myself.

And what do fathers do, when they are the breadwinners and a wife at home is emotionally suffering? They do what they must, they work. What does anyone do when life at home is fraught? They continue to give to the world the gifts they have.

But the mission world was even more conservative than my church environment in Portland. The mothers of Jesse and Kenny's classmates were all Southern Baptist, Mennonite, and Assembly of God. I could feel them wondering about me—*Could someone from liberal PCUSA actually be a missionary?* There was no verse or chapter in the Bible that justified leaving my family at home to take care of itself. I had no objectivity, no ground from which to give myself a break, to appreciate what I was doing for my family. I only had my raw stubbornness, and the now faint words of my feminist writer friends in the Souix Falls library.

At dawn the next day in Loki, the roar of huge Hercules planes woke me, rattling the windows and corrugated iron roof of my room. Operation Lifeline Sudan was running food aid into South Sudan again; no matter what we did, what the UN did to try to save the South Sudan from itself, the unending tragedy continued.

On my way to breakfast at the mess hall, sun flashed off pickup windshields, and a hot breeze blew grit into my eyes. Behind the camp rose a treeless butte of red and gray rocks.

I chose porridge and fruit salad for breakfast at the UN mess hall—fresh pineapple, sliced bananas, mangoes, and papaya. I closed my eyes as each bite of fruit burst with delicious juice in my mouth. I'd done before what I was about to do—I knew full well this would be my last fruit for two weeks.

I slipped a fried egg between two pieces of toast, wrapped it in a napkin, pocketed it for my lunch, and walked through early morning heat to the cinder block home of friends who were gone for the day. Free for a day before flying in, I had decided to do a spiritual retreat.

Palm leaves lay over the corrugated iron of their veranda roof. That shade would give me some relief from the blazing heat of the sun in its bleached blue sky. My hosts were using dishwater to nurse young bougainvillea vines, and tiny ants swarmed over bits of food at the corner posts of the veranda. The blossoms nodded in a hot breeze, magenta against dark shining green. To the south lay the Turkana desert, dun-colored as far as I could see.

After devotions and prayer, I was planning to memorize the 121st Psalm—the, *To the Hills I Lift Mine Eyes*, psalm. When I was a girl, we sang that hymn, calling it the Maji song. Then, lifting my eyes to the Maji mountains meant *My help cometh from the Lord, who made heaven and earth.* That's what hills still meant to me, even though I'd learned that the psalmist was saying he did *not* look for help to hilltops of Judah where his countrymen had built their shrines to Baal.

There were no hills in Loki, but no matter, what drew me to Psalm 121 now was its final promise, *The LORD will keep your going out and your coming in from this day forth.* It felt like a promise just for me, for safety in South Sudan—which we called *going in*.

I had come back to Ethiopia, and then to Kenya and South Sudan, with such hopes of serving this beautiful world, with its beautiful people. I needed a work permit to be there, unlike during my innocent, careless childhood, when I hadn't questioned belonging. The hope I'd had in exchanging my skills for a work permit was more ragged now. The price was growing steeper with every passing month.

In Loki that day on the veranda, I prayed and rested and read, bracketed by the bougainvillea, surrounded by the desert, thinking about hills.

Sunday, the day before I'd left Nairobi, the sermon had been about tithing. *A tenth to the church. Gifts and offerings above and beyond that.* On one side of me, ten-year-old Kenny had peeled silly putty off the hymnbook page and reached across to show it to Jesse, whose shoulder pressed against my arm. He was fifteen, almost the age Mark was when he sat beside me in boarding school church services in Ethiopia, his arm warm against mine through the scratchy shoulder of his dark green suit.

Give your first fruits.

Through open stained-glass side windows three rows up, I watched the eucalyptus trees wave like upright pendulums in the sunlight and wind. Mark sat, grim and scowling, on the other side of Kenny. I didn't have to look at him to know that. Icy non-verbals emanated off him, and my receptors were sensitive as a thermometer. Tears splattered onto the backs of my glasses when I blinked. I looked at people's heads—Kenyans and foreigners—as they listened in the pews in front of me, and I wondered how they managed their lives so they didn't sit in church and cry.

The Lord loves a cheerful giver.

I was supposed to be the heart of the family, Mark the head. My boys, Mark, my Sudanese students: was I failing them all? Stubbornness, like willingness, can falter under pressure.

Every time I traveled to South Sudan, or to the refugee camp in Kakuma, it seemed obvious that life itself was a blessing. I always reassured myself: my boys were happy at school. But I was afraid they would be scarred by the unhappiness sucking at Mark, spilling over on me.

The debate raged in my head. Surely, if they were wounded, they could heal. Wouldn't it be worse if I pulled the plug and said we had to go to the States and get help for Mark? We'd have no jobs. We'd plunge into unimaginable chaos. The boys would lose everything: their sense of family, their neighborhood, their school, their house, their friends. And what if they took losing Kenya as hard as I'd taken losing Ethiopia at age eighteen?

I had never taken full stock of dislocation in my life. Alone all day in Loki, nostalgic as I was for the hills and cedars and fog of Maji, Ethiopia on that veranda in the Turkana desert, reverberations of loss rattled my heart. I had trouble separating my life from my sons' lives. I couldn't think clearly about what was good for them. It wasn't surprising, anchor-less as I felt, that I'd gone back to cling to the Maji psalm. I had idealized Maji. I had first lost Maji when I was ten and went to boarding school.

Some of our friends, sent off to school in Jeeps and bush planes like I was, believed their parents loved the Ethiopian people more than them. Some of them never did make good transitions to adulthood. Would they have gone crazy-bitter, would they have tried to kill themselves, if they'd been raised in the States? It seems impossible to sort out, once a life is lived, what led to what.

I did know when each of the four oldest Kurtz girls left Ethiopia for college, that's when our lives shuddered and shook. We could never talk about how hard that was without our emotional Dad crying.

"Maybe I should never have gone to Ethiopia and put you girls through that," he would say.

It was years before I could tell him to stop. "It makes our struggles random and meaningless when you sound like you could have just as well stayed in the States." We had loved our Ethiopian childhoods. We needed to have our pain as well. We needed to have our troubles without throwing Dad into guilt and self-doubt. Without having to take care of him.

I had coped with all my childhood losses. I thought I had done well, but that day on the veranda in Loki, I wondered.

Maybe I was like a table, whose one leg had been sawed off, a saw-blade's width at a time, until now it sat off balance and wobbly. *You have no excuse*, I had lectured myself. *With all your advantages, you should be in better shape.* I had demanded uncomplaining responsibility from myself until I was left making the same mistakes Mom and Dad did, with fatigue, rigidity, denial instead of empathy. Was I as blind to my children's needs as my parents had sometimes been to mine, all under the banner of doing good in the world?

I had become an unwelcome foreigner in my marriage. In South

Sudan, I was equally helpless to make things better, but at least I was welcome there. I still had hope I could make a difference, even in the smallest way. And I was the only member of our family who could work.

In Loki on the cusp of going incommunicado, I reassured myself that the boys already knew they had a moody father. What he showed them was silence, not anger. Only with me did he bring out both. Only close in, did we each react as though the other could snuff out our existence.

The boys would be fine.

I prayed, that afternoon on the veranda in the desert in Loki. I asked God to take care of my family. Since I didn't know how to.

The next day I flew in, the only foreigner in a team of Sudanese, as the English teacher for a UN-sponsored teacher's training course in Nyal.

CHAPTER 13

Nyal was one of those villages where all traces of the 20th century had been erased. One of those places where schools now met under trees. After rogue commanders swept through, looting the people, the clinic, and the development projects, only dust and straw were left.

I walked with Kuong and the other Sudanese men from the landing strip to the usual sorghum-fenced church compound, where the pastors showed me to a grass-roofed *tukel*, empty except for a hand adzed bed with leather strapping. I set my duffle bag on the dirt floor. Its one small window was a hole in the mud plaster, latticed with sticks running across it; the light coming through made striped shadows on the floor. A tattered Kenyan *khanga* cloth bellied from the ceiling over the bed to catch the termite droppings. The doorway was low and open, with no door at all, not even a curtain.

Mud plaster walls radiate daylight heat for hours into the night. I lay spreadeagle on the bed so that no sweaty limb would touch any other. Still, I didn't sleep until a pre-dawn breeze finally brought relief.

The next night, Pastor John Both, a man so thin his skull joints showed at his forehead and temples, helped me carry my bed outside. He cut four thin whips off a tree and showed me how to lash one whip to each of the hewn legs of my cowhide bed and cross them in the middle. I tied my mosquito net corners from the whips and tucked the edges under my camp mat. The Sudanese men sat nearby in the moonlight, their stories, their soft laughter soothing me like a lullaby.

I prayed for Mark and the boys and fell deeply asleep.

Over our breakfast tea served in glasses, deep brown with un-stirred sugar in the bottom, Kuong told me we'd been invited to another village for Good Friday services. "You will preach," he said. "The women—and the men—need to see a woman church leader."

I worked uncertainly on a sermon. What could I, a foreigner with so many lucky advantages, say to these people that would give them hope? And then, in the middle of Maundy Thursday night, a population explosion of bacteria turned my guts to water. I ran, unbuckled sandals flapping, to the leaning outhouse. It was just me and nature, there in the dark of night—the moon was setting. A bat swooped across my path. In the outhouse, the circle of light from my flashlight woke a sausage bug and a dozen moths.

For the rest of the night, between dashes, I shivered in the warm air and curled up around stomach cramps. By dawn, I'd evacuated everything foreign. I slept until Kuong called my name softly.

Sipping as much sweet tea as I could hold, I wished for hills, from whence some help could come. I was going to need strength.

There was dew on the dust of the path, and the huge yellow sun was rising over the horizon as we left Nyal. By leaving early, we were ahead of the heat. The Sudanese had laughed—with an American along, the path would take over an hour. For them, long legged, born to the heat, raised on walking, maybe forty-five minutes.

The distance didn't worry me as much as the lack of shelter for restroom stops along the way. The Sudanese talk about their wide sky. Nothing breaks it from one horizon to the other. I worried that the tea would run straight through me. Or I might have another bout with the next generation of my foreign invader. My guts still felt like they might just as soon cramp as not.

We walked for half an hour. In this land, so flat and barren, there was no need to walk single file. Sandy soil stretched, flat, in every direction. In some spots the sunlight struck at just the right angle and the sand sparkled. Here and there a hot-climate tree, with its minimal, dull green foliage, stuck up to break up the brown. Our group spread out in a ragged, forward moving line. The men joked with each other in soft Nuer. The sunlight felt weighted, a too-warm quilt, so early.

Then a dull pain began in one knee. When I favored that leg, the other knee started to hurt, and I lost the luxury of limping. I knew just what to do when trouble struck: Dad had raised his girls on bearing-up and teeth gritting. I clamped my mouth tight and marched on, pain in every step.

Kuong was striding across the dusty golden land. He looked inches taller than in Nairobi, out there on the Sudanese plains. If I stayed close, maybe some of his sturdiness would sweep me along, a wounded bird in his slipstream.

I said nothing about the pain. It drilled deeper into both knees. When I learned years later that my intermittent knee pain came from bones grinding together, I thought, *Yeah. That's exactly what it felt like.* I chewed up the inside of my mouth. I whined, yammered, and whimpered inside my head. Scanning that naked horizon for signs of a village, my heart lifted when a thatched hall came into view—homes are round. Maybe that was the church.

"Catholic church," Kuong said. I squinted onward.

When we arrived, I dropped into the hand-hewn, hand-pegged chair offered me as an honored guest. The pain stopped, but my knees felt tight. My pulse throbbed in the puffy flesh.

How often do we, from an easier life, set out in Africa, motivated by some combination of adventure and wanting to be helpful—or just wanting to participate—and suddenly find ourselves a burden in a place where there's nothing to spare. I always assumed nothing bad would happen. I'd always been so hardy. And just this fast, I was three or four barren miles away from a bed, sick and in pain. Bearing it alone, because I didn't want to burden anyone else.

After a couple of hours of rest, a congregation of about thirty gathered under the shade of a tall, spreading flame tree, as high above us as a vaulted cathedral. I preached. They sat on the ground. I stood on stiff, tight knees. Kuong towered beside me like an ebony carving, larger than life. He translated. He may have preached his own sermon for all I know. Now and then I caught the word *Kwoth*, God.

In the middle of the service, goats bounded into the sorghum enclosure and foraged for fallen blossoms—fleshy red petals and the fuzzy brown calyx that held them together. I was happy for people to be distracted. I spoke about giving thanks even in suffering, one of St. Paul's themes for the persecuted church in the first century. But what did I know about how to actually do such a thing? I was having enough trouble facing Mark's anger; they faced violence, death, hunger and a completely uncertain future. I felt embarrassed to be admonishing them about giving thanks.

The Nuer congregation responded to my sermon with two hymns, smiling and clapping, songs of faith, something that seemed positively heroic. Songs they'd written, in the middle of a civil war that had lasted for two generations. Songs in their own language, their own style of music, neither of which I could really understand. But I could hear the heart in their singing. The pain. The hope. Their high, nasal musical tones, that usually seemed screechy to me, sounded sweet under the tree, where the notes could float through the open air and dissipate.

The church women, like church women everywhere in the world, insisted on hospitality for us, their guests. They had cooked up a mess of dried fish soup, all they had to offer this late in the year. In communities near big tributaries of the Nile, men fish in the dry season, when the water level is low. It's safe then, because the crocodiles have moved to deeper rivers.

Women dry the fish on the banks, amid the sun, dust, and flies, and store the meat to get them through until the next harvest. When grain is low and it's time to use the stores of dried fish, women boil a handful of dried fish until it reconstitutes into a slimy, charcoal gray soup. The one time I'd eaten dried fish soup, its rank smell on my fingers lasted through days of scrubbing with soap.

Now my stomach churned at the first whiff. I was grateful that the bacteria gave me a reason to decline, but felt guilty about having the luxury to gag at food that keeps people alive. If it were fish soup or starvation, surely, I'd eat it, too. Maybe I'd even learn to like it. But now I buried my guilty nose in the sharp fragrance of my tea.

In the early afternoon heat, Kuong visited with the young men that were probably leaders of the congregation there. I was not part of the conversation—no one but Kuong spoke English, I'm sure. I dozed in the chair, and ignored flies that landed on my arms, my hair. When Kuong stood, I looked up, knowing the dreaded time had come. I stood, and steadied a moment of dizziness with the chair back—it had been eighteen hot, dry hours since I'd eaten.

The men drifted away to pee in the sorghum stubble of a field behind the church. No one offered me such an option, a much more complicated operation for a woman when there is no privacy. Maybe I could wander through the shrubby trees, their trunks no bigger around than my forearm, and eventually get far enough away to squat on the sand. I gave it a moment's thought, and then decided to save my strength. Maybe dehydration would get me home. Most of all I hoped that the hours of resting would give me at least that first half-hour of painless walking. My water bottle, almost empty now, bumped in my nylon backpack with my sermon notes as we set out. I was filtering the well water every morning in my tukel. I had no way to know where water in this village came from, or how safe it was.

I walked gingerly. My knees still felt tight, as though Ace bandages were stretched around them. And stepping lightly is only a figure of speech.

Within minutes my knees were gone again. No relief vans. No taxi or rental car. No rescue helicopter. I wanted to moan. If I sat down and cried, Kuong and the Sudanese elders—what could they do? Carry me?

Pastor John Both came up from behind and lifted the backpack off my shoulders.

"*Gua*," I said. I wanted to hug him. I said *good* again, with as much thanks as I could put in my voice and smiled my best. It felt like a gesture of true love, and John Both, thin as a walking stick, strode on, not slowed down a bit by sharing my small burden. Now a sweat-soaked, navy silk, Goodwill blouse, with the sleeves cut off, fluttered cool against my back. And with the slight breeze came the 121st Psalm.

The Lord is thy shade upon thy right hand.

I could see, at the very inner edge of my vision, a tiny circle of shade from the brim of my hat. At this hour, it didn't even extend as far as my shoulders. The sun radiated on my bare arms, and my sweat prickled. The dun soil extended endlessly around me. Around the edges of my sunglasses light shimmered.

So really, there was no shade. There was only sun. There was only pain. But the eleventh chapter in the book of Hebrews says *Faith is the substance of things hoped for, the evidence of things not seen.* Could God somehow give me relief, walking at my right hand, throwing a shadow over me?

The sun shall not smite thee by day nor the moon by night.

I'd memorized the Revised Standard Version, which uses *you*. But the verb *smite* begged to be paired with *thee* from the King James Bible, the music of it comforting and old, like Shakespeare. The words sounded true, even if I didn't fully comprehend them.

Kuong was setting a fast pace. The bones behind my kneecaps ground. Pain radiated up from my knees and seemed to fill my body. I clamped my teeth against it. I knew someone would fall back with me if I slowed down or rested. Their gracious Sudanese hospitality wouldn't allow a word of reproach, even if it took me three hours to get home. But the afternoon sun would only get hotter. Slow steps, fast steps, it was going to take me the same number of steps to get home. Even now, my body was moving automatically, step by step by step, in spite of pain. Why drag it out?

Could I believe in shade? In not being smitten by the sun? I fell in behind Kuong. I stretched my legs to match his long-legged stride.

The soles of his desert boots flashed in front of me, right, left, right, left. The rest of the scene blurred. Faded. My world narrowed to sandy dust and crepe soles. Step, step, step.

The LORD will keep thy going out and thy coming in, from this day forth and forever more.

The pain never went away. I knew it was there, at every step, for the next hour. But what went away was any sense of suffering. I felt the pain, but in a mysterious way the pain didn't hurt. I entered a space where time—did it pass quickly or slowly? I couldn't tell. Time was immaterial. Distance was nothing. I floated above my body. Below me, it moved like light moves, like the circle of a spotlight advances without touching the material world. The rhythm of walking generated its own energy and carried me along. Step, step, step, I walked in a quiet, personal miracle.

I wanted the experience to last: pain present, faith transforming it. I wanted to live unchained like this, beyond my ordinary perceptions of life, the hard line between my physical and spiritual beings dissolved. I wanted to take this with me back to Nairobi and apply to the the suffering in our marriage: the difference between walking in pain and suffering in pain. I wish I could have moved forward peacefully from then on, my emotions silent as my pain had been, above Mark's anger. But I didn't know how I'd done it. I didn't know that I hadn't done anything, I had let something bigger than me happen. And I didn't know how to let it happen again.

The outskirts of Nyal appeared; grass and wattle tukels the beige of the land, because they had been raised up out of the land. Children, dark against the earth, ran out to shout and wave at us. Adults called out to James and John Both and shouted to us, "*Malay, peace!* Is it a good peace? Is it a wide peace?" I laughed with the pastors and elders and called out that my body was enjoying a good, wide peace.

Kuong looked at his watch. "We came back faster than we went out this morning," he said. "You are a good walker." I laughed again. Miraculously, it was true.

Flying back to Loki from that trip to Nyal, afternoon heat currents rising off the vast savannah bucked the plane. The face of a young boy I'd seen, his Kalashnikov rifle almost as big as he was tall, floated back through my mind. I sobbed suddenly, my fist digging into my cheek, my face toward the small, smeared window.

I shook my head and gave myself a bracing talk. The same God who had created in me the ability to rise above my pain would be with the people of Nyal, to help them bear their pain. It was my rightful job to go back to my home. And I had the promise of a reserved seat to Nairobi on a Medicins Sans Frontiers flight. A rare thing, now that the UN wouldn't fly us back and forth. I'd be home in Nairobi tomorrow. Maybe Mark would be having a moment of relief. Maybe he would give me a warm hug. Jesse and Kenny would be happy to see me. I'd be fine.

CHAPTER 14

Tabitha welcomed me to Loki with that longed-for hug. Average height for a Nuer, much taller than me, she was as soft, warm, and blue-black beautiful as always. The church officials had assigned her to run the New Sudan Council of Churches guesthouse, living in the dust and heat, apart from her husband in Nairobi because she'd never been able to have kids. It made me mad how they treated her. But she was only one move to the city, one opportunity for education away from traditional times, when her husband would have just sent her home to her father, gotten his dowry back, and taken another wife. The pastors thought they were being generous. They thought she should be grateful.

After supper at the UN mess, Tabitha and I sat together on the veranda. We smelled of sweat and OFF.

Her flashlight lit up spots in the dust around our flip-flops, checking for scorpions. "Before I married my husband, I asked if he had any other wives. Now I find pictures of children on his dresser. They are so young. How can I be angry? He was a commander. He thought his wife and children had been killed. I am trying to bring the children to Nairobi. They need to be in school."

"And their mother?" Maybe Tabitha, a childless second wife, didn't reply. I couldn't see her reaction in the dark, but I didn't press the question. It seemed too private. The cement porch felt rough through my crinkle skirt. The two-by-four edge of the post dug into my back. I changed the subject. "So when's the MSF flight leaving?"

"Chocolate?" Tabitha said. She held out a Hershey bar. "I told my husband to send me money and he sent me chocolate. Take the whole thing. I have more." We both laughed. Husbands!

Actually, I didn't talk about my husband with her. And she didn't talk about her dad. It was an agreement we had made without words. Her dad was Rev. X, the moderator who'd lost his position after the financial report in cows.

Nobody knew how badly Mark's state of mind had fallen apart with his job, and I wasn't telling. Now I know I was clinging to a dream: he would realize I couldn't do anything to change his feelings; he would regain his own hold on hope and self-respect; we would live and work in East Africa for years.

I didn't have any loyalty to the Sudanese men in the Nairobi office. I was *keeping the partnership alive* by being present with the people in South Sudan on behalf of Presbyterians in the US. Bearing witness. Being the body that proved to them that somewhere in the outside world, someone knew their suffering, someone cared. I couldn't do much but I could do that. From my work I also enjoyed fleeting moments of relief, living in a peaceful and appreciative community, even if it was only with strangers in the swirl of village life.

Since there was no such thing as progress in South Sudan, it was better not to have goals and objectives anyway. As soon as anyone set up a school, a clinic, or an ox-plowing food security project, liberation armies came through, looting and burning.

In Nyal I had relaxed into what I observed in the South Sudanese a sense of hope with no heart of desperation to see what we hoped for. I hadn't fretted when World Food Program didn't deliver the food to Nyal that they promised. Kuong never did call together the students we were going to teach, all of them waiting in villages around, because we couldn't feed them. Instead, the Nuer team and I ate sorghum, and waited day after day for the World Food Program flight. No radio response to our queries about why it wasn't coming.

I drew sketches of the hand-hewn chairs and beds. I read. I fell asleep under my mosquito net, under the Sudanese moon, full, then shrinking and rising later and later. In an African village at peace. *Mal mi chum-chum, sweet peace.*

It was this that I needed to carry home, an ability to find my own peace in the face of utter dysfunction. To find the faith that would carry me through pain. If the Sudanese could do it facing death, hunger and mortal uncertainty, surely I could learn to do better with my emotional turmoil.

During my bout with the stomach bugs, Kuong had the women make *madida* for me—sorghum porridge. With classic African graciousness, he gave me the only mango each day at lunch even after I felt better. I cut it into slices to share with everyone else on the team. I sucked the juice out of each bite before chewing it up.

To keep ourselves busy while we waited for the UN food, Kuong and Pastor John Both taught Bible classes to the local church leaders, and I taught women to crochet. They walked hours to learn to crochet, many of them with babies in baskets on their heads or tied to their backs. We sat in the shade and dust behind the church together, *Chain five, two double crochet.* I counted in Nuer, *kel, rew, diok, nguan, dhiesh,* and they laughed at me, a white woman speaking Nuer. They made crocheted doilies to cover their gourd bowls and keep flies off their food. Even in civil war, a woman wants to create beauty.

I hadn't minded spending two weeks there, accomplishing nothing much, just doilies and being. Dad always said good missiology on trips was, *Don't just do something, sit there.*

But now I was an American again, in the town of Loki again, a town built for and dedicated to transition. Now it was time to go.

Thank you, God, for that seat on the flight to Nairobi.

Jimmy was the one who broke the bad news to me. We were sitting at lunch, Jimmy, Tabitha, and me, in the UN mess hall. "A bishop from the Sudanese Anglican Church took your seat." Jimmy didn't look up. He worked *ugali* corn mush and scooped up goat stew.

The rotation of the earth slowed. I stabbed the prongs of my fork through glistening eggplant skin.

Not that it was Jimmy's fault. He was the logistician for the New Sudan Council of Churches base camp. It was a thankless job, and Jimmy was chronically homesick for his family in Uganda. Loki was where American and European kids came to taste that heady mix of deprivation and idealism that we can call adventure. Loki was no place for a young Ugandan, hardly more than a kid, brought up in community. Hot, dusty, lonely Loki. Six weeks on and one week off—but he couldn't get home and back in one week. Loki looked more like punishment than adventure to Jimmy.

"I can get you on the Turkana Shuttle," he said, his gap-toothed smile trying to make it better. "It's not bad. Loki to Nairobi by nightfall."

If the Turkana Shuttle was so great, I'd have heard of it before.

Jimmy's thumb and fingers were red with goat stew and flecked with white. His voice turned mournful. "When you get back to Nairobi, remember Jimmy, if anything happens to Mark," he said.

"I tell you, I'm old enough to be your mother."

He hunched over his plate, pouting, playing to Tabitha and me. "I'm looking for someone to marry Jimmy and take him away from here," he said. In went another bite of *ugali* and goat. "A white woman, no matter what conditions she might set."

"No matter what condition she's in?"

Beside me, Tabitha spluttered Orange Crush back into her glass. Jimmy pressed his lips together to keep the goat stew in as he laughed.

"Anyway, nothing is going to happen to Mark."

Mark and I communicated by the no-news-is-good-news method when I traveled. I'd had lots of good news from home in the last two weeks. My ETA, as we used to say in Ethiopia, waiting for the bush-pilots to take me off to boarding school—my Estimated Time of Arrival home would be good news, too. Mark didn't know I thought I had a place on the plane. He didn't know I'd lost it. He would know I was coming when I got there.

I lay on my bed in the evening heat. The generator's *thunk-thunk-*

thunk stilled. The quiet chirping of desert insects and a mosquito outside my net swelled up to fill the sudden silence. There was nothing to distract me—I'd finished my only book in Nyal. I stared into the darkness of my room long into the night.

Remembering the road trip to Loki was part of what kept me awake. Eighteen hours to go five hundred miles. The seats with springs poking through. Crammed in with more sweaty bodies than the van was created to hold. No bathroom stops.

And then, suddenly, in the hot darkness, I saw visions: *me in one of those Kenyan road accidents—the brakes give out and we end up a mangled mess at the bottom of some ravine, headlines the next day in Nairobi's* East African Standard.

Mark lying on the road, his motorcycle crumpled on the shoulder, his blood bright red against the black asphalt, while I hurtle along the highway home, oblivious.

Kenny's pale face under pale hair hovering by Jesse's shoulder. Jesse holding it together for the two of them, parentless, clueless, frantic. Tender Jesse, who'd held out hope to Mark the year before. The son who tried to help me carry the world on my shoulders.

Mark had moved us to a flat near the office, right off Westlands. So many moves in the last two years. So much disruption. But this had been a good one, because the boys were closer to their school, and because Mark's drive across town had been so hard on him.

Mark had been prone to road-rage in the best of Portland-polite driving. In Nairobi, gridlock jammed the streets the minute there was a slow-down. Drivers of matatus were daredevil scoff-laws who passed on the right, on the left, full in the face of ongoing traffic, on the sidewalks—horns blaring, lights flashing—whatever it took to inch ahead.

Moving closer to the office had helped Mark's mood some. Buying a motorcycle to weave through gridlock helped more, though it made my stomach clench any time I thought of him out there in traffic. On balance, I was grateful, and I held my tongue about the motorcycle.

I had finally called Duda Suzic, the UN counselor who'd promised to help us with our post-traumatic stress disorder after we were taken hostage in South Sudan. Or got caught in crossfire. Or burned out trying to alleviate the vast human suffering. I figured this counted, Mark's despair that he had lost the Financial Advisor battle.

Duda counseled Mark for a couple of months, and I could see the relief on his face when he came home from their sessions. She was in the perfectly right job—who wouldn't fall in love with her cropped honey blond hair, her warm smile, and her Czech vowels?

I asked her over one afternoon to evaluate Jesse and Kenny. She walked in the back yard with them, one at a time. She came in, sat with me at the dining room table, and told me they were doing fine, they were good kids.

I waited for Duda to ask, *And how are you doing?* When she didn't, I walked her to the front door blinking back the tears that were always hovering under my bottom eyelids. I didn't know support was my birthright. I thought my failures had left me bankrupt in the commerce of love.

I turned to what had worked before: I was a boarding school kid. They learn to get by with no one to turn to for help. I held myself together by being resolutely gutsy in South Sudan. By trusting that I was on the other end of the UN radio system if my family needed me. I knew that word of an emergency at home really would get to me by radio in Nyal or Loki. But as soon as I stepped foot on a bus, no one could reach me. Getting on a bus for two days felt like descending into an abyss of the unknown.

It was hours later when I finally fell into sleep that night in Loki.

The next morning, I counted my shilling bills one more time. They lay limp on the sheet, and so dirty you could hardly see the colors. I'd go through them pretty fast eating at the UN mess, and no telling when another flight would open up. I couldn't borrow anything from Tabitha but chocolate. It would have to be the Turkana Shuttle for me.

CHAPTER 15

Early morning smelled of dew on the desert dust. It was already hot. Jimmy took my shillings and paid the driver.

He handed me small change. "See, all the way to Nairobi."

The driver was stocky and lighter brown than the Sudanese, probably a Kikuyu from the central Kenyan highlands. He shook my hand. "Sit in the front," he said.

I tucked my bags between my feet and the gearshift. Tabitha ran to get me something to eat. Dust turned her flip-flops and ankles tan. My ten shillings—twenty cents—bought six hard-boiled eggs and a loaf of bread. Tabitha tipped her head and shifted her eyes toward a woman struggling into the back with a small child and a large gray bundle.

"A Sudanese pastor's wife," she whispered.

Here comes one more family for the donor money to support, I thought. But I had no ill-will for this woman and her baby, fresh out of South Sudan. Who knows what trauma she'd come through?

I waited until she and Jimmy got her bundle jammed under her seat. The child stopped shrieking and settled at her breast. Then I reached back with three eggs and half the bread, jagged and white where I'd broken it.

"*Asante,*" she whispered. The child stopped suckling and reached for the bread. The woman's breast slipped slowly back into the top of her dress.

Dry white bread for breakfast on the Turkana Shuttle. Each bite grew sweeter as I chewed it. In my head I could hear my boys singing the radio jingle, *"Nev-a say brr-ead, Say Supa-loaf."* Mark and me laughing at them in a happy moment. I couldn't get home soon enough.

I leaned out to wave to Tabitha and Jimmy, and squinted against the grit as the bus pulled out. Next stop, UN camp. Bags thumped into the hold, voices murmured, the driver licked his thumb and finger and counted shilling bills. The bus rocked, as people climbed in and got settled.

Now that the trip was upon me, I felt content. My body jiggled against rough seat fabric with the uneven idling. Nairobi by nightfall, Jimmy had said; that would be a mere twelve hours for that five hundred miles. How many miles per hour was that, dodging pot holes on our side and vehicles coming the other way in our lane dodging pot holes on their side? I asked the driver what time we would arrive.

"*Hakuna matata,*" he said cheerfully. "We will reach Kitale before dark."

This was not *no worries*. Kitale wasn't even halfway. I stared at him.

He smiled a weak smile. It had the look of not wanting to break bad news. Or maybe the smile of pretending not to understand me. Or maybe I was the one who misunderstood.

For hours we drove the one paved street of Lokichoggio, horn blaring. It slowly sank in: all itineraries aside, the driver was not going to leave Loki until the bus was full. I worked on relaxing my shoulders. Every time I remembered my shoulders, they had climbed halfway up to my ears again. Again and again, we pulled into the UN Camp.

Another white woman stood waiting with her faded backpack at Kate Camp. I knew her. Rhoda—she worked at the Wycliffe office, and we met when they printed my manual for teaching preschool English in South Sudan. Her straight brown hair hung in strands to her shoulders. Faded denim skirt, thick leather sandals, she looked like a real missionary.

I wished again that I was a Wycliffe translator, you live with people, learn their language, design a system for writing it, and translate the Bible. It would have been perfect for me. So straightforward.

When we'd been in Ethiopia, when I took Mark and the kids to see Maji, when we stayed in a little mud brick house that was waiting for someone to live in, learn Dizi and lead a translation team, I was sure I belonged in that house. A half wall lifted up as a window on sunset right over the table. I wanted to learn the Dizi language. As a girl, I'd thought Dizi was my destiny. I'd started a little note-book dictionary.

But my actual destiny had taken a different fork in the road, so I left Maji again and went back to Addis Ababa to teach English to my three hundred eager but naughty little students.

At Trackmark Camp, white South African pilots in khaki uniforms sat under trailing bougainvillea drinking coffee and rubbing sleep out of their eyes. Clipboards lay on the plastic tablecloths beside them: food-drop assignments for the second rotation of the day.

They would swoop the big bellied Hercs down over drop sites and workers would push maize and rice out flaps in the back. Hungry people would be crowding the ropes. As the Hurcs climbed back into cloudless skies over South Sudan, the Sudanese would swarm the target site. Men would carry the intact sacks of grain and stack them. Women would salvage sacks that split. Children would crawl in the dust and pick up the spilt grains before the birds could get them. Then the UN logistician would distribute the food according to family size. They would all take a share and begin the walk home, carrying the loads on their heads.

Somewhere along the path, likely as not, a commander of some liberation army would liberate the food. The people would return home hungrier than they left, after walking for two days. But they had to try. The UN had to try. That's all anybody could figure out to do in South Sudan. Keep trying things that weren't working.

If I thought about it too much, I'd be like my Mom, who always said, *If I start crying, I'll never stop.* She'd climbed out of her destitute and abusive childhood into a good life. It hadn't left her much margin for feeling the sorrows.

I had better hopes for myself and my children than any of the

South Sudanese did for theirs, whether in South Sudan or in Nairobi. But I couldn't stand up in the flood of Mark's anger. I couldn't keep my balance. All I could do at home, too, was try what never worked.

At ten o'clock, four hours after settling myself on the bus, we finally turned left, out of town. We lined up behind two trucks, their aid organization name painted bold and red on the bright blue sides, heading back to Nairobi for more South Sudan aid. In front of the trucks, the roadblock was down. Our driver banged his door behind him. I shifted in the sweaty seat. My *khanga* tucked into the top of the closed window would keep the sun off my arm, but the price would be no fresh air. I left it open.

People shuffled and stretched in the back seats.

A young boy reached up from the asphalt and tapped on my door. He held up an egg in one hand and a *pili-pili* Tabasco bottle full of salt, with holes pierced in the red plastic top. I smiled and held up one of my eggs. The first had choked me, going down with no salt. I extended my palm. He grinned and shook grains of salt like coarse sand into it.

"*Asante,*" I said, and he saluted.

When the driver banged back in, we all sat straighter in our seats. The trucks ahead of us belched diesel fumes and picked up speed. Kenyan soldiers, Kalashnikov rifle straps brown across their army green chests, waved us to a stop, and the roadblock swung back down.

We piled out, piled back in, sat some more. I should have seen right then and there that *Nairobi by nightfall* was a fairytale.

When we finally got on the road, wind coming through my window lifted my bangs off my forehead and dried the sweat on my face to a crusty layer. The sine wave of my mood ticked up just a little.

Turkana huts passed by out the window, four-feet tall domes of skins and pieces of old blue UN plastic tarps stretched over thin bent wood frames. Children in dingy t-shirts with nothing on their bottom halves jumped up and down and waved. Under scrubby acacias, men clustered in the lacy shade, their almost-white cloths wrapped around their waists and tucked in. Turkana women wore thick collections of bead necklaces, stacked from shoulders to chin. Doctors say the beads end up supporting their neck vertebrae, which become elongated by all the necklaces. They carried water and cloth-wrapped packages on their heads, down dusty paths be tween the huts.

We passed the turn for the tarmac, handling more flights of Sudan aid than Jumo Kennyata International Airport handled flights of tourists. On our way, a bit before noon. Maybe there was still time to get to Nairobi by dark.

And at least I was going home. Home crossed the backs of my eyelids, closed against the glare. I'd filled our flat with plants and beautiful colors. Outside, bougainvillea ran up over the trees and strung itself along the fence, crepe blossoms in magenta, fuchsia, gold, white, and scarlet. If I had to choose only one flower to festoon the world, I would choose bougainvillea.

After South Sudan and Loki, my eyes hurt for the first few days at home—the bougainvillea, the red and blue rug, my navy curtains with African geometrics in white. It always took me a while to lose the guilt that clung to me as I claimed my right to fly out and leave war behind instead of staying back, begging for a t-shirt, a bit of unused soap, the tea leaves in the bottom of the bag.

It would take me a few days to unwind, but I was ready for my more orderly life back in Nairobi. One in which Mark kept things working and created systems that off-set my absent-mindedness, off-set the Kenyan and Sudanese ways of living at the tip edge of chaos. When he wasn't swamped by his own emotional chaos, that was a sweet gift Mark gave me.

Then I sighed. If I got home and found him unstable, I'd be exchanging the tension of deprivation and possible danger for the chaos of emotions at war.

By Lodwar at lunchtime, my arm was splotched red and white

and tingled when I moved, as though the sun had shrunk my skin. It glistened with sweat. The Brits had built their political prison in Lodwar, below sea level, where a man was welcome to escape. If he left the safety of prison, he would die of sunstroke before he reached shelter.

I stood in line for the toilet, in a sweltering hallway dark with soot and smelling of sewage, mold and dust. I imagined I was breathing only the oxygen.

After my turn on a fetid squat toilet, I opened a Handi-wipe. It had gone dry, so I held it under the spigot of a galvanized tin can hanging on the wall, Lodwar's version of running water. I jiggled the can and a few drops of water wetted the wipe.

Lunch—scrambled eggs and *chapatis*, both glistening with lard, washed down with two passionfruit Fantas. The red and green plaid plastic tablecloth pulled up along my sweaty arm when I moved.

Rhoda was dipping fingers into stew and *ugali* at another table with her African travel companion. The thought of goat stew in that heat...Rhoda was definitely more acculturated than I was.

The server, his apron covered with splotchy stains, picked up my plate with one hand and my two pop bottles between two fingers of the other. He returned and swung a dark gray rag over the area in front of me. He said something in Swahili.

"*Baas*," I answered, though I didn't understand whatever he'd said. *Enough*. Though I could hardly swallow, my throat was so dry. Surely we would go soon. I didn't want hours of rough road on a full bladder.

The air was still and thick with grease. I walked out onto the stone veranda. *Let's go, let's go, let's go.*

The bus had disappeared, and so had the rest of the passengers. I dragged a chair into a triangle of shade, though every stone, every lateral and upright of mortar blasted heat. A young boy tried to sell me a necklace: circles punched out of ostrich eggshells strung on green nylon.

To my left, a boy shouted. Suddenly, every vendor on his bicycle, every bored passer-by, every tepid-soda-drinker from inside the hotel crowded around, pushing and cheering. A black fist swung above the crowd, and I heard thuds and grunts through the shouting.

By my elbow, a fat woman in dingy white with a green leaf pattern appeared. She launched into sustained cursing. I couldn't actually understand her, but there was no question about the gist. The crowd pulled away. The boys picked themselves up and dusted gray billows off their clothes. Everyone laughed. One boy wiped a drip of blood from below his nose with his wrist. The other mumbled something, picked up his bike, and peddled away, head low between his shoulders.

"*Something, something* soda?" the boy in the gray apron asked, as everyone else drifted back to their hot, sleepy spots. But I didn't dare. Surely the bus would show up any minute. I tucked my feet between the straps of my backpack and rested my head against the hot stones.

Someone tapped my knee. Rhoda's voice said, near my ear, "I know an Africa Inland Mission family in Lodwar. We're thinking of going to visit them. Would you like a walk?"

My eyes wouldn't open. "Aren't we leaving?"

"The bus won't leave Lodwar until sunset. It's too hot to travel now. We'll drive by dark to Kitale."

Oh, Jimmy. So much for Nairobi by nightfall. So much even for what the driver promised me: Kitale by dark.

What if the driver left us behind? Would he sell the ratty contents of my duffle: the navy silk shirt with the rust stain down the back where a shower at Kakuma refugee camp, another hot dusty place, another English course, had dripped on it all night; my crinkle skirt; the emerald green silk blouse that looked dusted with powdered sugar where the sun had faded it? That blouse didn't match anything, but in South Sudan, the more colors the merrier. When I came out of my *tukel* one morning in Nyal wearing that emerald green on top, the brown-gold-burgundy skirt and a lavender and turquoise bandana, Kuong had said, "You're looking especially smart this morning."

I heaved myself out of my chair, feeling drugged.

At the house, I let the conversation between real missionaries wash over me. I had always keenly felt the spiritual dimension of life. But what I cared deeply about was not souls and beliefs, but people's lives. Justice. Mercy. Peace. The redemption and regeneration love can bring.

In that moment, what I gave deep and grateful thanks for was cold water in a glass. The cold on my hands, holding it. The chill all the way down my throat.

Later, back on the baking hot veranda, I watched the sun drift toward the flat, dun-colored horizon, growing bigger and more orange. Twelve hours since I'd left the base camp, and we'd gone about one hundred miles. Tensing my shoulders and grinding my teeth was all I'd come up with to do about it.

Rhoda and Durgo ordered supper. Jesus said some demons couldn't be cast out without prayer and fasting. The same could be said for some trips, I decided. Prayer and fasting on the Turkana Shuttle to Nairobi.

The bus roared up. People appeared from nowhere and loaded on in the peachy-gray light of the Kenyan dusk. We would enter the southern hemisphere in the middle of the night and follow the Southern Cross all the way home.

CHAPTER 16

Sunlight fades fast near the equator. It was almost dark when we stopped at the roadblock on the way out of town. Police boots clumped up the steps and men flashed their lights in the faces behind me. Rhoda, Durgo, and the Somalis were herded, blinking and squinting, out of the bus. It's never too late in Kenya to shake down foreigners.

My own special officer came to the front window. "Passport," he said. He shined his flashlight in my face.

I winced, dug out my passport, and leaned to watch in the spot of light as the officer paged through. He found a blue triangle, Government of Kenya. Never mind it was my exit visa from five years before, not my entry permit. He probably didn't even know what he was looking for; there couldn't be many tourists coming by road through Lodwar. Maybe he couldn't read English. Maybe he had just hoped this would be his big chance to score tea money.

He shut my passport and handed it back with a flick of his wrist. "How do you find Kenya?"

I looked into his brown eyes in the dim light, at his cheeks, taut over his bones, with red glowing through the brown. *Kenya is a magnificent country mismanaged, oppressed, violent, and corrupt. That's how I find Kenya.*

I'd never tested the veneer that covered violence in Kenya. One of Jesse's teachers almost bled to death right on the street downtown, when a thief stabbed his arm. He wasn't getting his watch off fast enough.

Guard my lips. They felt thin and tight.

I managed to turn them up at the corners. "Kenya is beautiful.

Mount Kili. The bougainvillea.Mombassa."

His smile disappeared into darkness as he turned and strutted away.

I found my own small red flashlight, warm and heavy in the bottom of my bag. My fingers discovered the last two squishy squares of chocolate from Tabitha. I opened the foil carefully and licked off the chocolate. A crease in the foil slit my tongue; the taste of blood mixed with the chocolate. I should have remembered my fast.

Rhoda's face appeared at my window looking broad and sweaty. "Will you do me a favor?" She lifted her hair off her neck. "Have the Wycliffe office send my passport up to Loki? We'll go back tomorrow and wait there."

"Don't you have your work permit?"

"Well, yes." Her smile was not as tight as mine felt. Her work permit should have been enough, but in Kenya, as I'd learned, every policeman was a law unto himself. "My passport's in the corner of my top dresser drawer. If not there, look in the desk. Tell them Durgo's with me, I'm fine."

I pressed my stinging tongue against the top of my mouth, rolled my head back and forth against the back of my seat. Could I be more frustrated? I stretched my legs at an angle across my duffle. Sweat tickled down the side of my face. The air was still, with windows now closed tight against mosquitoes.

Finally, the driver banged, muttering, into the seat beside me and turned on the engine. Rhoda, Durgo, and two police climbed into the back and were barely inside before we k-turned and roared back into town.

"Lodwar police station," Rhoda said behind me.

Don't do this to me, Rhoda. Just don't. "I thought you were going back to Loki?"

"So did I."

What the police didn't know was that Rhoda was one of those missionaries who wouldn't pay. She'd just keep pleasantly saying she'd be glad to go back to Loki and wait there for her passport, if that's what they wanted to see. The police thought the threat of the police station would change her mind. They didn't have the sense to give in now rather than later.

Rhoda seemed unflapped by the rest of us—murmuring in clear vowels from the Kenyans, the Somali gutturals, the murmuring in my head, all of us mad because she was holding up the whole bus. She had greater moral certitude than I would have had. Of course, I'd gone to criminal court, making the same kind of moral stand, but that had only inconvenienced me. I didn't like the thought of how vulnerable to peer pressure I might have been.

But in the bus on the outskirts of Lodwar, I was not Mother Teresa. I was a mother who'd been two weeks away from home. Any more delay felt excruciating. The Ethiopians tell a story: an angel gives a blind man a gift—he will receive his sight the next morning. As evening falls, he cries out. "How can I bear one more night blind?"

Surrounded by the night sounds of crickets and desert creatures, the Swahili and Somali voices behind me soft and fatalistic now, with yellow glowing out of the police station, I bunched the khanga against the window as a pillow.

The driver's door banged and woke me. The instrument panel under-lit his scowl. Rhoda, Durgo, and the police climbed into the bus again, and this time gravel sprayed all the way out the police compound driveway. No one spoke. Cleats on the policemen's boots clattered on the metal steps as they exited at the check point. One policeman reappeared in the headlights to lift the roadblock. I looked back at Rhoda, my question in my eyes.

"They just dropped it."

Our headlights created a tunnel. Black shapes on the verge turned green in the light as we passed. I rebunched the khanga and fell asleep.

Somewhere, sometime in the middle of the night, we stopped. We must have climbed into the highlands. Cool night air soothed my sunburned arm as I followed the crowd into a chai house. I nodded to the waiter and he brought a cup of *chai* steaming from the pot on the stove. On the top floated a dead fly. It rocked on the sloshing *chai*. I squeezed my itching eyes tight.

Did it fly into the cup and die on the way to the table? Was the rest of the tea in the pot okay? It had all been boiled, anyway. I waved to the waiter and he replaced my cup. Or scooped out the fly. I didn't need to know.

The bus driver chattered to me, glad to get out of the desert, maybe. I nodded and sipped hot *chai*. I don't remember a thing he said. He paid for my *chai* and I thanked him by not saying anything about Kitale by nightfall.

I woke once again in my seat. The bus was still. The bus driver's body was black in the night, hunched over and sleeping on the steering wheel. Kitale.

I woke to the driver tapping my knee. He held out two blue bills and an orange. The light hurt my eyes. They gritted when I blinked. I stared, hands in my lap. He reached back and gave the money to Rhoda.

"The shuttle heads back to Loki," she said. "Durgo will buy our tickets." My sleep-deprived brain worked on it. Not Nairobi by nightfall. Not even Kitale by nightfall. The day in Lodwar instead. And if I had it right, the Turkana Shuttle charges us for a trip to Nairobi fully intending to turn around in Kitale.

The Somalis shouted and refused to get out. When the driver tried to give their money back, they folded their arms, turned their shoulders away, and shouted some more. I considered that option.

Maybe it was spending all day and night on the Turkana Shuttle that made me so mellow. I just shook the driver's hand and gathered my bags together. Not one word of reproach crossed my lips.

"Stay close to me," Durgo said. He held onto his bag with both hands and stepped into a crowd of young boys. Yelling erupted. I hesitated on the bottom step. One boy shoved another and grabbed at my bags. I hung on tight. Rhoda held another boy off with her shoulder. Between the shouting boys and the shouting Somalis, I could hardly hear her voice. "They're bargaining. Durgo will figure out which bus."

"Twenty-one hundred," Durgo shouted and pointed. Rhoda and I nodded.

A boy pulled on Durgo's duffle with one hand and punched other boys off with the other. We shuffled behind, jostled by the shouting boys, as close to Durgo and each other as we could walk, slipping in Kitale's rainy season mud.

Durgo counted bills into the bus driver's hand. They shouted at each other.

I needed a latrine.

"Three hundred more each," Durgo said.

This trip was going to make my frown lines permanent. "What happened to twenty-one hundred?"

Rhoda dug through the pocket on the front of her backpack. "The driver doesn't care what the boys say. The only thing arguing with the boys does, it gives you time to figure out which bus is going to fill up and leave first."

Lying. Misrepresenting. Looking for a take. The Kenyan pastime. Mellow was completely gone again. For someone who supposedly loved living in Africa, I was getting fried by smaller and smaller incidents. I pulled my sweater and three hundred shillings out of my bag. "Don't let him leave without me. I'm going to look for a latrine."

"We are going, we are going," the driver shouted. I waved my hand and jumped over a puddle. Who was he kidding? The bus was only half full.

A girl was sweeping out a gray wooden barbershop.

"*Cho?*" I asked, in my best Swahili.

She shook her head, "*Hakuna cho.*"

Across the road, two women shied their eyes away from me. "*Habari*," they said.

"*Msuri*," I said, only it wasn't going to be *msuri* if I couldn't find a *cho*.

Finally, a woman pointed, and when I got close, the smell led me on. I stepped around the corner. The breakfast I hadn't had turned over in my stomach. I held my hand over my mouth and tried to smell only my own sweat. I held my skirt up in a bundle and stepped between piles of human excrement.

I'm one of those people who, as a courtesy to the next passenger, wipes out the airplane sink with her paper towel. I pick up bits of toilet paper and trash from the floor of public restrooms. In strangers' bathrooms and the restrooms of gas stations, I change TP rolls that seem to have run out just before I came along. It's the *leave it in better shape* philosophy I got from Dad. But even I know when to stop. I dragged my feet in the muddy grass all the way back to the bus.

The converted school bus to Nairobi had straight gray seats and sliding windows. I yanked my duffle up the narrow aisle. A muscle in my back knotted. I stopped. Breathed deep. Straightened.

I mashed my duffle into the space where I might have expected my feet to go. My knees grazed the seat in front of me. I slowly stretched my back. It clutched. I tried resting my arms and head on the backpack on my lap, fetal position upright. I tried sitting ram-rod straight. Leaning against the window. Nothing felt any better.

We left an hour later. Before the other buses.

Dripping branches whipped by the window. How had twenty-four hours gone by and we were still only half way? *Jimmy, if you ever want a white woman to marry you, don't make promises to her about the Turkana Shuttle.*

"It'll go fast now," Rhoda said. "Only eight more hours."

Jesus said, *To whom much has been given, much will be required.* This pain sure proved it. How many people are willing to work in South Sudan? I wanted some kind of credit for my willingness, not eight more hours. Not pain.

Maybe my own brand of fatality drove me to hang on to working in South Sudan even when sometimes I could hardly bear it. Maybe fatality, not hope, kept me suffering on and on with Mark. Or maybe I carried an unexamined conviction that I just had to suffer—*to whom much is given, more will be required*, and I had so many undeserved advantages. Maybe suffering was my coinage of exchange for love. But where was the love?

I give up, I thought. But what does *that* mean, eight hours from home? I could hide my face in my *khanga* and cry myself to sleep and not wake up until we got to Nairobi. Or maybe if I did that, I'd snap. I'd start to scream and pull out my hair. They'd put me off, to sit with my aching back in the bushes on the side of the road. Maybe I could die there among the drips and cow pies.

But you don't die just because you feel like it. And isn't it interesting that there's really no such thing as relative suffering. When we're suffering, we can't imagine a moment when we won't be; we can't imagine someone else's suffering and compare it usefully. We can't save someone else from their suffering and when we are lost in our own.

In a muddy little town, tin shed roofs ahead gave a bit of shine to a market scene of dingy clothes, brown skin and damp produce. A boy ran alongside the bus as it slowed. He held up roasted corn, husks pulled back for handles, three ears in each hand like sprouts of grass on a child's drawing.

As the bus stopped, I waved to him and tried to open my sliding window. The cramp shot up my backbone. The window wedged itself at an angle. The boy's face tilted up, glowing with his smile.

The bus driver shouted at a woman dragging a bundle, big as a cotton bale, down the aisle. People pushed forward on each step of the bus behind her. I got coins out, and the boy and I both pushed on the window.

"Do you want some, Rhoda?" She'd become a silent zombie beside me. *"Mbili,"* I said. The boy pushed two ears of corn up over the edge of the window. The air outside was wet and chilly. The cold aluminum window frame scraped my sweater up to my elbow as I lay two big brass coins in the boy's thin palm. My smile matched his.

"*Asante sana.*" Ears of field corn, roasted over charcoal, charred and chewy sweet, they were so hot I had to drop them again onto my lap. "Here." I pushed one over to Rhoda. How could she not want roasted corn?

The bus roared away and I tossed my corn back and forth, burning one palm and then the other, blessed heat, the smell nutty in my nose.

When I finished my corn, the ache in my back was gone. It felt like another personal miracle. Or something the Preacher might have said in Ecclesiastes: *Vanity, vanity, all is vanity, but take heart. There is a boy. There is his smile. There is hot roasted corn.*

I woke once and sat still to enjoy the bliss of no pain. Rhoda breathed deeply, her head fallen heavy against my shoulder. Rain pelted the windows, front and side. The windshield wipers beat across the glass.

On the corner in Westlands, I stood in pouring rain as the bus pulled away. Naphtha and benzene exhaust rankled my sinuses. I crossed the street. Water sluiced through my sandals, and the hem of my skirt flapped wet against the backs of my calves. I found a pay phone and a coin. "Mark? It's me. I'm at the bakery. I made it this far, can you come get me?"

His bass voice always sounded high and sweet over the phone. He seemed happy I was home.

I set my soggy bags on a metal chair. The waitress smiled.

"*Msuri?*" she said, *Fine?* She set down silverware rolled up in torn-in-half napkins.

I smiled back from under my drowned-rat bangs. "*Msuri,*" I said, and ordered the usual for Mark and me: fresh squeezed passion juice and raisin sweet rolls.

CHAPTER 17

Before Mark and I started in Nairobi, we had settled Miriam in our house in Portland for college. She called us in the spring of 1998, as we struggled along, to say her boyfriend had flown out from Ohio and surprised her with a ring—could we come home that summer for her wedding?

Duda Suzek had stepped away from Mark's care. I'd found him another counselor, who put him on Zoloft. He was a little calmer.

So far, what Elizabeth had accomplished with her Women's Director's salary was two maternity leaves. I met with the new moderator and told him I wouldn't endorse a renewal for the grant. He lunged over his desk at me. He shouted, pounded on the desk and called me a spy. I knew pastors sometimes got in fist fights with each other during staff meetings. I left the office trembling.

We bought tickets for the day after the boys finished their school year, anxious to see Miriam, eager for a break from tension and failure with the Nuers.

Air France, our carrier, went on strike the week of our departure. We were so immured to chaos we didn't even question the agent who put us on Lufthansa with nothing but a piece of paper on Air France letterhead. It got us home.

A few weeks after we settled in for the summer, Mark's prescription of Zoloft ran out. "I don't need it any more," he said when he told me. Over the next weeks he went grim and silent. He talked only to me, only in a low voice, only in our bedroom at night.

On Father's Day, I gave him a back door with a lovely glass light that I'd found at the door and window outlet store. I thought a project might help him regain his balance. It was a brilliant gift for a man who only ever wanted tools. We'd always talked about converting the kitchen window to a door and building a deck for a bistro table on the east side of the house. I imagined drinking our morning coffee there, in the cool, fresh morning air.

When I unveiled the gift, the project to keep Mark pleasantly busy until the wedding, I looked expectantly at his face. I couldn't read the look he gave me. It wasn't gratitude. It wasn't joy.

In our room that night he accused me again of loving him only for what he could do around the house. "I'm just your drone," he said again. Unspoken was what happens to drones when they've done their duty with the queen. Mark was going dark. My Ethiopian friends might have suggested he was possessed by an evil spirit.

He said he would never be happy. He said he might as well die. He accused me of not caring. He seemed to believe I could say or do something to make him feel better. I tried to say what he wanted, in the tone of voice he prescribed. It was never quite right.

I reminded Mark, over and over, how happy we'd been to meet again after high school; what good partners we'd become in Portland; how sweet we'd been working together in Addis Ababa. I promised when these feelings lifted, as they'd done before, then if he thought some other life would make him happy, I wouldn't hold onto him.

Our tense conversations went late into the nights. Mark thought if I didn't do something about how bad he felt, it meant I didn't love him.

Mark was *flang* and I was back to dragging him in before dawn so no one else would know. I didn't want Miriam, the boys and our new son-in-law to think badly of him. Deeper, hidden by shame for unwomanly selfishness, I didn't want them to think badly of me for choosing him as their father. Lurking so deeply it's taken me years to see it there in the shadows, the ghost of unworthiness always whispered its warning.

I was exhausted from the travel into South Sudan. I was exhausted from the emotions the pain in South Sudan stirred up in me, and the hopelessness of doing anything to relieve the suffering I saw. I was exhausted by the emotional roller-coaster Mark and I had been on for two years. And now, I had a wedding to plan.

Miriam said food was the only place we could save money. I wanted to weep at the thought of catering her reception. Mark complained about costs, but he wouldn't sit down and talk to Miriam directly. Besides being a failure of a wife, I might be a failure as a mother, if this pillar of womanhood crumbled under the load.

Day after day, I pulled myself, sandy-eyed, out of bed on hot Portland summer mornings, the bright sunny days such a jarring contrast to my mood. I girded myself once again with that boot-strap-hoisting I'd learned as a child. Miriam and I planned, made phone calls, compared prices and went over lists and menus. I looked up pastry recipes. I baked and froze dozens of puffs for Boston cream pies. I rolled out, shaped and pinched the rims of shells for little tarts, doing it all in a haze.

Mark got more and more grimly silent. He retreated to his shop every day. But not to put in a new door. Later, Miriam told me that when I took responsibility for things Mark did so he wouldn't look like a jerk, I made myself look like the jerk.

Three weeks before the wedding, we left the boys at home and went to our favorite micro-brew for its hamburger special. On the way, both of us staring straight ahead at the road, Mark said, "I'm done. I need a new life."

I pulled into the parking lot. We sat in silence in the dimming light of a long summer dusk. Mark closed his eyes and laid his head back on the headrest. Random thoughts drifted through fear-tingled blankness in my head. I would never find a job in Portland, now that my favorite work skills involved speaking Amharic and Nuer. I would never again see the photo albums we left in Nairobi. Jesse would never forgive us for ripping him away from Rosslyn Academy. Miriam would be shattered by our crisis clouding her wedding.

I suddenly remembered the Zoloft. "Mark," I said, "You ruin Miriam's wedding, and I will never, ever forgive you." I told him to get back on the meds. After the wedding, if he still wanted to bail on our lives in Nairobi, we could figure that out. For one moment, I imagined how peaceful it would be, living alone.

"Who should I call?" His voice sounded plaintive.

"That's your problem." I got out of the car and went into the restaurant. He meekly followed.

I laughed about this later—to myself, never to Mark. How strange it was that, when he was threatening to sever our connection forever, my vowing not to forgive him galvanized him to action. We must have both known, deep inside, that his misery was not really mine to solve.

I also remembered a crisis-intervention counselor in Nairobi I'd found when looking for some support for myself. All he offered me was sleeping pills. He was high on adrenaline and sleep deprivation and it was Mark who intensely interested him. He said Mark's threats were manipulative.

I was horrified at the time. I thought manipulation must imply malice. But I eventually wondered whether maybe, after all, Mark's blaming and raging, his threatening over and over to leave me—all were different expressions of his misery. All pleading for me to do something to save him from it. And I, in my hope of earning love, could never just firmly but kindly say that was not my job.

I never asked Mark how he got himself resupplied with Zoloft. By the week before the wedding, he began to smile more, to talk again, to answer the boys' questions at supper. I was awash with relief.

Late on the evening before Miriam's wedding, as I tacked the tulle of her veil to her barrette, her in-laws-to-be called and told us to turn on our TV. There was a disaster in Nairobi.

It was August 7th, the eighth anniversary of the deployment of American troops to the Saudi Arabian Peninsula. Al Qaeda and the Egyptian Islamic Jihad had joined to punish the US for their incursion: they had bombed two US Embassies simultaneously, one in Nairobi and the other in Dar es Salam, Tanzania.

By the time we got our TV turned on, the building next to the embassy in downtown Nairobi had collapsed into a pile of rubble. Billows of dust and smoke had turned the air gray. We watched from Portland in disbelief, footage of mayhem unfolding in crowded streets.

The next morning, I took Miriam to get her hair done. On the radio, NPR spoke the words *Al-Qaeda* for the first time. The newscaster read the fax that Osama Bin Laden had sent to London. That was the first time we ordinary people in the US heard his name.

After I left Miriam in the care of the hairdresser, I wandered the mall, numb.

We lived in a rough global neighborhood. That's what the US ambassador had said in Addis Ababa, on the eve of guerillas marching in to topple the communist regime.

But I had grown up feeling compassion for the poverty of Ethiopia peasants, not fear for my own safety. This felt the same. We would return to Nairobi. We knew, as foreigners we would be safe from all but the most random of dangerous circumstances. But everyone in Nairobi, including us, would be more tense, knowing Kenya might be targeted for allying with the US.

I'd always believed that if I tried hard enough, I could make the world a better place. Someone should have given me a medallion of St. Jude, the patron saint of lost causes. No matter how I tried, the world was getting worse before my eyes, and I couldn't even bring peace in my own marriage.

I returned to the hairdresser's. I sat on a bench for a few minutes and smiled at how Miriam was going to emerge, glorious and radiant in her up-do. She had been growing her hair for months, and she'd shown the hairdresser her clippings of glamorous stars' hairdos when we set up the appointment. But when she walked out, one look at her face, and I braced myself. "What's wrong?"

"Mom! Look!" Miriam buried her face in her hands, and tears dripped between her fingers. "Touch it."

I did. With that much hairspray, Mark would have been safe on his motorcycle on the Nairobi streets. "What happened?"

"He was mean. He did it on purpose. He didn't even cut my hair. He just pinned it up and then sprayed and sprayed and sprayed."

We had a few hours left before she needed to be at the church, to zip up her size 2 wedding dress and become the tiny but sophisticated bride she'd dreamed of being. I sat with Miriam as she wept, stroking her back gently. I remembered how she'd come home as a newborn from the hospital in Ethiopia with impetigo. Remembered how I'd cried about her watery blisters, seeing the future, seeing how I would not be able to protect her from harm. Seeing that I had given her life, but I could not give her health or happiness.

"There is a salon over there that's open," I said.

"Remember? They don't do up-dos."

I don't know where my brainstorm came from at that moment. I reminded Miriam of the cute, chin-length bob she'd worn before she started growing her hair. I reminded her of our conversations on the couch in our living room in Addis Ababa, when she came home from boarding school and wanted to talk about boyfriends. About her blond friend who seemed so much more popular and attractive. About her fears that she would never find love or happiness.

"You're like me," I'd told her then. "We're granola. It may take us longer to find what we're looking for, but we stick to the ribs. We're the kind of woman men are looking for when they want a partner."

Miriam cried some more on that bench in the mall, grieving the loss of the dream that, on this day at least, she could be glamorous. She went through the collections of crumpled Kleenexes in both our purses. Then she wiped her eyes. She wadded up the clippings of models in up-dos along with the Kleenex.

"My nose must be red," she said, and started to cry again.

We walked down to the other hairdresser, the only other one

open on a Sunday afternoon. Miriam sniffled and blinked her eyes quickly.

An hour later, she came out smiling, a beautiful young woman who had made a new peace with who she was. She laughed, telling me about it on the way home. "The hairspray came out in solid lumps when she washed my hair!"

I wish I'd listened to my own wisdom about hair at weddings. But I was also seduced by fantasies of what I should look like— my one chance to be mother of the bride. I had bought a set of heat rollers, being too frugal to go to a hairdresser myself. In the pictures I wear curls that look less than glamorous and more like one of the many perms Mom gave me as a young girl in remotest Ethiopia. She had packed dozens of Tonys in barrels and trunks— enough to last a five-year term in Maji—because she thought her blond daughter needed curls to be beautiful. Mom slept on rollers every night and taught me to do the same. That stripped-down life in South Sudanese villages gave me something precious: chances to fully inhabit my own body as it was.

When we'd first gone to Ethiopia, Miriam had been twelve, still a child. Kissing her good-bye as she left for her honeymoon, I forced back my always-easy tears. I had lost her over and over as she flew from Ethiopia to her boarding high school in Kenya. Now it felt like I was losing her forever. Would her young man love her better than I had? I might never have had the courage to go overseas to work if I'd thought about all the separations the passing years would bring us.

I knew what separations from home felt like from the other side—sent from beautiful and beloved Maji to boarding school in Addis Ababa; then to Egypt when I was fifteen; off to college half-way around the world to Illinois when I was eighteen—it fitted me for trudging through the pain of leaving Miriam now. There was no more talk of Mark leaving me and our quitting our jobs, so by the time Miriam got back to Portland, a married woman, we'd be back in shell-shocked Nairobi. I packed for our return with the energy of someone on the run from grief.

Home in Nairobi, we learned more about the bombing. A delivery truck had driven up behind the US embassy carrying more than four hundred pop-can size cylinders filled with TNT—a full ton of the stuff. It got past the first checkpoint. It was speeding toward the underground parking lot, when a guard lowered the second gate and asked for ID. The driver jumped out and ran. The truck exploded.

Seismologists say if it had gotten into the basement parking lot, the pressure of that much TNT exploding underground would have rocked Nairobi like an earthquake. It would have leveled downtown.

Some analysts now think that Osama bin Laden planned the embassy attacks in Kenya and Tanzania expressly to lure the US into war in Afghanistan, the *Graveyard of Empires*. In Afghanistan, Al Qaeda could take on the West and have a fighting chance.

The saddest part of all is that Prudence Bushnell, the US Ambassador, had said that the downtown embassy in Nairobi was dangerously exposed. Her request that it be moved was denied.

And even worse, investigators had been watching the anti-American cells forming, were working on breaking them up, and had seen credible reports of plans to attack the embassy in Nairobi. But something, maybe a major-power sense of invulnerability, had lulled the CIA. They didn't even order security to be beefed up.

A dozen American Embassy employees died in the blast.

But it was Kenyans who took the most damage. Knowing the downtown Nairobi scene, it was easy to see why. Gridlock lasted all day there. Crowded buses and vans honked their way around private vehicles double- and triple-parked; office workers in suits squeezed past people in ragged clothes hustling a few cents a day to live on—hawkers of mirrors, key chains, ersatz designer watches, lottery tickets, medallions of St. Mary or St. Patrick, Chiclets, Kleenex. After the explosion, the hulk of cement that had been the embassy towered over screaming people, all of them bloodied, some being led by the hand, their faces slashed by flying glass.

Two hundred and one Kenyans died in the buildings that collapsed and in the two city buses struck by the blast of heat that funneled between buildings. Another four thousand Kenyans were injured, most of them blinded or maimed by exploding windows. People ten miles away heard the blast. People close enough to be cut were also permanently deafened.

I felt, rising up in me again, that impotent anger I'd fed on in Chicago. Collateral damage in the conflict between empires, it is always the little people that take the brunt. I was so like those Old Testament prophets, I could almost feel the straggly white hair growing, the long stringy beard. I needed only a walking stick, untanned leather sandals, and long, dust-covered Middle Eastern desert garb. Inside, I was railing, like they had, against violence and poverty. *Woe, woe, woe unto you!* Each of the victims had a mother and father. Sisters. Children.

In Nairobi, Mark was also back where he had to look failure full in the face. Even on Zoloft, he got harsh and bitter again. This time I found a marriage counselor. I pressured Mark into going to see him with me. Mark finally agreed, but he sat in his woven jute chair with his jaw set.

I sat in the chair opposite, pulling on wisps of jute as I listened to the counselor talk with him. Often, Mark was as rude to the counselor as he was to me during the week. Often, I wept as I sat there. I could tell the counselor was about to fire us; he couldn't get through to Mark.

The Al Qaeda attack and Mark's anger shadowed me through that fall in Nairobi. Despair threatened to move in, as softly as the fog that used to come over the Gap in Maji and roll up the valley, blurring all the colors and darkening the sky.

Paradoxically, that winter, 1998, I began the most important and hope-inspiring work I did in all my years in Africa. Looking back, it seems only right. Hope and despair, peace and war, reconciliation and violence—these contradictions lie side-by-side so starkly in South Sudan.

CHAPTER 18

My new assignment began with a surprise phone call from Bill Lowrey. Bill had written his PhD thesis on traditional peace-making rituals that had helped the Sudanese manage their cattle raids and flare-ups over grazing land and fishing rights. Now he wanted to help the chiefs apply those rituals to their modern conflict on the West Bank of the White Nile.

Bill called Thanksgiving Day. It was midnight his time in Vienna, Virginia. He said paramount chiefs had signed a peace agreement in Loki in June, while we were in the States with Miriam. They proposed to Bill and church leaders a follow-up conference in South Sudan, one that all the lower chiefs could attend. I nodded, wondering what it had to do with me.

Bill said, "If we do this bigger conference, we need someone credible to do logistical organizing. We'll need a lot of support from nongovernmental organizations, and they're going to want careful accounting. Would you be willing to take it on?"

Careful accounting? I should have said, and I know just the tone of disbelief I should have used. But it counts for a lot with me to be needed, so I smiled.

Organizing a peace conference felt like The Right Thing to do. Imagine if everyone helped organize at least one peace conference. I didn't think of danger or failure. When Moses was talking to his burning bush, he didn't imagine God would let him wander forty years in the wilderness, either. Maybe Moses felt as I did at that moment, that if God called, I had God's guarantee of success. Of course, that's also what Mark had assumed when he took his doomed assignment.

And maybe despair over conditions in South Sudan was feeding Mark's and my hopelessness at home. If hope for peace sprang up somewhere, might it flood hope and peace into our marriage?

I fell immediately under Bill's spell—if Bill thought I could organize a peace conference, who was I to doubt? He was short, stocky, and quiet-spoken. He always sounded like he'd thought through what he was saying and was choosing his words carefully. He had a gift for bringing out the best in people. Every time he came to meet with the Sudanese church leaders and Mark, they responded to his thoughtfulness by becoming temporarily thoughtful themselves.

Surely, peace work would help me pay that price for worthiness. I could actually be the *instrument of peace* I'd prayed for at our wedding—now in the world's longest running civil war. Surely it would spill back into my life and wash away all my failings. Mark would see that I had the best of intentions toward him too; the warmest heart, the truest love. What I'd been looking for all my life was a way to pay enough to qualify for unconditional love, one of those contradictions that gets set up so early we're slow to recognize the irony.

I was especially susceptible to longing that winter, running before despair over my marriage, like a boat in a high wind with its sails let out, unresisting.

I began by channeling Bill's stirring words into a proposal I could use to raise money from aid organizations. Bill said to start with the US Agency for International Development, USAID. They could be our biggest supporter if we played our cards right, he said. He said to get in touch with Telar Deng, a Dinka lawyer and judge, and then call USAID for an appointment.

When I met Telar, I only knew what Bill had said—he would be a big help talking with USAID. When I met him, what I thought was that he was one of the thinnest people I'd ever seen, almost concave, startling, like one side of a human parenthesis.

Telar and I drove across town together. By this time, four

months after the bomb attack, USAID had resettled the whole US Embassy on the third floor of its office building, and the embassy had brought in heavy security. As we rounded the corner from our parking spot, we came face to face with two machine guns. Marines, one white and one black, hardly older than Jesse, stood behind sandbags. They aimed their weapons at our chests.

I felt suddenly, hotly sticky with sweat. With the twitch of a finger, my life, which usually seemed so robust, could be snuffed out. I was an American. At the American Embassy. How could they be aiming guns at me? I checked my face muscles, hoping I looked innocent. Telar dropped back, behind my left shoulder. Trust, I was learning, had to be earned one moment at a time.

"We have an appointment," I said. My voice wavered. The Marines didn't take their fingers off the triggers, but one nodded toward the door. Telar swung it open and held it for me.

From inside a bulletproof glass box, a young man confirmed our appointment by phone. A grim-faced Kenyan policewoman frisked me, her fingers bumping over the hooks and underwire of my bra, the elastic of my panties. I stood frozen in the forced intimacy, not breathing.

We're used to it now, but I was shocked when they made me take off my belt and shoes. What lethal weapon could I hide in the soles of my shoes? The policewoman took the Swiss Army knife, small as my pinky, from my key chain and gave me a stern look, as though I should have known better than to bring a weapon onto the premises.

YOU ARE REQUIRED TO HAVE AN ESCORT AT ALL TIMES, the sign in the elevator read in bold caps. EVEN WHEN USING THE REST ROOM. My doubts pushed toward the surface. I was the token American representing Generally Accepted Accounting Procedures, but I didn't know a thing about accounting, and I was not even gifted—I was a *bad* choice, in fact—to organize a million details for a peace conference in the middle of nowhere in South Sudan. I was nothing more than a naive do-gooder, desperate to prove her life was worth something even as it fell apart around her.

Light from three high windows lit up the USAID lobby. The red, loose-woven slipcovers glowed on Kenyan pine chairs. Telar pushed back the corners of his suit jacket and jammed his hands into his pockets. He paced around the small room studying UNICEF posters of dancing rainbow children. His nervousness didn't reassure me.

A dishwater blond man burst from the elevator dressed in a blue Oxford shirt and striped tie. "Telar!" he said.

"Paul!" They pounded each other on the back like long lost friends. I felt a stranger in my own embassy, just as out of place as I'd felt in my own country when I left Ethiopia for the US and college. I smiled awkwardly and waited. A meeting with all the high-ups in the aid galaxy—I wished I had some of Telar's history, whatever that was. Or Bill Lowrey's optimism. Or Mark's attention to detail.

Paul McDermott opened the flimsy wooden door. "You wouldn't believe how cramped we are since the embassy moved in," he said. Conference tables had been pushed together like Tetris pieces, and a room had been built to fit, with fiberboard walls notched around fluorescent light fixtures.

More men entered the conference room. They shook hands with Telar and me, nodded to each other, shuffled their chairs around. They were all dressed for success. I'd dug out a blazer, too, an un-constructed rayon fuchsia number that had hung in the back of my closet, passed up to me by a sister. It had seemed that morning like just the thing. Now it seemed like a pretty lame substitute for a blue oxford shirt and a regiment-stripe tie. Maybe I shouldn't have brought attention to my gender by wearing reddish-pink. And if I had telegraphed my ignorance of the dress code, they could now guess how many reams of other things I was missing. I'd completely underestimated how big a deal this meeting was—this proposal, this conference.

I passed copies of my proposal, hoping my good intentions and Bill's coaching would show up. For all my idealistic talk of social change, beginning in Chicago, I had never had any training for changing a neighborhood, stopping a war, making the world better.

Of course, if my jacket had startled some of the men, the minute a proposal for peace fell into their hands, they laser-focused. They also wanted to intervene in one of the world's messiest, most intractable problems, a nested conflict: South Sudanese tribes fighting each other in the middle of their big war against the government of North Sudan.

The problem was one of many that overtook Africa as a result of colonialism overlaid on traditional ethnic animosities. It spread like a noxious weed that starts with one invasive plant going to seed. In the 1800s, when the British grabbed thousands of square miles along the Nile to protect precious waters for its colony in Egypt, it created the largest African country, almost the size of the US east of the Mississippi River, home to people from over eighty tribes. The British threw together Arabs in the north and Sub-Saharan Africans in the south with no intention of giving the country autonomy. The name they gave this country, Anglo-Egyptian Sudan, said it all.

To feed the fabric mills in Manchester, the British ran huge cotton plantations on the plains of the South. They let missionaries start a few schools and clinics there. Otherwise, they empowered the Arab northern half and ignored the African southern half. In the 1960's, when the British walked away, Islam was declared the state religion, Arabic the uniting language, and Sharia the law. The Southerners were maneuvered out of any power sharing in the new government. Christian and animistic Southerners rebelled.

The Arabs announced *jihad*. Land could be claimed by the warrior who cleared it of the Infadel. Long before Americans heard of Darfur, the *jinjaweed*—mounted militias—descended like whirlwinds of destruction on border villages in the South. The conflict in Darfur has uncovered the recurring reason for war in Sudan—not religion, but race and fertile farmland. The Darfurians are Muslims. They should be part of the Muslim family; they should be brothers. But other Muslims covet their land.

Then, as if power, land, water rights, language, race, and religion weren't enough reasons for North Sudanese to fight in the South,

Chevron discovered millions of gallons of oil under the South Sudan savannah in 1978. Sudan is on the US list of no-trade countries but senators proposed an exception so Chevron could drill. It was Bill Lowrey who had led the campaign to oppose the exception.

No one has clean hands when it comes to South Sudan violence; our enlightened neighbors in Canada offered to stand in for Chevron. As Bill and the other observers feared, the government of North Sudan sent attack helicopters to clear South Sudanese villages along the border so the Canadian oil company Talisman and their Chinese pipe layers could operate safely.

A few years later, the government of North Sudan had started taking a cool million dollars a day in oil proceeds to spend on their war against the South. And conveniently for them, the Antonov bombers burning A-1 jet fuel pumped and refined in South Sudan could take off from pipeline service airstrips in South Sudan to drop their bombs on South Sudan. North Sudan bombed Southern churches on Sunday mornings, Southern schools on weekdays, Southern hospitals and grass roofed *tukels* every day.

That was the civil war part of the problem, and none of us in that Nairobi meeting room could do anything about it. But when Colonal Mengistu fled Ethiopia in 1991 and left Sudanese refugees with no safe haven; when they poured back across the Baro River into South Sudan like what they call themselves, *black ants in the eyes of God*; when Commander Riek Machar mutanied, and fighting broke out between the Dinkas and Nuers—a close-in conflict—it killed and displaced more people than Northern bombs ever could have done. Southerners had to make peace with each other to have any hope of winning the war for independence from the North.

The two most powerful commanders both had doctorates— Commander Reik Machar's from London University, and Commander John Garang's from Iowa State. Common people had begun to call the ethnic conflict *The War of the Doctors*.

Bill's angle was to sidestep the doctors. The meeting of chiefs in Loki that he had told me about on the phone had been his first experiment. Now he was working with people like Telar to call in lesser chiefs and community leaders. He would also create a facilitation team of educated Southerners from the diaspora for the conference. Partner churches and nongovernmental organizations would help fund it: Christian Aid UK, the Dutch Reformed Church, Church of the Brethren, PCUSA, World Vision, and the UN World Food Program. If they succeeded on the West Bank, Bill said he and his team would take the process to other hot spots in the South-South conflict.

In that dingy USAID room, as soon as everyone had had time to skim my proposal, one of the men said, "This grass roots effort by the church is the only credible work toward peace we see right now. You know IGAD."

IGAD nations—the Inter-Governmental Authority on Development —all postured about peace in the Horn of Africa at expensive summit meetings. Back home, they supported guerrilla armies that raided each other's borders. They plotted to overthrow each other's regimes.

"We're interested in your proposal." Paul McDermott said. He seemed to be the big cheese in the room. He tapped the papers with his index finger. "But we've tried supporting programs with the Sudanese before. The money..." He fluttered his hand.

Well. Mark and I knew all about, *The Sudanese and money flutter, flutter.*

I squared my shoulders. My cheeks flushed with self-conscious earnestness, and I sat up straight. "That's why I've been seconded to New Sudan Council of Churches," I said. "I'm going to organize the logistics of the conference. I'll track the accounting. We'll be raising funds from other organizations, too. What we're asking USAID for is help with transport."

Bill had told me to calculate the transport costs and then ask high, so I had doubled my numbers and figured on bargaining down, the Ethiopian way. If I looked straight into their eyes, maybe they wouldn't know I thought our ask was exorbitant.

Neither Telar nor I blinked.

We agreed to open a special bank account just for the USAID money.

Sure, we could write checks payable only to transport companies.

I would be happy to give them reports every month.

USAID not only didn't blink, they accepted my whole number, $95,000. Maybe some Africa savvy would get me through this uncharted wilderness after all.

When I told him over the phone, Bill's voice went up a pitch. "We just might pull this off!"

CHAPTER 19

Suddenly I had a full-time job, a wonderful change from drifting along in pain. When Mark and I had vowed to stay together for better or for worse, I thought we were talking about better or worse circumstances. We'd managed plenty of those. But now it was our worse selves causing our suffering. I told myself that in a twenty-six-year marriage there were bound to be things—things either from inside or outside the marriage that would try to spin us apart. I didn't dare say that to Mark. But isn't that what grace is for? I thought when we did fail, grace would be there to heal us from the destruction we'd been hell bent on.

Mark was convinced that if I would agree it was all my fault he was so unhappy, it would help. But no empathy, no reflecting statements, no humble apologies ever made him feel better. That became my fault, too—I was doing it wrong.

If you hadn't said that, he said. *If you'd said it this way.*

It didn't make sense to me, that I had so much power over his feelings. But the Godly Woman in me couldn't walk out, bemused and sorry he was so unhappy, and leave him to it. I stayed to listen. He reproached and criticized me until I lost my patience. Then I snapped at him and proved how uncaring and disrespectful I was.

But now, with peace work to do, I was too busy to obsess on improving all the ways I was still getting it wrong. Lutheran World Service donated office space and I started going to work every morning, sometimes rested, sometimes sandy-eyed and battling a tension headache. At supper, if Mark was grim, I had more to work with. I covered his silence and entertained the boys with tales of my daily adventures.

My new Dinka-judge friend Telar told me Commander Mario Muor Muor had offered to mobilize his Youth for Peace for the conference. I didn't know who Mario was, but I did know that *youth* in South Sudan were men who were not yet elders—unmarried men through age thirty. Three hundred of them would build the peace village with Commander Mario, Telar said. They would build near X, suggested by the chiefs of Bahr el Gazahl Province.

X was a village too small to show up on a map. For weeks even I didn't know its real name; Bill and the Southerners kept a news black-out for fear the government of North Sudan might hear rumors of the plan and bomb the site.

Filling out requisition forms and local purchase orders at the office gave me something constructive to think about. The young Sudanese men in X needed axes to cut wood for framing the tukels; shovels to dig and mix mud plaster for the walls; machetes to cut thatch; picks to dig outhouses. I sent New Sudan Council of Church's Kikuyu logistician running around Nairobi buying lentils, rice, and cans of beef stew to feed the youth teams. He requisitioned cases of soap, bales of used clothing and blankets, twenty-five-kilo bags of salt, and quintals of sugar to pay them with.

Bill flew from Virginia to Khartoum to meet with Commander Reik Machar, who was not happy about being by-passed early and brought in late. He finally gave the Nuer chiefs permission to travel to Dinkaland.

Telar and other Dinkas met with representatives of the SPLA and wrangled promises for security, supplied by the 11th and 12th battalions under Commander Salva Kiir. That was the first time I heard of Commander Kiir. I had no idea what a big place in history he would end up filling. But then, it was only 1998, and he was still just a high-level commander in the SPLA.

When Telar told me about the commander giving us security, he also sounded surprised, as surprised as Bill had been about USAID's support. Light shining off the dark cheekbones of Telar's smile showed that he also felt stirrings of hope for peace.

And hope, an unfamiliar feeling for so long, began to seep into my life. *This peace conference is for real*, I told myself, surprised that after so many years of chasing after something important to do with my life, something important had found me.

Bill flew back to Virginia from Khartoum and coached me by phone. "Five hundred delegates, better figure...over a thousand people," he said. "And give us ten to fourteen days to get it all done."

How many kilos of sugar would eight hundred to a thousand people stir into how many kilos of tea leaves in ten to fourteen days? How many goats and cows would we eat; how many bags of dried fish? How many pieces of soap or bags of salt would each cow cost? If I'd been a detail thinker, all the unknowns would have driven me crazy. My globalist brain just made up the best formulas I could, and figured we'd all manage with what we had when the time came, as Africans do so well.

On the tangled web of Nairobi phonelines, I dialed ten times for every call that went through. World Food Program said no to sugar and salt. I wrote *sugar, salt* on my purchase list. They agreed to donate 1,200 calories of food per person per day—their estimation of caloric need for a sedentary person. No wonder the tall Nilotics are as thin as their walking sticks. People couldn't make peace sitting around feeling hungry for two weeks: I added *rice. Lentils.*

The mythical Commander Mario Muor Muor came to Nairobi to meet with our planning team. More even than Bill, more than Telar, one meeting with Commander Mario and I believed in him. Lean, ageless, unsmiling, he carried himself with a grave dignity that explained how he could leave the liberation army to organize for peace and live to tell the story. If he ever thanked me, it would be all the payment I could want.

"We are building five villages, each with thirty *tukels*," he said. "We will assign local youth and women to assist each village. They will cook and carry water."

That helped; I could picture thirty *tukels*. Back in my office I divided a thousand people into five villages. Seven people for every *tukel*, each maybe fifteen feet in diameter. Of course, people wouldn't sleep inside. Around each *tukel* at night, they'd brace walking sticks and saplings against each other as I'd been taught in Nyal. They would lash them together (*twine, check*) to hold up unbleached muslin mosquito net tents (*check*). As they did at home, the Sudanese would sleep on the dust on tarps and blankets (*check, check*).

I filled out requisition forms in triplicate: for every village, large *soferias* for cooking rice (aluminum tubs with wide rims and no handles); medium *soferias* for beef, dried fish, and lentil stews; and small *soferias*, relatively speaking, for tea water. Teapots, cooking spoons, serving spoons, eating spoons, and teaspoons; cups, trays, buckets, bathing basins. *Check, check, check, check, check.*

And every Thursday afternoon, Mark and I went to see the marriage counselor.

Mark described his meek grandfather Abe, his disdainful Grandma Eula. I remembered Abe's question-mark posture. Was meek the right word—how resentful was he, really? It had the look of another badgering family, with gender roles reversed.

Mark talked about his own dad, who always bent to accommodate Mark's mom.

Mark saw, for the first time in his life, that he hadn't had a happy childhood.

He remembered raising his hand to his mother once, when he was about five years old. Maybe he was just trying to stop one of her scathing rants. Or maybe he really did want to hit her.

She slapped him. The blow knocked Mark through the basement door. He clung to the railing and stumbled down the stairs. She followed, slapping and kicking him. They sat on the bottom step, Mark sobbing. In a soft voice his mother said, "Don't you *ever* do that again."

"You've conflated your wife and your mother," the counselor said.

I clung gratefully to that word from outside our war zone. *Conflated.* Surely Mark would recalibrate. But within a week, he had forgotten and I had lost my grip on *conflated* as well. I thought Mark should to change his behavior. And why would he change, when I was obviously willing to go on, being the good woman, putting up with behavior that was not good for me, not good for him, not good for our family? I walled off my disappointment at home and focused on work; the drop-off from disappointment into despair looked too sharp and sudden.

A volunteer couple from Church of the Brethren flew from the States to Nairobi to help me with the organizing. The wife suggested we pack delegate supplies into bins like the UN's displaced-refugee kits. The plastic bins could double as buckets and bathing tubs. Small things, like bags of salt, soap, and spoons, could go inside and wouldn't have to be handed out in a chaotic mob scene, threatening peace before the conference could even begin.

"I don't know. The bins won't nest if they're full," her husband said.

So I calculated the cubic footage of five hundred blue plastic bins. Mrs. Grimsted in seventh grade had promised I'd use all those word problems in real life someday. But then I called and found that no one in real life knew the cubic footage of a plane vs. that of a truck, so I just wadded up my scratch paper, reverted to my it-will-be-fine calculation method, and ordered the kits.

Like a version of Groucho Marx, who didn't want to be part of any club that would have him, I bounced back and forth from hope to disbelief—this peace conference couldn't be history-making if *I* were helping organize it. But what I put on when I set out for donor offices with my reports was hope with a dash of confidence. I wore shiny cheeks, a fresh haircut, and always the bright rayon jacket, like a Dumbo feather. I dressed to look my part: rugged but honest, committed, transparent and above all, responsible.

A chief works his way toward a decision in South Sudan by putting it out for everyone to have their say. Especially among the

Nuers, people choose leaders for what they can provide—goods, prosperity, peace. Chiefs are replaced if they don't deliver. And if they move out too far ahead of their people, no one follows. The paramount Nuer and Dinka chiefs had signed their thumbprints for peace in Loki. Now, to have community buy-in for peace, they had to gather their people.

Most importantly, they had to get buy-in for the question of restitution.

Traditional law was based on restitution—everyone knew the price in cattle for a canoe destroyed, a *tukel* burned, a person abducted or killed. That worked great, back when raids happened in face-to-face fighting. This war-within-the-war had been so widespread, so traumatic that all thousand representatives at a peace conference could claim restitution for something. But who would they accuse?

There was no way to calculate restitution for the kind of destruction modern weapons had brought to South Sudan. Whole villages had been burned when one anonymous soldier tossed a grenade into a thatched roof. Unimaginable bitterness would be stirred up, trying to calculate the losses, haggling over cattle that had been stolen, "stolen" back, taken again—and yet, Bill Lowrey had convinced everyone that the only kind of peace that would stick had to be rooted in tradition.

The only way to frame restitution, Bill and the circle of Sudanese collaborators like Telar said, was to propose amnesty: damage so close to equal on each side, that they effectively cancelled out. This one issue was essential. If the chiefs couldn't agree on amnesty, organizers would scuttle the conference.

And it had to be worked out ahead of time—descending into conflict over amnesty would plunge the conference into its own civil war.

Word went out. Mario, Telar, and others from New Sudan Conference of Churches flew into South Sudan and sat with the chiefs in their villages.

I felt as though we were collectively holding our breath. Out on those wide plains, the chiefs were observing, negotiating, calculating what they could propose, what their people would accept. The whole peace-making process focused down to one slow dance toward amnesty.

In Chicago I'd learned the term *as-if organizing*: working on an event with conviction, even with no guarantee it's actually going to happen. I'd known it as a concept; now I was getting my apprenticeship as we waited for the chiefs and their consensus. I sat in my office listening to dial tones, wondering if I could learn *as-if living*. What would that look like? Living with conviction of an outcome before it ever showed up in my life?

Finally, word began to come in from South Sudan—the chiefs were falling in line behind this radical idea. But in order to hold, a negotiation this important had to be finalized face to face. I wrote *Chiefs' Visit* across the top of my To Do List: Thursday, February 11, 1999.

I signed the first charter contract, wrote out the first check, sent a thank you to USAID. Bill flew into Nairobi again from Virginia. After he took a day to get over jet lag, I sent him off with Telar and Tabitha's father—the Rev. X ousted by Mark's financial report in cows, now in the New Sudan Conference of Churches Peace Office.

In the major Nuer town of Ler, the charter picked up five chiefs and a woman delegate. They flew across miles of lush no man's grassland to the peace village. Bill felt sure that seeing one hundred fifty *tukels* rising up on the wide-open Dinka land would prove to the Nuers that the Dinkas sincerely wanted peace.

As the plane circled down, Bill saw X, the half-finished *tukels*, and a grassy airstrip surrounded by hand-tilled sorghum plots. They landed, and the dark faces of a crowd flashed by.

To the Dinkas there, who had waited at the landing strip, searching the sky for the silver flash of the *sky canoe*, laying eyes on Nuers from up-river in enemy territory would prove that *they* were serious.

Bill and Nuer leaders stepped onto the brown soil. Paramount chief Chief Madut, over six feet tall, emerged from the crowd of Dinkas. He wore a bright red fake fur hat he must have claimed like a prize out of some bundle of used clothing from the temperate zone. He embraced Nuer Paramount Chief Isaac with a shout and a hug that lifted him right off the ground. The soles of Chief Isaac's Keds spun in a slow circle. Their paramount chief sashes of red and white pressed together.

Chief Isaac was slight for a Nuer, maybe five ten. He laughed. His ceremonial scars beaded with sweat across his forehead. He waved his cow-tail staff at the Dinka women. Their joy cries rolled in waves. Chief Madut's red-orange pompoms dangled from the earflaps of his hat into Chief Isaac's face.

Chief Isaac and Chief Madut had once cooperated over the rich *toich*, the flood plains of the White Nile, which Bill and the Nuers had just flown over. Those plains gave everyone year-round grazing land so essential for the survival of their cattle—their wealth and livelihood. Hotheaded young men and the greed for bride-price cattle had led to cattle raids between them for centuries.

Chiefs like Isaac and Madut had always settled peace, paid restitution, created a safe zone there. But now, fear of Kalashnikov raids, dangerous as forest fires, had exiled both tribes from the *toich* for seven years. Fishing holes had been abandoned. No cattle grazed the rich bottomlands. They had all lived hungry.

The crowd walked under the blazing Sudanese sun from the airstrip to the village in a noisy, sweaty procession.

In South Sudan, it's not the white dove that brings peace. It's the white bull, Mabior, and he brings it with his blood. He stood waiting in the center of town, tethered with a thick, frayed rope knotted a dozen times to a stake three feet high.

Mabior's horns arched wide, shaped by a Dinka boy, shaped when they both were young; shaped in a cattle camp, where the youth had cared for the cattle, living on milk during the dry season, painting their naked bodies with ashes to keep off the mosquitoes, spending their days shaping the horns of their favorites, their nights around the fire composing songs extolling them.

Mabior was sacrificed. The chiefs split his carcass down the middle. They stepped one by one over his body, just like Abraham did in Genesis, when God covenanted with him.

May the body of anyone who breaks this peace be split like the body of Mabior.

CHAPTER 20

Dinka chiefs climbed with the Nuers and Bill into the plane and flew back up river to the Nuer village of Ler. Nuer women there lifted Chief Madut, sweating in his fake fur hat, to their shoulders. The air reverberated with joy cries and singing. His scarlet pom-poms bobbed above the women's heads.

The Dinka chiefs were hosted by Nuers now, under the trees in sweltering heat. All the chiefs had risked visiting enemy territory. It was time to talk about restitution.

Telar brought up the question. Protestations, accusations, negotiations flowed around Bill in two languages he couldn't understand. Telar, fluent in both, cajoled and translated. He whispered enough English in Bill's ear to keep him current. Bill channeled his anxious energy into prayer. He held before God the need for peace. Softened hearts. Forgiveness.

Finally, one by one, the chiefs began to agree. "The pain has been equal," Rev. X, said. Around the circle, now thoughtful, considering it, the others clucked in their throats. But everyone was still waiting for Chief Madut. He finally looked up, directly at Chief Isaac's face. "Let us lay our claims aside. Let us go from here in peace," he said.

Bill took a huge breath of the hot air. Women trilled the joy cry.

Chief Isaac held a handful of sesame seeds high over a large gourd of water. He poured them in. He nodded to a *biny bith*, a Nuer Earth Master, who lifted the gourd and walked around the circle, holding it out to the chiefs. Each chief spat into the water. The *biny bith* dipped his fingers in the water. Everyone jumped up and crowded in—chiefs and children, men and women.

The *biny bith* sprinkled the water. People raised their faces to receive the drops. Women trilled. *We have become each other. We are one.*

The negotiating circle turned into a party. The chiefs danced. Sweat shone on the flying arms of drummers squatting in the shade. Chief Isaac pulled Bill into the circle, an American among the Nilotics, short where they were tall, pale where they were dark, blond where their hair was black and tightly curled. Someone pressed a staff into his hand. The sunset glowed orange on one horizon and the moon rose silver on the other. The circle thundered with drums and laughter and cheers.

Bill leapt higher than he had ever thought possible.

Now the conference really was going to happen. I had to get serious about the details. The radical concept of amnesty wouldn't hold unless the people—the lesser chiefs and community, youth, women's and church leaders—confirmed the paramount chiefs' consensus that it would work.

Telar radioed villages, told people to choose their delegates and start them walking to the conference. But they sent word back that rivers and marshlands were still in flood.

I laid a map of South Sudan on my desk. I hovered over it with my lists of towns, delegates, and chiefs.

I called Kevin Ashley. A man running charters into South Sudan had to believe he could do anything, and Kevin burst into my office like sunshine, the bleached ends of his brown hair flying. There was the Let, his favorite, he said, from Czech Republic; there was the Antonov; there was Canada's boxcar of a plane, the DeHaveland; and there was the sixteen-passenger Caravan. There were airstrips that were landable with full payload; there were airstrips that were too short. My head was spinning.

Kevin Ashley said landings and take-offs are what eat up fuel, and none of our landing strips had depots. Tropical days have hours and hours of light for flying, but with full payloads, the planes couldn't carry fuel for many rotations, he said. Every flight would cost a minimum $3,000. I breathed thanks for USAID's full $95,000.

I lay at night and listened to the nightjar trill outside our window. Mark, often as not, lay with his back to me. I lay and recalculated charters in my head, endlessly subtracting from $95,000.

I didn't tell anyone what else I thought about when I lay awake like that. Maybe I could help bring peace by wanting it so badly. Maybe my prayers and my hard work would move God's heart. The Almighty would intervene. Banish the hounds of war. Bind the spirits of conflict and revenge. It had to stop sometime.

After all, France, Germany, Italy, and England didn't spring up pristine from European soil either. Peasant boys were slaughtered, mothers and sisters raped, villages plundered. There had been no United Nations to airdrop food. There had been no Geneva Conventions. Even so, the Hundred Years' War had finally ended.

By that count, though, we were only one third of the way to the end in Sudan. I was afraid to hope as much as I did. If only historians would look back and say, *That was the beginning of peace in the Sudan.* They would write, *From that grass roots peace conference, momentum spread to the warlords.* Or even, *It took another decade for the peace negotiated in Wunlit* (I could say the name of the village in my prayers) *to be spread throughout South Sudan.*

They wouldn't have to know my name, those historians writing years from now. If only I could help start real peace, I'd happily go down in oblivion.

My prayers included Mark. Surely it was possible for us to work our way clear to a place where we could connect sweetly again. Where we could feel each other as partners when life buffeted us. But I worried. Mark had worked so hard for so long to keep his resentment and anger repressed. Now that the volcano had erupted, would it ever go dormant?

I wished he could see things my way, how pointless it was to destroy any hope of joy in the present by obsessing on what lay in the shadows of the past.

"It's easier for you," he said. And that was true, because in the world of things, my practical streak loved to simplify. I liked to move on.

But I didn't want to move on from Mark. I had collected experiences with him, thirty years' worth, since we'd met in boarding school. They included the dramatic—a miscarriage during a Portland ice storm and our two revolutions in Ethiopia. They included many tender moments. And they included difficulties that we laughed with the kids about later, but that weren't funny at the time, such as when a thief cut through our tent in Ethiopia and stole all my clothes except the t-shirt I had worn to bed.

If the ropes lashing Mark's and my raft together frayed and we separated, how thin any new relationship would seem to me. A new love would never fully understand me, not understanding Ethiopia—never having seen sun and rain jostle each other over the ridge that shelters Addis Ababa to the north—never having watched the fog roll up to Maji.

I also held onto compassion for that ferocious, insecure woman in her twenties who'd been floundering so desperately. Who'd objected to how shame and confusion about being female had undermined her. Who kept trying to earn love, but was never perfect enough. She was always with me, like a friend whose failings I observed with a mixture of regret and tenderness.

I grieved to think that if Mark and I weren't together, I would lose not only him but his witness to someone else I loved—the bright, indomitable sixteen-year-old even further in the past, a girl we both remembered running through dewy African crabgrass to practice piano in the boarding school library—a girl full of joy, who might still live somewhere inside me.

In the office cafeteria I had met Messiah, an Eritrean born and raised in Ethiopia. After the communist regime fell, Eritrea held a referendum and seceded from Ethiopia (a promise from the guerilla leader, now Prime Minister, in exchange for training and support in their fight against the Ethiopian army). After all that, the two now-separate countries fell out over a rocky triangle of land and a village on the border between them. They marched to war. Hundreds of thousands of young men died. The Prime Ministers each expelled all citizens of the other country, and Messiah fled to Kenya.

He introduced me to the owner of a trucking company, and I sent three trucks off to Wunlit with barrels of diesel, the delegate kits, and quintal bags of salt and sugar, lentils and rice.

The next day Messiah treated me when I went in for tea and *sambusas* at his cafeteria. He read my mind, my insomniac prayers. "You are a good woman," he said. "Working with these people for peace? You will be famous someday for this conference."

We talked about Ethiopia and Eritrea. "When will *they* stop fighting?" I asked. The spirits seemed bent on pain. He crossed himself, a devout Orthodox Christian, and slurped his tea loudly.

Ethnic explosions overlaid on colonial borders was a story all over Africa. Our geography books haven't done Americans any service when it comes to understanding this. When Western map-makers drop the equator down and put the US and Europe in the middle, it makes them look bigger than they are. Africa shrinks away under what should be the midpoint bulge of the globe, like a fat man's belt buckle disappearing under his belly. Westerners grow up with visual evidence for believing that Africa isn't much bigger than the US. We're not taught that Africa is the second largest and the most genetically diverse continent, with ethnic groups that speak over two thousand distinct languages and prac-tice dozens of different religions. In fact, the US could fit into the Sahara Desert, and Africa could swallow India, China, Argentina, New Zealand and the whole continent of Europe, and still have room for dessert.

I held my hot glass by the rim and breathed sweet, spicy fumes. There wasn't anything more to say, Messiah and me, both heartsick for our huge, suffering continent.

In one of his calls, Bill told me the obvious, if I'd thought about it—delegates would come to the conference sick with untreated infections and sores, diarrhea, malaria, typhoid, STD's, pneumonia, TB, guinea worm, and whatever they'd been living with in a land without hospitals or clinics. He wrote a grant request to the Presbyterian mission department: the people of South Sudan needed to experience the fruit of peace immediately. He called me from back in Virginia after the Chief's Visit, ecstatic. "PCUSA came through with money for a peace conference clinic!"

I met with a doctor from Medicins Sans Frontiers Belgium, who ordered me a metric ton of medicines. Only when it came time to transport the medicine did I learn it filled seventy-two boxes: pills, ointments, dressings, bandages, and syringes. The boxes covered the entire corner of Medicins Sans Frontiers' warehouse—enough medicine to keep a village clinic supplied for two years.

Disgusted, I decided to send one truckload to Loki immediately, and figure out later what to do with the rest. If I got a truck on the road the following Thursday, the meds would make the Saturday charter to Wunlit. Every day I checked with the Kenyan logistician. Every day he assured me he had a trucker ready to sign.

At closing time Wednesday, he knocked softly on my office door. I looked up and smiled, expecting to hear that the medicines were on their way. He leaned into the room, but came no further. "I'm sorry, madam. All my contacts...they refuse."

After he left, I pounded on my desk, on the piles of papers and phone numbers, on the dozens of invoices. I walked home without seeing the jacaranda and bottle-brush trees, the piles of composting garbage mixed with plastic—the classic beauty and squalor of Nairobi. I stewed all night. Every time I turned over, I pulled the flannel sheets to my chin, and battled self-reproach. *What should I have known? What should I have done?*

It wasn't until years later that I saw how my habit of constantly taking personal responsibility for anything that went wrong— the chorus of self-reproach taught by a badgering mother—also kept the dark dance going with Mark. The power I accepted over his feelings was a symptom of the power I expected myself to have over every happening in the world. Doing well to keep shame at bay.

I dashed to the office in the morning. Above my desk hung a calendar from an Asian broker, left behind by the last tenant. Before phone lines could fill up, at eight o'clock on the dot, I called the broker.

He showed up an hour later, emanating a sweet-smelling cloud from the product that slicked back his hair. Yes, he said with a big smile, definitely he had a truck. It could load up immediately and arrive in Loki in time for Saturday's charter.

Words were easy. I'd beat myself up all night; I wasn't going to be taken for a fool over those medicines again. In the grip of a brilliant thought, I wrote into the contract a 10% deduction if his trucker for any reason at all missed the charter. The broker looked at me sad-eyed, and signed.

With three truckloads of supplies on the road to Wunlit and a truck full of medicine on its way to Loki, I went home that night light-hearted. Against all odds, I had won that round. Now I could concentrate on transport for the delegates.

We were in a season of electrical black-outs in Nairobi, and the newspapers helpfully notified us which neighborhoods would have non-service-ON (no power), and non-service-OFF (power), but in practice there was no system. Many evenings our table fell suddenly into dark before we could finish eating.

That night, as the boys took the candles off to do their homework, Mark and I sat in the dusk. He looked mournful, withdrawn.

"Maybe we had to be this raw before we could be stitched back together whole," I said. After my success of the afternoon, I could see a future full of potential. We hadn't been old enough or mature enough to be wise when we got married. In the end, maybe through this pain we would each redeem the other.

He glared.

"You could be bored," I said. If he had married someone less impatient, less willing to take risks, someone who never rocked the boat, mightn't he be in one of those stagnant marriages in the women's magazine articles, *Can This Marriage Be Saved?* "You could be just drifting along."

"Bored sounds great."

"Mark, I'm a good wife to you." I heard the humiliating note of pleading in my voice. I saw so clearly that I couldn't control his feelings, but I didn't see that I believed he could manage my fragile sense of worth.

Mark scraped his chair back and left me in the shadowed dining room. But in bed that night he pulled me close and got sentimental in a handyman's sort of way. "What I need is a lobotomy. Then our marriage would be almost perfect."

I lay silent, absorbing the warmth of his hard-muscled arms. For that moment, with the trucking end of transport taken care of and Mark holding me, I was content. Nothing could dim my optimism.

CHAPTER 21

When I arrived for work the next morning, the broker was waiting for me. I could tell he had bad news. I unlocked my office without looking him in the eyes and sat down. I crossed my arms over vital organs.

"There are bandits on the road to Loki." The broker's black eyes pleaded with me to understand. Bandits? My thoughts slowed, like a Jeep would, hitting mud.

"You can listen on the radio. The police are holding traffic. They sit for six hours. Maybe eight. Then they go in convoys. The Turkana desert is bad. Very bad."

"The truck?"

"I was afraid because of the 10%."

"It's still here?" That bad. I couldn't believe it. Even when he nodded, I could not believe it.

"What shall we do now?"

I sat still for a long time just looking at his worried face. It was too late for the medicine to get to Loki in time for the charter, or into Wunlit in time to start the conference. I could dial a hundred times and try to verify his story. I could cry. I could pitch a fit.

If I hadn't tried to control the outcome, the medicine would have been on the road, maybe in the hands of the bandits or the Kenyan police, but blessedly out of my hands. Somehow, we would have managed. But now instead, a truck fully loaded with medicine that should be in Loki, was camped on my doorstep. It all came down to this: I'd been too American. I'd pushed too hard. It doesn't pay in Kenya. Kenya pushes back.

"I also arrange charters," the broker said with a small, helpful smile. "For only ten thousand dollars, I'll fly the shipment straight to Loki."

I looked into his eyes. Had he done this on purpose?

Stewardship of the $95,000. People sick and waiting for the medicine. My fingers shook as I signed the check. I didn't know whether it was a brilliant ten-thousand-dollar solution, or a five-figure mistake.

Bill flew in again from Virginia. I sent him off with the rapporteur team to start the conference. I stayed to back things up. Bill told me about the Wunlit white bull of peace, and I later read the *Washington Post* story, stared at the pictures on the web, and listened to the song the young boys sang for peace, as it streamed through my computer.

Mabior's horns arched four feet wide. The *biny bith*, and Dinka Masters of the Fishing Spear circled, shouting—old men with wrinkled faces, dressed in dirty navy-blue jumpsuits, leaping as high as their waists. They threatened Mabior with their supple spears. He kicked up the dust in a tight circle around his post. The sounds and smells of a thousand people pressed around him. He rolled his eyes. His nostrils dripped. Women burst into song.

Mabior, take our message of peace to the spirits.

He snorted, braced his front hoofs. Meaty muscles bulged under his thick hide. He ducked his magnificent horns at the dancing men.

It took five men to bring him down. Two grabbed each horn. Behind him, another twisted his tail into a knot. Mabior dropped onto his knees in the dust.

Nuers and Dinkas shouted as one person. Mabior was fallen. He still bellowed, defiant. As they sawed through his neck, his bellow turned to gurgles and his blood poured out, thick and red, onto the dust. An earthquake of sound rose up.

May the blood of anyone who breaks the peace...

Women pushed into the dusty surf kicked up by hundreds of feet and Mabior's hoofs. They sang, shrill and high. They danced the lifelines of the Sudan, the Blue Nile, the Mountain Nile, the

White Nile twisting together through the *Bilad as-Sudan* of Arab geographers, the Land of the Blacks.

In Nairobi, during the first week of the conference, my office settled into a quiet calm. I sorted the papers that lay in drifts on my desk. I sent off a shipment of clothing—in-kind payment for the Dinka women and boys serving the various peace sub-villages. On Friday, New Sudan Council of Churches folks sent me a message— Bill wanted to talk to me on the radio-transmission system.

I went to the radio alcove and stood, smelling the faint tang of sweat and cement dust, while the Kenyan logistician finished his business. Then I heard Bill's voice. I smiled, took the speaker and greeted him as I slipped into the chair.

Countless people had written phone numbers and doodles directly onto the Kenyan pine desk. I was losing half of every sentence to static, but nothing could disguise Bill's enthusiasm—*see with your own eyes...want peace so badly...*

I didn't know anyone but Bill who could have pulled something like this together. I felt honored to be associated with it in any way. Then I scrambled a pencil out of my pocket. I'd be on the next flight in, and Bill had a list of things he needed me to bring.

Some of the kits were missing something. *Charlie—Utah—Papa.* Cups? What were people drinking tea out of, if cups hadn't made it into the kits? Tea for breakfast, tea boiled up at breaks. My shoulders tensed, braced against the predictable onslaught of guilt and responsibility. Mom's chorus, *You should have known better.* Had it been my job to go through five hundred kits, counting every-thing myself?

Bill continued. I started to jiggle my foot in frustration as I scrib-bled—the foreign journalists wanted all kinds of things like beer and cigarettes, batteries and video film. Rev. X wanted a sleeping bag. Someone needed Zoloft. Someone needed Lipitor.

"Bill," I said.

"Do your best, over."

After he signed off, I sighed and sat looking at the list under the bare bulb in the alcove. People had gone to South Sudan without sleeping bags and medications? Or were the Sudanese doing that old thing, looking to benefit from the largesse of wealthy donors? Corruption, opportunism, a slyness learned from the life-force that demands we survive in spite of desperate circumstances—I didn't know what to call it.

Usually we could just walk in and get prescription medication over the counter, but like everything in Kenya, the process was unpredictable. Sometimes the pharmacist would be seized by a developed-world moment and insist on all the legalities. Mark hated following rules—one of the big issues with his mom as a child—so when we needed medicines, he made bogus prescription forms and signed them himself. The dare, the possibility of getting in trouble gave him a thrill. I sent him to the pharmacy. I ran to the souk for the other requests.

I crossed the sleeping bag for Rev. X, Tabitha's dad, off the list though. He'd been in and out organizing chiefs for the last five months—he knew perfectly well how to equip himself for South Sudan. But it appeared he felt entitled to a sleeping bag I would buy him with conference money.

I thought of a joke Nuers tell on themselves, one that my translator and language tutor had told me: *The hardest work I ever did was finding a job with a salary. After that, the hardest work I ever did was going to the bank to cash my check.* Just the fact that this was a joke—there seemed no end to wrestling with Rev. X over differences in our world views about how resources can be used. So, no. No sleeping bag.

But there was the matter of the all-important cups. I chewed out my supplier, who was penitent. I told him to deliver cups to my office. But at four o'clock the afternoon before I left, they still had not shown up. I dialed and redialed. Finally, I got through.

"All my personnel have left," he said. "I thought you needed the cups tomorrow."

I pressed my temples between thumb and fingers. "Tomorrow. At the airport. At six in the morning." I was determined not to make his mistake my crisis, dashing all over Nairobi that evening buying cups. I had my own packing to do.

After supper that evening, I slipped my tent into its place in my duffle. Around it, I tucked in my usual Sudan wardrobe, some comfort food, re-hydration salts, aspirin, and a snakebite kit. By then I had learned what the mysterious Zairian black stone was. Cow bone turned to charcoal was so porous, so dry, it sucked venom right out of a wound. Then you boiled the stone in milk to cleanse it. When it dried, it was ready for the next snake or scorpion.

On one of my trips, a scorpion in the woodpile had stung the teen-aged boy tending our fire. I was in my *tukel* when it happened, and, like so much that swirled around me as a foreigner, missed my only chance to see a black stone. But when I came out and learned what all the hubub had been about, the boy didn't even bother with the aspirin I offered. The black stone had worked its magic.

Early the next morning, when Peter Kimani hooted lightly outside, I leaned over the bed and kissed Mark good-bye. He moaned, musty with sleep, threw his arm over my neck and squeezed. I kissed him again and waited for him to release me, but he just tightened his arm.

"Ouch," I finally said, and pulled away. I didn't have to feel guilty for a surge of relief—it was a peace conference that was going to give me a break from this way tenderness could turn in a flash into something else.

A peace conference also seemed big enough to free me from obsessing on Mark's depression—how my travel absences might be exacerbating in Mark what had been a lifetime of anxiety and tenuous connections with people he should have been able to depend on.

As Peter Kimani and I rattled to the airport, the sun rising over the savannah made lacy black silhouettes of the acacias.

The cups were waiting there for me in several pink and blue plastic bags tied together with white nylon twine. I wrapped my hand through loops of twine and held them tight. I followed the agent with a group of NGO observers out across the tarmac in golden sunlight. Their backpacks rattled with Nalgene bottles. The highland air was chilly, but I'd worn only a denim shirt over my black silk tank top and brown crinkle skirt, knowing that soon enough I'd shed even that, and my arms would film over with sweat in South Sudan.

I clambered up onto a bale of used clothes and lay back against another, my head a foot from the ceiling of the plane. The other passengers bumped and tripped past me, along the narrow aisle, and scrambled in among the piles of cargo.

We had a long list of observers: Michael duCille and Karl Vic from the *Washington Post*; a writer and photographer from *Life Magazine*; an anthropologist; two men from London papers; one from Danish Radio; a woman from Church Aid; someone from BBC; reps from Conference of German Churches, Life and Peace Institute, Human Rights Watch and Church of the Brethren. Half of them had gone in the first week and would come back out on this plane. The rest were going in with me.

Catholic Charities had reproached me for charging observers $450 a seat. I explained we had to charter larger planes than we'd be taking if we didn't have observers, but the woman at Catholic Charities was sure we were profiteering. Bill had recruited me to do exactly this—manage the tight spot between donors who wanted to conserve money and Sudanese who wanted sleeping bags.

My stomach made a mild protest against that old cargo-plane smell from my childhood, a mixture of aviation fumes and sweat, stale used clothes, and whiffs of countless other strange cargo loads. With no seat belt to fasten and no safety lecture about water landings to interrupt, I lay back. I added and re-added our flight contracts, subtracting always from $95,000.

Lucky Moses. Manna and quail and water from the rock...

I let the plane's vibrations massage my tense shoulders and neck as we taxied up the runway.

The plane rattled and bumped to a stop on Wunlit's grass landing strip. When the mechanic opened the door, hot air blasted into the plane. I took a deep breath, switching worlds.

As soon as we passengers were out of the way, young men, already sweaty, began unloading the plane. The observers clustered nervously behind me, squinting around at the tall grass, scrub trees, and shades of brown that colored dry-season South Sudan.

A Sudanese man with deep wrinkles in his face and corkscrews of white in his hair came forward, shook my hand, and waved toward an ancient Bedford sitting under a tree, off to the side. Its paint faded from red to splotchy orange. It looked held together with wire and loose rivets. Commander Mario Muor Muor had arranged for this truck to provide conference transport for the few miles from the airstrip to Wunlit. I told the journalists and observers to pile in the back. I led the Bedford owner to the cargo piling up on the ground and retrieved two cases of WD-30 motor oil—the payment we'd negotiated for two weeks of limo rent.

He bowed over the oil to thank me. He led me to the truck and gestured me into the front seat, where a square piece of torn cotton cloth, now brown, lay over a lumpy surface with straw poking out around the edges.

The truck lurched along at a couple miles an hour over tracks made in mud and dried into treaded ridges. I gripped the panic bar over a gaping glove compartment and braced my legs to ease the jarring on what were bare springs covered with straw.

We piled out near a sorghum stalk enclosure at the edge of the peace village. "Find a spot with some shade for your tents," I told the others. They scattered as though they were looking for the best hiding place in a kid's game.

CHAPTER 22

I stood for a minute at the gate of the sorghum enclosure to take in sprawling peace village, which I'd imagined so many times. The closest *tukels* stood twenty-five feet away in shade-less sunshine on that flat, flat, flat Sudanese plain. The other five peace-villages-in-one—each with thirty *tukels* housing a dozen or more delegates—stood in random row upon row, like mountain ranges behind them. My brain had been working with the concept of 150 tukels. It was another thing to see them.

To my left, at the side of the village, sat a thatch-roofed hall, longer than any I'd ever seen, swaybacked in the middle and bristling with dozens of thatch topknots.

A black wire draped over the tops of half a dozen walking sticks and ran a hundred feet from the hall to a boxy black speaker under a tree. Voices crackled. That was the solar-powered PA system I'd ordered. Men squatted in the shade of the tree with their knees up to their armpits, their walking sticks poking up at all angles. A few off-duty soldiers in camouflage stood around the edges at ease, leaning on their AK-47s to listen.

On the right edge of the village, opposite the long hall, sat a white tent—the conference clinic—and somewhere, the Red Cross had dug one well for the conference. I could faintly hear the pump handle squeaking, and my imagination supplied the line of women and boys I knew would be drawing water for the clusters of mini-villages, for the hundreds of us basically camping out.

I turned in the entrance of the sorghum-stalk enclosure. My duffle banged against one of my legs and the cups rattled in their plastic against each other. In the center of the enclosure stood an old neem tree. On the ground, branches rested in rows in the crotches of small tree trunks pounded into the dust. It was a Sudanese *al fresco church*, about thirty feet square, and those were the pews.

Across the front lay a narrow nave: three walls and a flat roof, all made from sorghum stalks lashed to sticks like the fence. The three water filters I'd ordered for the observer village sat on a small camp table beside the podium. A vertical stick rose up from the front edge of the nave. The lateral lashed to its middle created a dark, rustic cross against the bleached-blue sky.

Narrow, serrated leaves rustled from the living vaulted ceiling in this sorghum cathedral. Someone had pitched a tent in the right corner of the nave. I headed over to claim the open spot on the left.

A thin boy with a huge smile tugged on the handle of my duffle. "Shall I take?" I gave it to him, but shook my head when he reached for the bundled cups. Those, I'd deliver myself. The sound of chattering voices rose from the direction of the meeting hall—morning tea break. Bill came into the church and gave me a big, sweaty hug.

He talked as I set up my burgundy tent. "The Dinka delegates spoke yesterday and the day before. It was pretty tough stuff. But the Nuers took it well." This was why the conference needed two weeks—to settle a Sudanese dispute, each side had to first, as they put it, *vomit out* their pain. The Nuer speeches were just about to start.

There were problems, Bill said. The cups, of course. And food was limited everywhere. The worst food issues had been in the observer village, there at the church.

"What did people think they'd be eating in South Sudan?"

"It tastes fine," Bill said. "There just isn't a whole lot of it. In the other villages, people look out for each other. But here, some of the expats are digging in like there's no tomorrow. Come late, you don't eat. The worst offenders got on the plane, so hopefully that's taken care of."

We started over to the hall. My sandaled feet quickly turned brown with sweat and dust. A chattering crowd funneled through the one low door. We'd taken a risk, bringing unoriented expats along to observe and write about this conference. Hard enough for those of us with some experience to understand and accept all the cross-cultural differences, the uninitiated had even fewer tools to work with. They'd be just guessing at unspoken meanings, estimating how their actions might look or affect others. Or they might not even see how cultures are constructs for making sense of life as it flows along. Our ideas of what's real can be very different.

I was particularly worried about one of the women, the *Life Magazine* journalist. She'd called me from New York before she left to ask what to expect. I told her how hot it would be, and to make sure her sandals were sturdy. I told her to dress modestly and wear skirts. When she came to meet me in my office in Nairobi she was wearing a skin-tight lace t-shirt. I hoped she was doing better in the *dress-modestly* department here at the conference.

Ducking under the low edge of thatch, I was instantly surrounded by bush-conference sounds and smells: the cacophony of sounds in unknown languages, bare feet shuffling on packed earth, clothing rubbing against log benches, the pungent smell of bodies in the midday heat, and air that tasted as though it had been breathed by someone else before it got to me. I paused, giving my eyes time to adjust to the dim light.

Marc Nikkel, an Episcopal priest from Wisconsin, sat ready to take notes at a camp table in the middle of the hall. He was tall, but built big, twice as wide in the shoulders as the Nilotics. Under the table, a huge truck battery was sucking juice from a solar panel on the roof to feed his laptop and the small fluorescents over his head.

In the center of the room, holding a microphone, stood Paramount Chief Isaac from Ler—such a slight man to have so much presence. Telar Deng stood beside him, profile to me, thin as the post holding up the roof, ready to translate.

I figured I should sit on the Nuer side, being with Presbyterian Church of Sudan. But Dinkas and Nuers are so closely related— their language, their thinness, their height. I would usually look for the Nuer men's scarred foreheads, but in the dim light, I couldn't see that kind of detail. Then I recognized paramount chief Madut, with his red pompoms, and saw that his side was the larger half of the hall. Since the conference was being held in their territory, it made sense more Dinkas had gotten to Wunlit.

I slipped along the opposite side to join the rows of Nuer women. They gave me shy smiles, and women scooted over to give me room on one of the swaybacked branches suspended a foot off the ground between tree-fork benches.

Chief Isaac began, "I speak according to the direction I am facing. That is where death has spread. The most important thing we must do is determine to stop death."

Telar translated first into Dinka, then into English, a process that left lots of time to think. I settled in to understand only about half of the layers of what he would say. To watch for what I could understand beyond language.

Chief Isaac went on, his voice firm but not overly loud. "It was last year that I came to realize that the conflict and killing between Dinka and Nuer could end, when I saw the involvement of the New Sudan Council of Churches, with the commitment of our church leaders of Dinka and Nuer. But in April the Dinka raided our cattle at two places. Some of the Nuer chiefs took revenge, while others of us refused. You must know that the Nuers do not want to retaliate."

The Nuers don't want to retaliate?

"However, if you touch them, they will not forget it. They will respond. History reveals that the Dinka love cattle more than we Nuer do. As we discuss, it will be clear that it is not the Nuer, but you Dinka who are guilty."

My pulse picked up. Murmuring began on the Dinka side. I searched between the shifting heads in front of me for someone's face. The one I fixed on was impassive and stern, salt-and-pepper whiskers glinting in the dim light. When Telar finished translating, Isaac still didn't raise his voice over the murmuring.

"This is clear, in that even as we work toward this peace initiative, your men go to raid our cattle. You are very clever. If we make peace here, you Dinka will say the cattle that have just been raided do not need to be returned."

Someone on the Dinka side shouted. A Nuer jumped up and shouted back. Telar raised his hand. Isaac stood still, head high, looking at the brightness outside the door. The murmuring rose.

With a glance at Bill, Telar whirled to the Dinka side and his magnified voice rose over the noise. That part didn't get translated, but I could guess what he was saying.

Surely the Dinkas knew they'd also violated rules of engagement. Warriors should have been ashamed to kill women, elders and children the way these looting parties did. Besides their traditions, they had Geneva Conventions being pressed on all sides by the UN. And from what Bill had said, the Nuers had sat quietly through two days of being accused, having *their* motives impugned, having *their* integrity questioned. Now it was their turn to speak, and Chief Isaac's upright back told me—well, he had just said it, if you touch them, they will respond.

Telar's voice subsided, from harsh to sarcastic to gentle. People sat down. The hall grew quiet. He nodded to Chief Isaac.

Chief Isaac didn't say much more. Maybe he'd already accomplished what he wanted, establishing for all the lesser chiefs that they could speak freely. The backs of my legs were going numb on the six-inch branch. I stretched them out and rested them on my heels. Telar introduced another chief.

"I greet you all heartily in the name of God and in the name of the South," the chief said. "We once made a conference in 1987 between Dinka and Nuer with Telar Deng and Mony Luak." He said peace had held in that region for years. So that's where Telar's credibility with the USAID men came from.

The chief backed up Chief Isaac's accusation with another example of Dinka perfidy, and then reminded everyone that this was not a traditional war reparations court, where everyone would negotiate grievances. This was a peace conference. Everyone also knew that the paramount chiefs had agreed to lay aside restitution. To declare amnesty. This gathered community would either ratify or reject before they were done. The case was being made.

The chief went on. "What I want to say is that we must preserve the peace we agree on. This peace is from within ourselves, we chiefs, with our own effort. It does not come from others, like the Europeans who have come here. They are only observers."

Applause burst out like rain on a tin roof. I smiled. These chiefs, most of them illiterate in any language, were so politically astute. His comment about observers was not aimed at people like Bill and Marc and me, it was for the dozen Sudanese intellectuals. Men from the Sudanese diaspora in the US and Europe. Citizens of wealthy and peaceful countries, now foreigners in South Sudan. They would not be given a public platform to speak here, but they were meeting in the moonlit evenings. They were expressing strong opinions about things they were no longer going to experience. Like Irish who live in Chicago and Boston. They were the rapporteur team, there to take notes and observe for themselves. They had been invited so they saw for themselves and did not buy any warped rumors about what had happened in remote Wunlit.

"We have come as Dinka and Nuer chiefs to discuss our conflicts. The white bull has cleansed the evil from among us." Applause and joy cries almost drowned out the English translation.

Another Nuer chief began. "I ask you, children of my mother. We chiefs, each of us has our wife. If our wife tries to cook food with her pot she must have three stones. If there is only one, it will fall down."

With that, he launched into all the things that had destroyed their cooperation, and he refuted some accusations the Dinkas must have made earlier. "Finally, what I ask you, chiefs," he said, "is this our conflict? The people who are destroying our land, those are soldiers, and we don't know them. For example, Commander Guy Tut was killed and buried. Then his body was exhumed and lashed with one hundred lashes by Commander Carbino. Also Commander Mien Kual killed people like chickens. These are the problems created by others that have drawn in Dinka and Nuer."

I smiled at the woman sitting next to me. Peace here depended on distancing themselves from their warlords and rogue commanders, their own tribe-mates. Not an easy task anywhere, when tribalism takes hold.

The next chief stood. I sat forward, anticipating more of this amazing, practical wisdom, more of these African metaphors, thrilled at this process. I was forgetting to breathe, being there to learn from this graduate-level course on Nuer culture.

"You Dinka and Nuer," he said. "I caution you to be careful of what you observed in Mabior. The bull was very wild. I have never seen a bull as wild as that bull. Anyone who resumes these conflicts, Mabior will take revenge on him, because Mabior died for our reconciliation.

"We the chiefs, we are like a python. When there is conflict, the snake will cover its children so that they will not be burnt by fire. For the present, let us be calm. We civilians, let us separate ourselves from the soldiers and refrain from looting. Finally, the soldiers will be ashamed. The looting of cows goes on and on because we civilians participate. If we stop supporting it, it will cease.

"Let us stop seeking after cattle, for if we obtain peace, then we will have our cattle; we will cultivate and make good use of our land. If conflict continues, we will end up with nothing. In concluding my speech, I pray that our meeting will be blessed by God."

Amen, I wanted to say. Amen and amen.

By the time we broke for lunch, my legs were so stiff I could hardly hobble out of the hall, which had only gotten hotter and stuffier as the sun swung overhead.

I couldn't bear to go back in for the afternoon session, but walked around the outside of the hall, looking for another option. A breeze blew hot over my face and I shook my hair away from my scalp. At the Nuer end of the building lay a stripe of afternoon shade; I decided to listen from there, sitting on the ground with my back against the mud plaster wall.

As the speeches began again, a young woman came around the corner of the hall. Her smile said she'd been looking for me. She grabbed my offered hand, flung herself down beside me. She tucked my arm under hers and wove her dusty fingers through mine. "I am Deborah Nyandien. I am from Ler." Her two missing bottom front teeth gave her English a lisp. "I was the Nuer woman chosen to give greetings this morning. I told the men if they don't make peace, we will no longer bear children for them to kill in their war."

My eyebrows went up and I smiled, thinking of the Greek women boycotting sex. But a Nuer woman *exists* for the children she will bear. Boys to keep the memory of their father alive, girls to bring him dowry wealth.

Nyandien's short braids quivered all over her head. "Yes, I said that. Awut Deng Achuil from Dinka said it is not for a woman to cause a disturbance at a peace conference." I looked into her eyes, mock solemn, and then we both burst out laughing, Deborah "Lysistrata" Nyandien hid her gappy mouth with one hand. We settled back against the mud plaster, shoulder-to-shoulder, to listen to the men make peace.

CHAPTER 23

Late that afternoon, I sat on Bill's camp mat and leaned against another mud wall, the wall of his and Marc Nikkel's dim *tukel*. The air pressed hot around me. Sticks from inside the framework of the *tukel* crisscrossed the tiny window, splitting the brightness of the sinking sun into geometric slivers of light on the floor. Bill and Marc's camp mats lay on either side of a low door, backpacks gaping at the foot, jumbled with clothes.

Marc passed me a *Common Book of Prayer*. He read the liturgy as though he knew it by heart. Bill and I read our parts in unison. At the end we prayed together, "Make your face to shine upon us and give us peace."

I sat with my eyes closed, my head against the rough mud wall, my legs stretched out, in the heat and the quiet and the sense of God. Another observer who spoke that afternoon, a chief from the Boma people to the east, began by saying, "I greet you black people in your black land, with your black water, with your black fish. Peace be with you."

That was the single prayer. Peace. What it takes. Who should make it. Who must not disturb it. The fighting was driven by land rights and cattle, not so different, really, from Western civilization wars driven by national boundary disputes and competition for resources.

My mind drifted home. Calling the problem between Mark and me a war seemed confusing, suddenly. Love isn't a zero-sum resource like cattle or oil. The more you give, the more you have—isn't that the cliché? But it wasn't working that way. I was giving as much as I could and wasn't earning the love that was supposed to follow. Mark just kept saying he couldn't love me because he didn't trust me anymore.

Forgiveness and hope that the future can be different from the past—spiritual matters—lie at the center of peace. Mark wasn't able to manage them. And where would he have learned? He'd written a letter home about the early abuses. Instead of apologizing, his mom had refused to come to Miriam's wedding.

Now we were asking the Dinkas and Nuers to forgive rape and murder and trust each other again. What an act of faith, this peace conference. As aggressive as Nuers and Dinkas can be, as cheap as life had become in the Kalashnikov age, bringing people face to face to hash it out seemed almost foolhardy. Only respect for Bill, Telar, and chiefs like Isaac would keep the war, thinly buried, from flaring up on site.

The next morning, our breakfast thermoses of tea crowded the tray sitting on a stump. On the corner sat a stack of thin plastic glasses, the kind you use to serve punch at a reception.

"What are these?" I asked, when the boy came with hot milk.

"Cups," he said. He shrugged a smile into his shoulder.

This is what the supplier ran out and got when I demanded he come through with the missing cups? A wave of impotent rage rose up in me. More than anything else about Kenya, I hated what seemed like sneaky cheating. My supplier put together displaced-person kits for South Sudan all the time, he knew the kind of heavy-duty cups the Sudanese need for their tea. And he knew there was nothing I could do about his *misunderstanding*, once I left for South Sudan.

I picked up a punch-glass. We would just have to use these as cups until they all cracked and broke, and then we'd have to share whatever cups had made it into the kits. Hopefully it would work itself out. Imagine holding a peace conference in Northern Ireland and having only enough cups for half the delegates! In a hot spot, the littlest thing could become a crisis.

And no one could predict what small thing would suddenly break the delicate trust that was building and endanger us all there in Wunlit. Tens of thousands of people had been killed in an area to the east after two men from different Nuer clans got into a fight over a fish. And it wasn't even the fish that people began brawling about. It was because the thief threw the fish down *disdainfully*.

"I pour for you?" the boy said. I held the punch glass by the rim, but it softened as he filled it with scalding tea. I sucked in my breath and got my cup to the ground before it slipped through my fingers. I was drinking out of the end of it, a heat-softened oval, when Bill walked through the gate. I held it up and twisted my mouth ironically.

"I heard," he said. He shook his head and laughed. That's one of the things I loved about Bill. He didn't judge or criticize. He didn't say I should have known better.

After another day of pain-purging speeches, after soothing liturgy and prayers in English in Marc and Bill's *tukel*, Marc stretched. "Anyone for a walk before dark?"

"Telar and I need to work the bugs out of tomorrow's agenda," Bill said.

I'd met Marc Nikkel first in Ethiopia, when he came through Addis with his Dinka fiancé, a university student he'd met in England, a woman as tall as he was. But when he got to the Sudan to negotiate with her parents, they thought they'd struck gold—a bridegroom from America! He couldn't afford the number of dowry cows they demanded, converted to cash. It seemed shocking to me, at the end of the 20th Century, but that was the end of the relationship.

Marc spoke Dinka fluently and had come back to work with the South Sudan Episcopal Church. Then abdominal pain turned out to be cancer and put him in the hospital in Nairobi.

"How're you doing?" I asked.

He pulled up his pant legs to show me thick splotchy ankles. "My circulation's shot. I need as much exercise as I can get."

As he loped along out on the road, his dark hair across his forehead flopped a little in my peripheral vision. "The doctors found so much cancer they just sewed me back up. Everyone thought it was the end," he said. "But I asked my Dinka friends to pray, and the doctor put me on this twenty-four-hour drip." Marc patted the khaki packet hanging around his neck. Its rubber tube disappeared between two buttons. "I think God let me come back one more time to make peace." He was walking so fast I was out of breath trying to keep up.

I couldn't speak or look at him. I hadn't realized how bad it was. How heroic he was being. Or how crushed he might be if, after all our efforts, no peace came.

A beehive *tukel* rose out of the brush on our left. Dinka-style thatching, three even ridges like tilted steps bumped down the side of the roof. Two young children stood in the doorway, naked, with shaved heads.

We waved as we passed. Marc called, *"Sheebok."* They stared, silent. We must have looked weird and ghostly to them; no other white people could ever have come to Wunlit.

Dust lay in layers on scrubby brush along the roadway. Fresh tire tracks wide apart told me heavy equipment had gone by. Marc Nikkel stopped. "This is as far as we can go. Commander Salva Kiir's camp is up that way."

In Wunlit, commanding battalions Eleven and Twelve to guard the Wunlit Peace Conference, Salva Kiir hadn't yet been given the Stetson by President Bush or made the black hat his trademark. And John Garang, the larger-than-life doctor, commander, warlord hadn't yet died in a helicopter crash. Kiir was still John Garang's deputy.

Rifts opened up between them before Garang died. When Garang didn't leave him, or anyone else, in charge when he made international trips, Kiir complained. "Who is in charge of the Movement? Or does John Garang take it with him in his briefcase?"

Kiir and Garang also disagreed about whether South Sudan was better off independent or as a province of greater Sudan. "Better a free citizen in our own country than a second-class citizen in someone else's country," Salva Kiir said.

That comment was quoted in every corner of South Sudan.

In 2005, when John Garang's helicopter crashed, Commander Salva Kiir took his place as vice president of the Sudanese government in Khartoum. When South Sudan's status was finally put to a referendum in 2011, southerners embraced Kiir's opinion about freedom with a 98% yes vote. Salva Kiir earned a place in history as the political midwife to a newborn nation.

He'd been just a teenager when he joined the rebel army in the late 1960s, and probably didn't finish high school. BBC called him an *accidental politician*, a man with a monotone public speaking style and an unlikely rise up the ranks of the SPLA.

Did he rise to a position he cannot sustain? Has he made the transition from the military—with its ethos of subordinate obedience—to politics, which requires negotiation with peers? He seems to still be on the lookout for slights, or reminders of his inadequacies. And the primary person he has to negotiate with is Doctor Riek Machar, a peer who even John Garang couldn't keep under control.

In 2013, two years after the referendum that brought South Sudanese independence, President Salva Kiir reorganized the military and dismissed over a hundred generals—generals that, admittedly, were accused of extrajudicial killings and corruption. Then he also sacked his cabinet and his Vice President, Riek Machar. Kiir being Dinka, Riek being Nuer, the new capital city of Juba erupted in an ethnic blood bath that spread to towns where Dinka and Nuer border each other.

A couple years later, Kiir accused the UN of supporting Riek. Then five journalists were murdered. The world's newest nation raced headlong into its own civil war, one that eventually displaced over two million civilians, and led officials in Washington to say Kiir was an *unfit partner for peace.*

But Salva Kiir hung on.

In April 2019, the pope called a South Sudan retreat at the Vatican. Salva Kiir flew in; John Garang's widow; Riek Machar, who'd taken refuge in Khartoum—all the lead actors through decades of conflict in South Sudan.

Pope Francis pleaded with them. "I beg you as a brother to stay the course of peace."

Salva Kiir later told his parliament, "I was shocked, and trembled when His Holiness the Pope kissed our feet. It was a blessing and can be a curse if we play games with the lives of our people."

He publicly invited Riek Machar back to Juba. He swore all was forgiven. But peace in South Sudan is a story whose ending has not yet been written. I'm glad I didn't know, when I was in Wunlit, how rocky the road to peace would yet be for South Sudan.

Walking west, back to camp with Marc Nikkel that evening, the wide Sudanese sky glowed pink above a flat horizon until the peaks of ragged thatching in silhouette appeared.

Inside the golden sorghum compound, under the neem tree, dusk had already fallen. Supper would be late, the boy with the big smile told me. No water yet, to cook the rice. I slathered my ankles with OFF and used a towelette to wash the dust and Deet off my hands.

In the middle of the night, my hip woke me, aching against the ground. My camp mat had developed a slow leak. I blew it back up without opening my eyes.

The next morning, when I held one of the thin plastic glasses under a water filter spigot and turned the handle, there was no drinking water. All three filters were empty. The boys had filled them the night before, I was sure, when they finally got water. I lifted one of the lids. Unfiltered water rocked in a cloudy circle above ceramic cylinders fuzzy with impurities.

"Hun gora peu," I told women in the smoky, sorghum-thatched cooking hut behind the church. I want water, one of my first phrases in the language, and a bumper sticker for life in South Sudan. The longer the conference took, the more that was everyone's refrain. We wanted water. It also never took long in South Sudan for the stress of fragile subsistence to wear people down. Fights had begun at the well.

Mario Muor Muor had known one well wouldn't be enough for our crowd. He had asked Red Cross to drill two wells. They must have looked at all the empty *tukels* and thought he was crazy. They drilled one well and moved on.

Now women from nearby Wunlit village, who had been walking five kilometers to a river, were coming to the well. It was an early fruit of peace for them, and no one wanted to exclude them. These were the mothers at the center of their families. Wealth had been exchanged, they had come at a price, and their contribution was to provide: bearing the children who bring that immortality and wealth back to their husbands, growing the sorghum, gathering the wood, cooking, carrying the water.

The soldiers guarding the conference also came several times a week for water, and soldiers don't wait in lines. The women and boys sat for eight, ten hours in the sun, or sometimes all night, to draw water for cooking, but even so, peace-villages here and there began to miss lunch, lacking water to cook with. Basins for washing our faces and hands sat empty. Nilotics are used to missing meals, but going days and days between the ritual of an evening bath was pushing people over the limits of emotional deprivation. Bill fretted that the whole peace process could fall apart at the well. Only Mario's tight reins on the water line was keeping the situation under control.

If the women didn't have water for me to wash the filters, we wouldn't have drinking water. But a woman brought me a *soferia* of water, and I squatted as she would have, to wash the ceramic filters. The dirt and minerals that clung to them were so fine they felt slimy. The morning hadn't gotten unbearably hot yet. I was alone in the church, feeling peaceful. As I scrubbed, I realized that when I was done, I would have clean hands for the first time in three days. That small thought gave me joy.

I faintly heard morning devotions over at the hall, *A Mighty Fortress is Our God* by Martin Luther. Luther might not have recognized it, tune-warped in translation, with a plodding single drumbeat. The Dinkas and the Nuer women and youth wrote their own music—contrapuntal, call-and-response tunes. Teenaged boys accompanied them on drums with wildly complex rhythms. But the Nuer pastors stubbornly stuck to translated missionary hymns from the hymnbook *Golden Bells*. I was happy to have a useful job as an excuse to miss the Lutheran national anthem rendered by Nuer men.

After lunch, as I waited for my tea in the punch glass to cool, a Sudanese woman crept into the church enclosure holding her smallest aluminum *soferia*. "*Mal-ay,*" I said in Nuer.

"*Sheebok,*" she whispered in Dinka, and didn't look up. She twisted the faucets on the water filters, one after the other. Everyone knows everything in an African village; word must have gone out that the expatriate observers' camp had water. But there was no water, even though I had cleaned the filters.

A circle of mud in the dust below each faucet told me why. Once people had drained whatever the filters held, they were leaving the faucets open, letting the precious drips that filtered through to drip on out. I shut the faucets.

I thought about the woman, about people who don't have mechanical tools—they must assume if there's no water, there's no point in closing the faucets. Or maybe people who don't have mechanical tools don't know you have to close faucets to let the water fill up for next time. Or maybe they don't even think *open* and *closed* when they turn those little handles, trying for water. Maybe being faucet manager would be my best contribution to peace at that point. I'd heard enough; let the speeches go on without me.

CHAPTER 24

On faucet duty, I sat hunched over, elbow on my knee, and listened to the crackle of three languages over the speakers out under the big tree. My three-legged campstool sank into dust up to the rubber caps on the legs.

Every time I came back to South Sudan, I marveled at how people can live with nothing but what the earth produces. This was how the human race began. People in subsistence economies even today don't have easy, comfortable lives. Every individual doesn't live. But enough do. The Dinkas and Nuers had lived on those plains, with their sorghum, with their cattle, fighting over their rivers and grass, for generations upon generations. They'd figured out ways to keep enough peace to survive.

But now that they had guns, new ways of keeping peace had to be invented. The UN had tried all kinds of Western-style peace-making. Bill's genius was seeing that the new thing needed to be a mix of old and new.

Such a thing was bound to be beset by all kinds of set-backs. That day, Bill had come back from an early morning meeting with Mario and said, "He looks awful. No one knows what's wrong, but the Dinka doctor who's supposed to be running the clinic is making himself important trying to boss Mario around."

Throughout the day I turned my worry to prayer every time it drifted back to worry.

When Mario called Bill and me to see him the next afternoon, we walked over to his heavily guarded *tukel*, sitting at the outer edge of the village in a grove of young trees, each as thin as my forearm. Bill lifted the ragged cloth hanging in the doorway, and I ducked in. Mario lay on a hand-carved bed. He turned slowly onto his side to shake our hands. His skin was hot and dry.

"Why is the young white woman here?" he asked, straight to the point, as soon as we sat down.

Bill leaned forward, elbows on his thighs and hands clasped together. "She's a reporter. She is here to do a photo-journalism piece," he said.

"On the first day, she offended Commander Salva Kiir." Mario paused, as though he had to build up strength to go on. "Insisting to interview him when he was trying to open the conference...he is next in authority behind Dr. John Garang...does she not understand?"

I breathed anxious, shallow breaths.

"Now I am told she blocks the doorway...she pushes her breasts into the hall. Our men can't go in or come out...they are embarrassed...these are chiefs...they must be treated with respect." Mario finished and closed his eyes.

"I am sorry," Bill said. "We'll take care of it."

Mario nodded.

I ducked out the low door and waited for Bill at the edge of the grove. I'd gone so hot all over that even the warm South Sudan breeze felt refreshing.

Ms. Lace T-shirt had miscalculated the formality of the peace conference, maybe because it was out in the bush and people here were poor. The Sudanese women were wearing their best clothes, but she crawled out of her tent every morning in baggy shorts, her shirt tied in front so her belly button and a roll of pale flesh above her waistband showed. As she came and went in the meeting hall, she lounged in the doorway, blocking the exit *and* one of the only sources of light and air.

Even now, it's the word *breasts* that brings a wave of shame— for her, for me. Shame as a woman. How deeply the glorification of all things male, the denigration of the female has penetrated my self-esteem. This is the kind of insight that comes to me only when I stand in another culture. Cushioned in my own culture, where a man wouldn't use the word *breasts* frankly like that, I would never have noticed how it could make me cringe.

And now, an awkward conversation with that young woman, with or without using the word *breasts*. We both knew Bill was the one who could find a tone that would change behavior and still soothe ruffled feelings.

As we walked through the clusters of peace village *tukels* to our camp in the church, I went back to worrying about Mario. It scared me to see him so sick, and all we had was a clinic—no lab, no IV fluids. Neither Bill nor I spoke, wrapped up, probably, in similar thoughts. *What did Mario need? Surely, he wouldn't die here, would he? What part in the delicate balance might that upset?* We passed the line of waiting boys and women, which only Mario could manage. A line that defied all cultural patterns of clustering. A line that snaked, in the blazing sunlight, all the way to the well. The pump's squeaky handle never stopped.

Throughout that day, I thought about the young American journalist. I felt so tolerant of tribal cuttings, bull sacrifices, and troubling things in Nuer and Dinka cultures and so condemning of her inappropriate behavior. It was because we were guests, she and I, I decided. We were witnessing something sacred at this conference. The quality of our presence could have an impact on the delicate balance of peace.

But I was more deeply unsettled than the conference warranted. I can see now that my reaction to the journalist came, in some part, out of my chronic wish to return to that simpler life of my childhood.

The people of Maji had welcomed our family with warmth and curiosity. They had been bemused by how different we were—our skin, our eyes, our hair, our home, our language. Like I was of the Nilotics. It was only when I went to the US that I had felt shunned for being strange.

By the time I traveled to Wunlit for the conference, my joy in finding again the crevice between cultures, had already been deeply threatened. I felt fierce about my fading chance to live not as an African bound by African culture, not as an American bound by American culture, but somewhere between the two. It led me into hypocrisies, excusing the dark side of cultures in Africa and condemning my own.

I didn't ask Bill what he said, how she reacted.

As the second week of the conference wore on, drama in the observer village escalated again. Most of the foreigners, with all of their good intentions, had come with unrealistic expectations of what *South Sudan adventure* would actually feel like day by day. One woman got more and more paranoid until she convinced herself she had been poisoned. I heard her retching in her tent, trying to vomit, hours after I thought my reassurances had calmed her.

And then the young journalist left her laptop in her backpack in the screen porch of her tent. Someone picked it up—probably some passing soldier, Bill speculated later. But she suggested to the guy who ran the observer camp that the boy with the big smile might have taken it. *You should question him and search his things.*

What things, I thought when she told me. The boy wore the same t-shirt every day.

She couldn't have imagined what would unfold. I would have had a clue, but even I didn't know that her suggestion would be taken so seriously, that in this culture, even the suggestion of theft would mar the reputation of his father, the brother of a chief, for generations.

The day after she pointed a finger at the boy, Commander Salva Kiir ordered soldiers to imprison him. His father ordered him beaten and threatened him with trial by poison when he didn't confess. (If he were innocent, the poison would be nullified by the spirits. If he were guilty, the poison would be poison.)

Telar, Bill, and Mario only saved the boy's life by convincing his father that this white woman was ignorant. No Dinkas would listen to her.

When the boy came back to work at our camp, he had lost that eager smile. I watched him go about his work now, eyes cast down. His exposure to Western culture at a peace conference had shown him our dark side. Every culture has one. We accept and excuse our own darkness. We are shocked by that of the Other.

I felt crushed. I forced myself to listen, to make empathetic noises as I sat with the young woman on one of the pew benches.

"He hung out with us," she said. "He asked if he could have my backpack when I left." She explained that in New York, it would have been a natural impulse, to grab it when he could. "I only want my computer back," she said. "It was my journal. I wrote stuff there that I can't replace."

I understood why, in the individualistic way an American would consider reasonable, the woman had taken things in her own hands instead of coming to Bill or me for advice. How could she be expected to guess the conventions of a communal culture?

It was time for us to wrap up the conference and go to our homes, where we knew how the signals we were giving would be taken. Where we could predict the ramifications of our actions.

The Nuers finished telling their stories of pain and outrage. The Dinkas meekly listened to the details of what they'd done to the Nuers, who had done the same to them. Now delegates split into mixed-tribe working groups. To cut translations down by one language, English-only expat observers were excused.

In the middle of that afternoon, the observer camp manager called me from filter watch. He gestured to two boys walking herky-jerky from the pickup carrying a sloshing jerry can of water between them. "We took a vehicle to the river. There is water for you to bathe."

I ran to get my blue nylon toiletry bag with all the things I hadn't used for days—soap, shampoo, deodorant. The floor in the tiny, low bathing *tukel* was slimy with mud. I carefully hung my kit and clothes on twigs in the wall. When a breeze fluttered the curtain, red with huge gray daisies, I stepped further back into the shadows. Even though I knew the boys would be Sudanese-polite and look away while I was in there, my naked body seemed so white it might glow right through the curtain like phosphorus.

"Good?" a boy asked, when I ducked out past the gray flowers again.

My wet hair felt cool as well as clean. *"Gua elong elong."* Very, very good. There is nothing more *good* than water in a dry, hot land.

Group reports began. We were finally on the downhill side of this marathon. Now only the big question about restitution was left. I went back to the hall for this, back to the still heat and the used air. The first group came forward from both sides of the hall and stood in a cluster while their reporter flipped through page after page of newsprint, reading into the microphone the names of three hundred seventy-two villages destroyed.

Their recommendation: people must move back. They called on aid organizations to help with wells, schools, maybe a clinic somewhere in the *toich*, one that would serve communities on both sides of the river. Fruits of peace, as Bill had called it. Such developments would not only be fruit, but guarantee of peace, if only the donors would see that.

The Peace Violations Working Group gave their recommendation: those who broke the peace should stand trial where they'd stirred things up. A woman's joy cry shrilled above the clapping. It meant violators would be punished by those they'd harmed, not let off with slapped wrists back home.

Recommendation from the Death Restitution Working Group: death had been equivalent and anonymous. No one on either side would pay death restitutions. I could see Bill's shoulders relax as joy cries ratified the decision.

The Working Group on Abductions gathered in the center, and their reporter announced they had several recommendations: first, abducted boys would be sent home. Second, men who had abducted girls and married them must choose—send them home, or pay the bride price, which would legitimize their children. A murmur of approval moved around the hall.

This was not the Middle East, where, if girls were sent home, they would be punished for having been violated. This was Sub-Saharan Africa, where most of them would probably be legitimized as full wives. Those who were sent home might become second or third wives, but even that—again, this was where sometimes, at least, more wives are welcomed because they share the burden of hoeing the fields by hand and carrying the water. It's also taboo among the Nuers for men to touch their pregnant or nursing wives, so polygamy helps with child spacing and keeps both mothers and babies healthier.

The reporter stepped forward to make his third recommendation. He raised his voice a little. Telar's lips had been parted, ready to translate. Instead, he turned his head and looked at the reporter, shocked. People on the Nuer side leapt up from their benches, shouting. The reporter shouted back. A man ran forward and grabbed the mic from Telar. He was shouting so loud his voice buzzed. Bill jumped up and ran to Telar's side. Men throughout the hall waved their fists in the air. A woman began to wail.

I sat up straight, adrenalin pumping. No one was armed—that had been part of the conference agreement. But five hundred people were suddenly shouting in two languages around me. What had happened to all that good will? How could it disappear so quickly?

Telar twisted the microphone out of the Nuer man's hands. He went on shouting. Telar spoke over him, lips against the black foam of the mic. "We will *not* discuss this here." He pushed the man's chest, held the mic out of reach, and turned another man away with his shoulder. The men still shouted at each other, both at the same time.

I had stood, in my spot by the twenty-foot-long pole-bench, just because everyone else had. I looked for someone to translate—Deborah from Ler was at the other end of the bench.

Telar's voice, magnified to distortion, pierced through the mayhem. "We will refer this matter to a committee—the facilitators plus the Restitution Working Group. They will report back after lunch."

The shouting died to a murmur. Telar softened his voice. "If we discuss this now, at this time, it will take many days. Our water is short. We will run out of food."

Then he adjourned the meeting. Babble erupted again, shrill with emotion. The acrid smell of angry sweat hung like a cloud in the air. I crowded my way to Marc Nikkel, who was pushing lanky hair off his forehead.

"What happened?"

"He said they decided men who abducted married women should pay compensation for adultery."

I thought about that as I ducked out the low doorway. Came up with nothing. "I still don't get it." The last flood of Sudanese from the hall had scattered, still talking intensely, out into the peace village. Quiet settled around us as we headed to the church under the Neem tree.

"If deaths are forgiven," Marc said, "but not adultery, those women cost more alive than dead." He paused for me to follow the logic. He finished softly. "They would go out to the forests to gather wood. Never be seen again. Maybe not the men themselves. Maybe someone in the family."

Even in the noon heat, my fingertips went cold. How vulnerable the women were. And how imbedded into everyone's psyches that vulnerability was. Even the men had known instantly what would happen. Abducted wives already lived as spoils of war, intimate with the very men who had burned their homes, maybe killed their husbands and children.

Marc Nikkel went on over my silence. "I know some of the men in that working group. They chose it because their married sisters were abducted. They want compensation. It won't pass. But opening it up to discussion would have undone everything."

Lunch was late again because there was no water to cook the rice. I crawled into my stifling tent and ate a sesame brittle. My mattress had deflated, so I just lay on the hard ground. I stretched my legs out. I spread my arms apart as well, so no part of my body touched another. I closed my aching eyes.

Women's lives. The complexity overwhelming. So central for life and survival. Counting for so little. It was tempting to judge the Nuer and Dinka men. To call them oppressors. But really, a delicate cultural dance had allowed men and women to survive together out on these plains under difficult conditions.

I didn't know how women fit into war in my own culture. Here, it was clear. Access to women was the post pinning the bull of peace in his circle—or breaking and setting him loose to rampage and kill.

The fight for cattle among the Nuer and Dinka was directly linked to a man's life in an uncertain world. Men collected cattle wealth to have access to women. Wives performed the work of physical survival—gathering firewood for cooking, doing the cooking, carrying water. A woman ensured that a man's DNA was represented in the community of the future.

Would the requirement that one third of the conference delegates be women like Deborah from Ler change the balance? Maybe that, alone, was so radical we could stop and wait for decades to pass, giving time for the culture to shift and adjust around disruptive speeches by a woman at a conference. The notion that just because men own the cattle doesn't mean men control women might take time to emerge into the culture as truth.

Maybe just my coming among them, being educated, ordained, and independent, was a radical act of women's development in South Sudan. Even if I never ran any programs. Who were aid organizations, from the outside, to say how fast women's status in another culture should change?

Anyway, look at me, I thought. My culture had believed in individual worth for generations—long enough to now extend that value even to women. But educated and independent as I was, I doubted myself a dozen times a day. I got tangled up, trying to be a good woman in my church and mission context. Worse, when Mark was angry, it opened up in my deepest soul the fear that I wasn't worthy of love.

And, like working women all over the USA, I worried about myself as a mother. Were my boys getting what they needed? They had a mother who disappeared regularly, for weeks at a time. When I traveled into South Sudan, I might as well have gone to the moon. Did their father give the boys what they needed when I was gone? How would they relate to women when they were men? Maybe they would resent forever that I wasn't there when they needed me at home, making *their* worlds better, but instead dashing off, trying to make worlds better in South Sudan.

Did fathers think about these things when they traveled?

I closed my eyes and brought my racing mind back. I needed to just feel sad for the women of South Sudan for a few minutes.

After lunch, Telar announced the Restitution Committee's new recommendation: amnesty for men who abducted married women. The women would be returned to their first husbands. If their husbands had been killed, they would be returned to their fathers and brothers, who would protect them and help them raise the generation below, still vulnerable, still valuable. People murmured, but this time no one shouted. Peace was assured.

CHAPTER 25

Bill was so relieved that he couldn't stop smiling. After the meeting, he put me to work feeding a hundred sheets of paper one by one into the tiny mobile printer, fueled by that panel on the thatched roof. Out came Articles of Agreement, written up by the rapporteur group led by Bill Lowrey. Delegates would take them back to their districts. Most of the delegates couldn't read, but they would know what the papers said, and the papers themselves would be sacraments: visible evidence of a spiritual reality. Peace.

Marc Nikkel leaned over the computer, making final corrections on the list of delegates. The tiny solar fluorescents, flickering against thatch above us, gave just enough light to see what we were doing as the light outside faded.

"You do have the inkpads, right?" Bill said.

A stack sat waiting in a corner of my tent—in my excitement over thumb-printing the peace covenant, I'd bought enough ink for thousands of chiefs. I ducked out of the dark hall, into dusk and shadows under a sunset sky. Stepping through the sorghum entry-way to the church, the air felt intimate. Stars winked in the navy and apricot sky around the edges of the neem tree roof.

Nuer men don't smile their *please* for a woman, even if that woman controls their transport home. As the conference wound down, demands peppered me whenever I stepped out of the sorghum-stalk church.

Put me on the first flight. Take me to Nairobi. Take my family to Loki.

I'd given my word to Kevin Ashley not to get him in trouble with

Kenyan authorities by letting the delegates use peace conference charters to sneak in illegally.

"Everyone must go back to where they came from," I said over and over. I tried to see it as an opportunity to practice spiritual disciplines: to stay gracious; to smile; to stay bemused at being ordered around.

James's family was the only exception. He was the new New Sudan Council of Churches field organizer for the village of Ler. NSCC had agreed to resettle his family in Kenya, and Telar had asked me to put them on a flight to Loki. That exception was all in order.

Rev. X, he of the re-purposed money and the hankering for a new sleeping bag, came to me. He was huge, his genetic Nuer height filled out with eating goat stew and *chapatis* in Nairobi. "When you land in Ler, take the commander's family to Loki. He is our friend. He has permission. They have been waiting for transport. After the looting of Ler, there was nothing."

With him, I would always smell a rat. "They have papers?"

"Yes, they have papers."

His smile was all reassurance. Which wasn't reassuring at all. What was he hiding, being so polite? Of course, he'd *say* they had papers.

"From the Kenyan government?"

He nodded and laughed, doing very well at being cross-examined by a mere woman.

"I'll think about it and check the passenger list." We both knew the plane would fly full to Ler, and almost empty from Ler to Loki. But even if the family had papers, I wasn't sure about this, using our flights to help a Sudan Liberation commander. I knew too much about commanders.

They raided the very villages they were supposed to protect. Or they promised protection in exchange for the most beautiful young women in town—commanders had wives by the dozens, all without paying dowry cattle. Which meant every Nilotic man wanted to be a commander. Which made it easy for North Sudan to buy them off with weapons and splinter the resistance. All that splintering is what had led to conflagration on the West Bank in the first place—those soldiers that the chiefs had accused of looting women and cattle, those commanders that the peace conference had distanced itself from.

And when the UN dropped off those logisticians who called civilians together around food drop sites, when they roped off the target areas to protect people, when hungry Sudanese families crowded the ropes, watching big-bellied Hercules aid planes swoop down with UN workers to push maize and rice out the back, those commanders and their troops were also watching.

The aid community knew that the commanders got much of the food dropped for women and children. Donors knew they were keeping the war going by feeding the troops. And of course, the troops were also the husbands, sons, and brothers of those women and children. The community and the troops couldn't ever be totally separated from each other.

I put aside the question of the commander's family. Sitting on my camp stool in the church, I worked on the lists; flight schedules penciled, erased, and rewritten; estimated costs in parentheses beside destinations; totals added and re-added at the bottom.

One afternoon, Mario Muor Muor sent a boy of about eight who spoke English to summon me. My little guide and I wove through the middle of the village, skirting the invisible circles of privacy around *tukels* and passing the noisy line of women and boys waiting their turns at the pump. As I entered through his gray curtain, Mario coughed weakly into his hand.

"I am worried about you," I said. "You've become so thin."

"I am not able to eat." He coughed again.

He was wasting away.

"They are going to bring me milk. That will make me strong."

Naturally a Dinka would put his hope in milk. I hoped he was right. Maybe milk was medicine to a Dinka. I said, "I could put you on the first flight with Bill and the Sudanese observers. Get you to the hospital in Loki."

"I am the only one who can distribute. Otherwise there will be fighting." He was talking about the bundles of used clothes and the bags of salt and sugar we'd brought in on that last flight as payment for the women and boys waiting in the water line, building fires, cooking for the delegates in the thirty mini-villages. Nilotics are famous for fighting over goods like that unless someone with unimpeachable credentials distributes them. Mario shifted, closed his eyes. "The delegation from Tuich. They are asking to be transported home by truck. I cannot do that. You must arrange a flight."

This was the delegation that Bill had tried to tell me about over the radio. With the roads cut off from Wunlit by high rivers, they'd walked, arriving exhausted, but to great acclaim, several days after the conference started. I pretended to look through my passenger lists.

Jesus said the Sabbath was made for man, not man for the Sabbath—the budget was for the peace conference. And it was a hundred times more Mario's peace conference than mine. I spoke slowly. "Everyone who came by truck is asking for a flight. The money is running out."

Mario pulled his knees toward his chest as he coughed again. "You are right. But this group walked. They wore out their shoes. They cannot carry their kits home. If they wait for the truck, I will have to wait with them. We will run out of food. I will die here."

I fiddled my pencil against the page of lists. "Let me work on it."

My guide came quickly when I ducked back out. We headed past the clinic, its line now as long as the water line. There'd been an outbreak of meningitis, and Red Cross had asked our permission to vaccinate using the peace clinic. People from villages all around had walked in to get shots. I felt a glow of joy, imagining how many hundreds of lives we were saving in one way or another with this conference.

Suddenly three chiefs stepped out into our path. They carried walking sticks and cow-tail fly whisks. One clamped a pipe, carved of wood and wrapped in pounded-bullet-shell brass, between his molars. We shook hands. The boy held his left hand to his right elbow as he shook, ultra-respectful, as a child should be to chiefs.

"They want to know who you are," he said.

I looked directly at the men, even though they couldn't understand me, knowing my eyes conveyed more than my words, anyway. "I am the one who arranged transport to bring you and take you home. I also ordered the food and the delegate kits."

The boy translated, "They are happy you did this. But there were no cups, they say."

I made a face. Before I had to answer that, the chief with the pipe took it out of his mouth and spoke with a gesture. The others laughed.

I smiled in anticipation. Standing in the middle, waiting to understand, that was a place I loved. Enough uncertainty to keep me alert. African generosity making it safe.

"This man wants you to be his wife," the boy said, smiling up at me. "He has six. But he is looking for another. He has many cows to give your father."

I grinned right back. "I am already married. I am the mother of three children."

When the chief spoke again, everyone laughed, and four or five more men gathered to listen in. "They have heard that white men have only one wife. Are you the only wife of your husband? They want to know."

"Yes, I am the only wife of my husband," I said.

White teeth shone through smiles in the circle all around me. The chief spoke. The men hooted. The boy poked in the dust with his bare toe. He opened his eyes wide at me and giggled. "How can one woman keep a man satisfied?"

So, it was truth or dare. Well, I could play, too. I drew myself up and lifted my chin as if I were also a chief. No smile. "I am a brave woman," I said.

We left them slapping bony knees covered by khaki slacks, jumpsuits or white *jalabiyas*. My young friend grabbed my hand and we laughed too, all the way across the village and through the sorghum gate.

The campstool in the dust made a fine office. At the top of the page, $95,000. It was a broad-strokes budget, approximately $5,000 for flights with two rotations, $3,000 for one. Add back in $450 per observer. That didn't help much. Oh well. There were undesignated gifts I could throw into the transport pot if I had to. It was up to me to get Mario out alive. What if I added a rotation to the Ler trip on the last day? Tuich wasn't far. There'd be daylight hours aplenty. Fuel would be the question. I'd have to set it up with Kevin Ashley in Nairobi at sunrise radio contact.

But it was a bad day up in the atmosphere between us and Nairobi the next morning. Kevin Ashley had left the office by the time the radio operator got through. I caught the name *Sebastian* behind the whistling and crackling. His voice said roger, the plane could go to Tuich. I wanted to believe him.

"Will they need to refuel? Over." I said.

"Please repeat. Please repeat. Over."

I shouted and spoke slowly. "Fu-el. Will they need fu-el. Ask Kevin. Over." I felt silly, the mechanical dweeb of the century, telling an airline employee we would need to refuel. And what an impossible word to shout.

"Not reading, please repeat."

"Check on fu-el. Foxtrot-Utah-Echo-Lima." I'd grown up hearing radio lingo through static on the shortwave radio in Maji, Mom leaning close, trying to hear if Ethiopian Air Lines had made it to Maji that week. "Fu-el. Over." I heard only static as Sebastian's answer.

In the thatch top-knotted conference hall, it was time to sign the articles of agreement. Telar read off names. "From Gogrial

County, State of Bahr el Gazahl, Chief Alfred Amet Kuol." Lots of the Christians used a baptism name, then their own given name and the given name of their father. They didn't have family names like we who come out of Europe. Traditionalists added their grand-father's given name as their third name. Telar called fourteen more spiritual leaders, chiefs, and commissioners from Gogrial county, and last, four women delegates.

The Sudanese rapporteurs helped them press their thumbs into the inkpads and leave their marks at the right line. Some also signed, if they could. But in these oral societies, where visible sym-bols verify the truth, the mark of their flesh on paper sealed the covenant more convincingly than any scribbles.

Around me, the Nuers and Dinkas clapped flat handed, palm against palm, fingers splayed, like they clap when they dance. A woman on the Dinka side sang out, and people sang back to her.

Chiefs had met around evening fires and agreed to turn the conference hall into a high school—a boarding school, with the *tukel*s ready for Nuer and Dinka students to move into. Bill had offered to leave the extra paper and pens. The newly dug well would help the village rebuild. We'd made peace and we were leaving blessings of peace behind. Bill's face shone like Moses's as he came down from Mt. Sinai.

My face didn't feel like his looked. I was too worried about hear-ing back from Kevin Ashley so we could get that group to Tuich.

As the rejoicing crowd flooded out of the hall, my would-be suitor and his friends pulled a translator through the crowd and asked me for the inkpads. "The judges will use them," they explained.

I ran back into the hall, glad I'd bought so many. I pressed ink-pads into these old man hands with their swollen joints and long gray nails. *"Gua, gua,"* I said, that word for everything good, clever, or beautiful; a word that had to mean all that was in my heart.

It had to mean, *Go in peace. Bring order. Punish your young men who kill for cows and abduct wives they don't pay for. Sit under your neem trees. Pronounce justice to restore your villages. Teach your old women to read. Make your young boys throw down their Kalashnikovs and pick up pencils. Let your girls and boys draw water for their elders from new wells. Let girls laugh with their friends and walk home unafraid, with water basins balanced on their heads.*

And let them grow up to teach, to heal, to make peace.

The next morning, I put Bill, Telar, Marc Nikkel and the Sudanese diaspora observers on the first flight to Loki, where they would finalize the official peace conference report. On the next flight, all the expat observers to Nairobi, several of them quite subdued. What we learn about ourselves in cross-cultural situations can be unwelcome and unsettling. I'd been humbled plenty of times. Had I learned enough yet?

Because now I was left as the only white person in Wunlit. Whenever I was part of a group of foreigners, it was impossible even for me, a hybrid, not to wrap Western habits around me. They could be so familiar and comfortable. Left alone, like I was now, I would unwrap. I would let the other culture become part of me as much as it was possible to do. And the people hosting me would go about their lives and stop accommodating me, because I was only one and they were so many, and my being with them hardly nudged the balance. They could be themselves without translation. It was my favorite way to be foreign: completely immersed. If it were Ethiopia, I would find people to hang out with, gossip, joke around with in Amharic. I wished my dream of learning to speak Nuer properly hadn't evaporated in the church office's financial chaos.

After the Bedford rattled away, I stood by the church entrance looking at the almost deserted peace villages. The white canvas of the clinic tent collapsed off to my right, sending up billows of dust. The extra medicines would stay, locked up in one of the supply sheds. Medicins Sans Frontiers was already negotiating with the elders of Wunlit to set up a clinic here. Even my big, expensive mistake had been redeemed. Another truck was loading up Dinka delegates from some of the nearer villages.

"Are the next delegations ready?" I asked James, Ler's new field organizer. He led me to stacks of blue plastic bins, the bottom ones softening in the heat and sagging under the weight.

Wow. They were ready and waiting. *"Gua elong, elong,"* I said. "James, tell them the truck will come when we hear on the radio that the plane is on the way."

CHAPTER 26

When radio word came, I ran out, holding up the corner of my skirt, and wove my way through to the center of the village. Men were already loading the Bedford, handing blue bins along a human chain and up over the edge. Even in remotest South Sudan, people must know that planes run on time.

The twenty-one delegates from Tuich, the men who had walked so far, had heard the rumor of a flight to take them home the next day. They crowded and jostled to shake my hand. They spoke in Dinka, louder than usual, maybe hoping I'd hear their appreciation in their voices.

I did. "Tell them to be ready in the morning. The plane will take them first," I told James. We didn't actually have the go-ahead yet, but my optimism had kicked in. I was as-iffing them home. Their rotation would only take an hour and a half. Plenty of time left for the last big two-village group: the rotation to Yirol, then Chief Isaac and his big delegation from Ler.

James and I would be on that plane, too. We'd drop everyone off, pick up James's family and head for Loki. From there, I'd be the only one left with the pilots, flying through to Nairobi and home.

I probed for some excitement about getting home, and found only a trace. For one thing, there would be my reverse culture shock, getting back to civilization. For another, how would I find Mark? Heat, dust, scanty food—the hardships of South Sudan were physical and easier to tolerate than the anxieties Mark's attacks kicked up.

The peace conference had been the best and biggest job I'd ever done to make the world a better place. And it had felt like the ultimate act of joining my life with the lives of people in Africa. Here, I'd felt like a quiet hero. I'd had my favorite rush: hard work in exchange for worth. At home, the ground under me was in constant upheaval.

Before dark fell, I blew up my mat. Mario would be able to distribute the pay-in-kind. He would get to Nairobi for medical help. Everyone would be home, safe. No matter how I felt about the home situation waiting for me, I should be relieved it was all working out.

But in the dark, I became anxious again. I lay with my eyes wide open in my pitch-dark tent. It shouldn't have been so easy. They couldn't do my three rotations without refueling. How had Kevin worked that out?

I said the twenty-third Psalm. The first Psalm. The twenty-fourth Psalm, the love chapter from First Corinthians, and what I could remember from Isaiah 40—all the long Bible passages I had learned as a child. The rhythms felt like prayer and gave me some relief from my otherwise obsessive prayer: *Work-it-out, work-it-out, please work-it-out.* I tried to relax. I reminded myself that God would be present the next day, whatever unfolded. But as soon as I approached that place of peace, my mind scampered back to frantic worry.

The water pump went silent sometime after midnight. My mat let me down. I blew it up. The hundred and twenty-first Psalm that I'd memorized before my trip to Nyal said, *The Lord will bless your going in and your coming out, from this time forth and forevermore.* I said that over and over like a mantra. I tried to relax the muscles in my neck and shoulders. This *going in* was almost done. Unfortunately, that just made me feel superstitious, as though the odds of disaster for the *going out* had now risen exponentially.

I never slept. The sky was still dark, only washed with the faintest rim of light through the sorghum stalks, when I heard through radio static that the plane had left Nairobi, on its way to us, on the West Bank of the White Nile.

My stash of granola was gone. Breakfast tea from a cracked plastic glass hit my empty stomach like acid.

I jounced out to the airstrip with the delegation from Tuich to talk to the pilots myself. With one hand, I held my skirt down against the blowing grit of the plane as it pulled up to the scrubby tree we used as a terminal building. With my other hand, I signaled the delegates to wait. I ran over to the plane. The propeller whipped my hair around my face. I squinted to keep the dust out.

The pilot's leg stretched from the ladder to the ground. Already his khaki shirt was dark under the arms and down the back. He leaned close to hear me over the engine and whirling propeller.

I shouted. "Will it work, adding a rotation to Tuich today?"

"Sebastian told us you have changes." Inside the pocket of the open door was a map of South Sudan and a ruler. He fought with the blowing map, got it refolded, and measured the distance. The copilot leaned in. They nodded. "We're here to do what you tell us," he shouted.

I waved the delegates aboard with a victory smile. They clapped. Then each man lifted his kit to his shoulder and ran to the ramp that led up under the tail, into the bowels of the empty plane.

Back at the peace village, the next two delegations were ready— Paramount Chief Isaac's group from Ler, and the small group from Yirol, where we would touch down on the way. The bins sat in a stack in their part of the village. "One hour." I held up my finger and looked around for someone to translate. *"Kel sa'at."* Was that right? The men grinned and nodded.

When I collapsed my tent, I found that white ants had eaten trails in the space blanket I'd used for a ground cover. I folded it up anyway, packed it away for next time. I turned those little handles and refilled my water bottle for the last time. I perched on a log pew to wait. Had the pilots actually said they could do all three rotations? Had I said anything about fuel? I wasn't that good at nailing down details, and the noise and whipping wind under an airplane wing weren't the best conditions. As I worried, I ate a sesame brittle.

James appeared around the sorghum gateway. "The truck is ready." He hoisted my dusty, faded duffle onto his shoulder. From the entrance, I looked back for a good-bye glimpse of my peace conference home. Only the filters were left, sitting on the ground now, because I was taking the fold-up table back with me. Only log pews, crispy brown leaves and bits of bark. Only, above them, the stick cross rose, its silhouette dark against the arch of a pale blue sky.

The passenger seat of the Bedford was reserved for Chief Isaac this time. He walked with dignity to the front. The red and white sash across his white *jalabiya* in the bright sunlight hurt my eyes. A dust devil billowed out my crinkle skirt. Many hands reached down to help me up over the sides. Deborah, my Lysistrata friend, found my face through a gap between the men's tall shoulders and smiled. We were crammed body to body in the back of the truck, the last two Nuer delegations and me, nearly a hundred of us.

Dinkas gathered around the truck, shouting and waving. Someone sang out. The rest chorused back. All around us they clapped, lifted their walking sticks and stamped a step dance. The hairs on my arm bristled up. How lucky I felt, the final witness. Pressed in among the Nuers—peacemakers, all of us, together breathing the Sudan village smells of smoke and sweaty bodies— this song in our honor felt like a blessing of peace from our Dinka brothers on our last day.

The truck billowed diesel exhaust and ground into gear. We headed out, to fly up the White Nile and home. Thorny trees along the road scratched the Bedford's sides. We lurched in and out of the ruts. On a rock, a foot-long lizard with a red head and blue tail sunned itself as we jolted past at walking speed. All the way to the airstrip, the Nuers continued to sing around me. Tears of joy dried along the edges of my eyelids.

When the plane landed, turned and stopped, we picked up bags and blue bins and surged forward in a mass. But the pilot jumped down, landed in a crouch in the dust. He held his hand up like a policeman stopping traffic. Eyes on mine, he motioned me over.

Ever since I'd said yes to Bill on Thanksgiving Day, I'd been watching out for this moment. The job was big. A big job meant big mistakes. I hated mistakes. I'd counted on my big mistake with the medicines taking care of my quota. Apparently, it hadn't. I walked to the pilot, tense as a child marching to punishment.

"You still want to make the rotations to Yirol and Ler on the way to Loki?"

I nodded, kept my eyes on his face, *Please.*

"We don't have fuel for a third landing," he said.

"Didn't Sebastian talk to you?" My voice sounded calm. I was glad for that. Inside I was hysterical. I wanted to grab his sweaty shirt and shake him, scream how hard I'd tried, how many times I'd shouted *fu-el* to Sebastian. Behind me, the silence of people waiting to hear their fate hung like a cloud. It was their turn to listen without understanding, to wonder what had gone wrong, to feel foreign and vulnerable.

The pilot mopped a drip of sweat off his eyebrow. "Nope. Haven't heard from him all morning."

I stood as still as a stone.

The pilot checked his clipboard. "We'll be back in the area for Medicins Sans Frontiers tomorrow. We could add a rotation. Is that what you want?"

What I wanted. That was not among the choices. What we wanted. The last Nuers in Dinkaland, dirty and tired, Chief Isaac and the Nuer men and women wanted home. I wanted home. A hug from the boys. A shower. Mark might even hold me. It was supposed to be that night.

But when the pilot says there isn't fuel, there's nothing more to say.

I nodded and turned away. The last pennies of $95,000 slipped through my fingers. The dollar signs rolled over and over, in the thousands, and the sum at the bottom of my column turned red as I walked over to the Nuers. With the last pennies went my sense of doing well. I had wrestled all night, like Jacob with the angel of the Lord, only instead of a blessing I'd come away face in the mud. My body was not at peace. The spirits reproached me: *You knew they couldn't do three rotations. Why didn't you try harder to talk to Kevin Ashley?*

Chief Isaac's eyes never left my face. With James at my elbow to translate, the crowd came around me like a pool of water. "I have bad news," I said. My voice sounded far away. "There is not enough fuel to make the rotation to Ler. The plane will go to Yirol and then to Loki for the night. It will come back tomorrow."

I put my hand on the warm, sweaty spot over my heart. I didn't know what I was going to say until I heard my own voice. "I will stay with you. I will not sleep in my own bed until you are safe in yours."

The Yirol delegation separated themselves out of the crowd. Their eyes avoided ours. They bent their tall, thin bodies and picked up their bins. They walked silently up the ramp into the plane.

I turned away with the Nuers from Ler. We covered our faces against the whirlwind of take-off. Grit pinged against my ankles and bare arms. As the roar faded, I wiped at what had been forced between my tight eyelids.

Silently the Nuers handed their bins back up. We climbed over the sides of the truck and bounced back to camp. I felt hollowed out and empty. My mind drifted back to my original African home in Maji. The Dizi people believed evil spirits lived in waterfalls, so they had given the haunted knoll that bulged out between two of them to the missionaries for their homes, clinic, church and school.

Behind the biggest cataract, which bounced and tumbled hundreds of feet off the side of the mountain, people showed Dad a huge cave that stretched into the darkness and held thousands of bats, squirming upside down on the ceiling. It was his favorite place to take guests.

When we hiked to the Bat Cave in Maji, I leaned to the side along the narrow path that hugged the edge of the mountain. I touched the hill on one side for reassurance, careful not to look down the thousands of feet on the other, ignoring my flip-flopping stomach, ignoring my shaking knees, ignoring the image of my body falling, falling, falling to death on the rocks below. I was trying to impress Dad with my courage. Dad was invariably unimpressed. He assumed that of course his daughters were behind him, courageous and obedient, as he led the way.

I'd spent my life like that, trying to *be therefore perfect*, as my boarding school dorm mother had exhorted me to be—a goal particularly idiotic in South Sudan. But knowing it was impossible had never sprung me loose from trying.

Back in the peace village, I climbed down the side of the truck, and James took my hand to balance me as I jumped from the back tire. I couldn't look at him.

I ducked into Mario's hot, dark *tukel*. He hardly moved. He listened to me without opening his eyes. The center of my chest hurt. My eyes and stomach burned. Why hadn't I listened to my anxiety and sent the Nuers home first, just in case? The Dinka group from Tuich could have happily waited an extra day. The Nuers and I would have been on our way home.

"Commander Salva Kiir and the battalions have not left," Mario said. "I will give the Nuers my word for their safety."

I'd been so stricken by my failure that I hadn't even thought of our safety. Adrenalin, shame, and a prayer of thanks, a painful mixture, shot through my heart.

"But I paid the women and boys. They have gone. There is no one to serve food or water."

That seemed completely minor. South Sudanese live through long hunger-times whenever the rains are light and the harvest is scanty. Their bodies know how to do that. I could certainly do the same. I thanked Mario and wandered back to the sorghum church.

I didn't have the energy to bother with my tent. I laid my mat and bedding on the chewed-up ground cloth in one corner of the rustling, yellow nave. The last melting piece of sesame brittle fell out of my bag. I ate it and licked every seed off the cellophane wrapper.

The boy who didn't smile any more came over and bowed. "The women have tea for you. They will cook rice."

James came in. He sat on the first-row bench, as silent as though he had come to sit with me at a wake.

"Will you take me to Chief Isaac?" I said.

We walked without speaking, through the blasting, early afternoon sun. Shreds of sorghum stalk and chips of bark, the last traces of cooking-fuel, littered the ground near *tukels*. Where another white ox had given his life to ratify the peace, an island of blood stained the oceans of dust.

Mario's military-style line to the well had broken down. It looked as though the women of Wunlit had all come to fetch water together, now that the conference was over. They crowded and chattered. Children darted in and out. Their laughter rose above the squeak of the pump.

Chief Isaac stooped out of the dark of his *tukel*. We squinted at each other in the glare. He shook my hand, and then held it. James translated. I hoped there was humility, respect, integrity in my apology.

Chief Isaac looked me straight in the eyes and nodded. "We came to make peace," he said. "That peace is worth a high price. Today is tomorrow. We are home."

Today is tomorrow. What grace. Chief Isaac had no need for perfection or the tyranny of the calendar. I bowed my head, blessed and exonerated.

CHAPTER 27

James walked with me back to the neem tree church. "You should not be alone," he said. "You stayed with us while your people have gone. Now I will stay with you."

I thanked him. A woman brought us tea in two plastic punch glasses.

We sat under the lashed-together cross through the hot, still afternoon. He told me his story—he was the youngest son of his father's fourth wife. One of his older brothers had raised him when his father died. "I am taking two of his children with me to Nairobi for schooling," he said. "It is my thanks to my brother."

His wife did not want to leave Ler and go to Nairobi, James told me. "I told her she must learn English. Someday peace will come and then we can be together again in Ler. She can teach if she learns English. She can work with me in development."

And while she studied English and the children went to school in Nairobi, James would stay in Ler to rebuild. "I will wear out my shoes," he said. That's how hard he would work between outbreaks of destruction. He would do what he could to bring some tools, some services, and some food to some people. He would have to take hope from the smallest signs of progress.

James admired my campstool. I showed him how the legs folded, how the elastic strap went over the shoulder. "I could carry this through the rivers," he said.

I should have given it to him then and there, but I was afraid. It took so little for Mark to flare up. If there was any sign of a welcome home from him, I didn't want to mar it with a disagreement over a camp stool. "I will ask my husband," I said. I was comforted that such wifely submission at least made perfect sense to James.

I lay on my mat in my clothes that night. When radio static, like wind in the sorghum, woke me, I slipped on my sandals and ran to the radio hut. The operator repeated Kevin Ashley's call numbers. He bent close to listen. Our plane had already left Loki, he said. In the pink and orange of sunrise, I went to tell Chief Isaac.

This trip to the airstrip was silent. No delegation came to see us off; no one sang. James's shoulder bumped against mine in the jostling truck bed. "They had no food for lunch or supper or to break fast," he said. "After the villagers finished, the soldiers used the well. At three in the morning, finally everyone finished. Then our youth delegates drew water and served the chiefs. They drank and washed. Now we will go home."

But somehow there had been tea and rice for me. Even when we had all been deprived of what we wanted they'd made sure their guest had been served. I, with a full stomach, suffered emotionally. They'd suffered physically. If I lived in Africa for one hundred years, I didn't know that I'd ever understand where deep reserves of generosity came from in people who have so little. Or where I could go to imbibe some of their long-suffering stamina. Their ability to keep hope alive in the most extreme circumstances. Surely I could figure out how to do the same at home.

The tracks that workers used to slide pallets of food out the tail ramp in famine emergencies ran down the middle of the floor of our charter. Chief Isaac and the other chiefs in their white tunics and red banners sat in the row of seats in the front. James, the delegates and I sat on our luggage, like so much cargo, on the floor. I leaned back against the vibrating metal side to rest.

The landing in Ler jarred me awake. We slowed down to taxi across the rough grass, and the delegates at the windows laughed and pushed.

The props revved. Out a smeary window, as the plane turned, a young man came into view. He danced, leading hundreds of

Nuers across the dusty grass toward us, his hands bouncing off a cowhide drum. The drummer's forehead sparkled with sweat, and his t-shirt had soaked through. Some of the clapping, dancing women wore dresses that had been washed in tributaries of the White Nile until they'd mellowed to shades of beige; some men wore nothing but gray emergency aid blankets tied over one shoulder, their sides long stripes of black flesh from armpits to ankles; some of the children wore ragged t-shirts. Others danced naked, their skin splotched with gray dust.

The ramp under the tail of the plane dropped open like a bridge over a moat. The Ler delegates poured out. For a moment, the backs of their heads were all I could see from where I stood by the window. As the props slowed, the tumult of the peacemakers' welcome party filled the plane, the drum vibrated in my body. The women's shrill joy cry bounced off metal and glass.

Finally I could relax. Finally I could smile. My mistakes were done and we had all survived. The Wunlit Peace Conference was over. I'd done my part.

Heat had blasted in with the sounds of rejoicing. I moved to the top of the ramp in the now empty plane and leaned against the aluminum, still cool from the flight. We were only on the ground long enough for the exchanges—delegates off and James's family quickly on—so the propellers idled, adding to the chaos.

Chief Isaac disappeared into the crowd and bobbed to the surface when women lifted him onto their shoulders. He waved his cow-tail fly whisk like a royal scepter. The crowd carried him in a circular dance, and I let their excitement lift my exhaustion. With him safely in Ler, I could fly home with a clear conscience.

For years, Ler had been the safest village in Unity Province. The people of Ler knew all about the fruits of peace: aid workers abounded; children went to school all the way through high school; people who were sick visited a clinic; organizations ran food-security projects, like convincing the Nuers that their precious oxen wouldn't be harmed by learning to pull plows, or teaching people to make fishnets with that bright green nylon twine I'd seen in coils piled as high as my waist on the Loki tarmac, waiting for the flights in.

But a rogue commander had rampaged through Ler just as the peace process with Bill began. The UN airlifted aid workers out, and Ler's schools collapsed into piles of smoking cinders. Several metric tons of textbooks were burned. Soldiers looted the clinic and carried off its tin roof. Medicines that would have kept people healthy for years were scattered in the ashy dust or pocketed in camo uniforms. The people celebrating Chief Isaac could hardly be more hungry for peace.

James had left the plane in the flood of delegates. Now he came pushing back through the crowd, his wife close behind. She carried a baby. A young child held onto her skirt, and two teens pressed in close, the niece and nephew, carrying bundles in knotted cloths.

I shook their hands, once they'd clambered onto the ramp; we had no language between us but the few words of Nuer I'd learned before the women's work had fallen apart. It didn't matter, the crowd was too loud to talk over. They walked forward, to the seats bolted to the floor in the front of the plane.

A lean man in khaki, his military boots unlaced, emerged from the crowd. He carried himself as confidently as Chief Isaac had, but he stood head and shoulders taller. A woman followed him closely, sheltering her baby with one shoulder, jostled by singers' elbows. A little girl in a stiff ruffled dress held her mother's hand on one side and her younger brother's on the other. They all wore shoes and sweaters, even in that heat. They carried no luggage. The woman's hair had been carefully braided.

This must be the commander who wanted to send his family to Loki. In the chaos of staying an extra day, I'd forgotten about Rev. X's request. I had chartered the planes based on my word the peace conference wouldn't become a funnel of unauthorized South Sudanese refugees into Kenya. That made me the agent at the gate, and activated all the law-abiding, ultra-responsible oldest daughter impulses in me.

So Rev. X had promised—but Mark and I had learned not to believe his word, nor count on reading his face. I had just one word, which I called above the noise to the commander, about three feet below me on the ground. "Papers?"

His daughter was climbing up over the end of the ramp, her fluffy dress catching under her knees. The commander bent down to lift his son up. Sweat shone on the back of his neck. The boy leaned off the ramp to cling to his father's neck. Fear shone in the little boy's eyes. The roar was overwhelming, and his feet, like mine, must be tickling with the vibration. He had surely never been so close to so great a machine before.

The commander held him with one arm and pulled an envelope carefully from his breast pocket. His tongue showed pink through the gap in his bottom teeth. The paper in the envelope had been folded into quarters and opened and refolded so many times it was soft like fabric and worn along the creases. The corners had rubbed off completely. I opened it. Government of Kenya. So Rev. X was on the up and up this time.

But then I saw the date. Kenya lists the day and month in reverse order from the US. For a moment I couldn't think. Under the roar of the plane, the thumping drum out in the crowd pounded my ears like a second, dancing pulse. The smell of sweat and dust filled my nostrils. I squinted at the faded lines of type. I looked down at the commander, the scars across his forehead giving him a slightly worried look, and said, "Expired?"

He looked at me in mute appeal.

I stood frozen for a few seconds. Rev. X had promised.

My brain screamed. *No! No hassle with passport control! No having to bribe Kenyans!* I was almost home, I hadn't slept well the last two nights on the hard Wunlit dust. I had let down my resistance. Exhaustion had leaked in.

Singing, shouting, joy cries rebounded from one side of the

plane to the other. The commander's wife climbed over the edge of the ramp on her knees and stood. The little boy ran from his father to her, his mouth open. I couldn't hear his voice.

I pointed to the date again. "Expired."

"Government of Kenya doesn't care," the commander shouted. He jumped up onto the ramp.

I raised my hand to block out the noise that was making a nerve in my left ear flutter. "I think the Government of Kenya *does* care." I could hear resentment and reproach in my voice. *This is illegal, do you think I'm a fool?*

The commander's wife stood on the foot of the ramp holding the baby in its thick blankets, patting her little boy's head with her other hand. Sweat was running down the sides of her face. Her braided head turned from her husband to me and back. Usually *he* gave orders. She was watching my face. She was listening to us shout above the singing—she didn't need English to read trouble. Her baby wailed. The sound was lost in the high song of joy, but his mouth was open and wet, his cheeks shiny with tears.

This wasn't about her; I stood at the top of the ramp, shaking my head. James shouted something from the ground. Women danced behind him, around the other delegates, clapping. The commander's frown lines and scars hatched his forehead. He opened his mouth as though to speak.

I looked him in the eyes. *This is not the South Sudan People's Liberation Army.*

Then the soles of my feet registered pounding footsteps coming from the cockpit. I turned. The pilot, red-faced and sweating, was thundering down on us. He was squeezing us in on a day that he'd promised to Medicin Sans Frontiers. I had used up every bit of my decision-making energy. "Expired," I said. I held the papers out to explain the shouting, the delay.

The little boy ran past me, to James's wife up in the front. The commander's wife screamed.

"Off," the pilot roared. He waved his sweaty arms. "I'm throwing *everyone* off if we aren't ready to go in two minutes." His footsteps back to the cockpit rocked the fuselage.

James's wife wiped a tear from the little boy's cheek. His sister ran and grabbed his hand to lead him back to the ramp. The commander jumped to the ground, shouted to his wife and lifted his son down. She gave him the crying baby. Then she jumped down. She turned to her daughter, whose skirt floated up for a second as her mother lifted her down.

The joy cry trilled again and again. The frown between James's eyebrows cut through his scars. James, my new friend! My teeth ached in my tense jaw. I felt chilled in spite of the heat.

The woman looked up at me with tears pouring down her cheeks. She was young, her features delicate. Was she a legit first wife, or a young woman pulled out of some intimidated village by this commander?

It didn't matter.

The ramp rumbled and lifted off the ground. It cut off my view of people's bodies, then their faces, then all but the blue Sudanese sky. The plane fell dark. Even the rejoicing voices faded.

The crowd ran from dust and grass and leaves whipped up by the propellers. I looked through the window for the commander's wife, but all I saw was a last glimpse of the welcome party, black legs and the tan soles of people's bare feet running away from noise and blowing grit. Women held their dresses down. Babies' heads bounced above their bundled bodies on their mothers' backs. My last sight of Ler was James, standing firm in the whirlwind, his face turned away.

I braced myself against the side of the fuselage, making my way to my duffle as the plane lurched into the air.

Surely a commander's wife doesn't work the land like a common woman, bent double, digging the farm plot one clod at a time with a fire-hardened stick; she doesn't carry her baby in a leather sling on her back, swinging him around to the front when he cries so he can nurse while she goes on digging under the hot sun.

But I was just excusing myself. Even in Ler, water had to be carried from the river, or from a well in the center of town. In Nairobi, water would have gushed from a tap. In Nairobi, the commander's wife would have sent her daughter to school. Maybe she dreamed of her daughter becoming a nurse. A teacher, or a businesswoman who could do sums without using her fingers in New Sudan, after peace came. That little girl in her fluffy dress.

I felt sorry for their dream delayed. I felt confused.

I felt angry, launched back into my childhood world, where I'd believed my value came from working hard enough. Wasn't all I had done for peace enough? I cycled through a list of self-reproaches: *I should have asked James back in Wunlit what the whole story was. I should have checked with Telar. I should have known to tell Rev. X the commander's papers would have to be current. I should have had enough presence of mind to think it all through there in the instant.*

And always that tingle of guilt: once again, I was on my way out and others were left behind. The day the reverend asked his favor floated back through my memory. Blazing sunshine. The front of the sorghum church. He'd said, *They have papers. There's been no transport out of Ler.* And suddenly I realized the other dimension of what had just happened.

I stumbled along the vibrating aluminum floor to where James's wife sat and leaned my hip against the metal of her seat. The nephew understood enough English to pull their papers out of his foster mother's pocket and unfold them.

Expired, of course: *There's been no transport out of Ler.* But because I'd trusted Telar about James, I hadn't even thought to check their papers.

James's worried face as the commander and I shouted at each other above the roar of the plane, the pilot gunning to get off the ground and back to Loki; James couldn't explain without getting his family kicked off the plane, too.

His wife glanced up at me and then looked down. She jiggled the baby and wiped translucent breast milk off his bottom lip.

CHAPTER 28

I folded the papers back up along the worn lines, gave them to James's nephew, smiled, and made my way back to my duffle. I'd only partially understood what had been asked of me in Ler. What happened was that the girl who had hated to get in trouble turned into a woman who honored the immigration laws of Kenya. And the commander was right—even the Kenyans didn't actually care about the laws of Kenya.

I thought of the school director in Ethiopia, and his comment when I was looking at politics through my foreigners' eyes: "You don't know the heart of these Africans," he'd said.

Rev. X had been completely honest for once—the commander's family had papers. Now that I had time to think, I understood that the date on those papers had no bearing on their legitimacy except in the mind of an American. The papers *were* the permission, just like the peace covenant everyone would honor even if no one could read it.

I'd worked in rural Africa often enough to know, if I'd thought of it, that there are no calendars in remote places. And remember, numbers are metaphors. A date just filled a spot on the papers. It was the papers themselves that meant, *You have permission to enter the Republic of Kenya whenever you can find a way to get there.* The papers went on to say something that was slow to penetrate, hard for my Western eyes to read, hard for my law-abiding mind to accept: *On that day, some lucky immigration official will make arrangements for you, and you will compensate him for working out the details.*

Self-reproach for confusion about laws and calendars and papers revved up again. *I should have been able to figure it out.* And my mother's voice, which had long ago become my own: *I should have known.*

I lay down on the vibrating floor that smelled of metal and feet, with my duffle for a pillow. My shoulder wasn't fleshy enough to protect the bony joint that ground against the aluminum. My body sagged with exhaustion. To comfort and distract myself, I imagined a redemptive scene: *"Ready," I say to the pilot. I fold the papers, smile at the commander, take his little girl's hand and walk her up to one of the seats bolted to the floor in the front. I help her fasten her seatbelt. Her hair smells of the sorghum-stalk fire where her mother cooked their morning meal.*

As time passes, as the voices quiet, humility creeps in. Like the *Life* Magazine journalist, I didn't understand enough.

Like Rev. X, I'd gotten lost in a cultural no-man's land that was neither Nuer culture nor Western, out on a frontier where there was no rule of law. Rev. X understood how the contempt of the thief who'd stolen the fish had started a war. Did he think respect was only important for Nuers? He should never have shamed Mark the way he had.

And now I had applied Western standards to those permission papers. Rev. X and I had both caused harm by not understanding the other. In some sad, horrible way, we were even.

On that flight home, buffeted by air pockets and heat currents, I had no perspective on what I'd done. I couldn't yet reassure myself that the little girl would get to Nairobi. Her father was a commander, for pity's sake. I couldn't yet hear a loving voice telling me that their situation really shouldn't have been in my hands, little ol' me. I couldn't see the faces of thousands of common people whose lives I'd saved by organizing food and transport for peace conference delegates—only the faces of one privileged but disappointed family not getting to Nairobi.

The sister who told me to leave Mark where Jesus *flang* him had fed me another line: *Stand for yourself with an open heart.*

Coming out of South Sudan I had not yet learned the lessons about standing—I only knew trying hard.

And an open heart? I thought of St. Paul's list, the gifts of God's Spirit: love, joy, peace, patience—the further along the list I went, the more depressed I got. Love didn't seem to be on offer in the currency I earned by trying.

Now, all I could do was to ask God for grace. *Take care of that little girl. Let my efforts bring peace, even with all my mistakes. Let my willingness to try be to my credit.* A tear ran hot across my temple and dropped onto the faded, blue canvas of my duffle bag. It smelled like the rain on dust.

I had thought I could make a contribution in Mother Africa. Ten years before, the Presbyterian Church had asked me to be an English teacher in Ethiopia—it had seemed so simple. As we flew to Loki without the commander's family, I felt completely humbled.

The problems of the Sudanese were enormous and urgent. It was so hard for me to stand quietly and be present. I was too quick to take responsibility for problems beyond my capacity—there it was, causing confusion with Mark, confusion with the South Sudanese. Isn't that how life unfolds? We face the same problems at home and at work because they come, not from our circumstances, but from the cracks inside.

I certainly wasn't wise enough to hold people's futures in my hands, and that's what South Sudanese required of an American sooner or later. Even of just a teacher. I had white skin. I had dollars. We all hoped I could do more. Whether people were asking me for skirts or medicine, to teach English or to get their families out of South Sudan, I was a disappointment.

It's taken me years to figure out what happened in Ler, and what it means. Even now the understanding can seem perfectly clear, and then perspective slips away from me in the night.

Maybe we are called to be willing, not to be successful. Maybe we never know what we're really there for. Maybe all we need is the courage to step forward with our gifts in hand, holding onto the knowledge that we will fail, but our failures will not cast us into outer darkness, *where there will be weeping and wailing and gnashing of teeth*, as my dad used to say in mock threats. The result has to be left to God.

It's taken me years to believe in the faces I'll never see, the lives that were lived but would have been lost. I raised money, bought food and medicines, sent in the kits (minus those cursed cups!), and wrote checks for all those flights. The Wunlit conference made history. Every once in a while I look it up online, and gaze again at the photos of the white bull, of Chief Isaac and Chief Madut.

My name is never mentioned. But I was an instrument of peace. Why did I let that little girl and her weeping mother blot out all that I did?

I did learn this: we can't see the future. We have to say yes with no guarantee but that we will be held onto in the chaos by some power beyond us.

It felt to me that the end of the peace conference was the end of something else. We were on the downhill slope of our four-year commitment to the South Sudanese. Where did we belong next?

Moses, that disjointed, wandering patriarch, my anti-hero, had a problem much like mine. A Hebrew boy raised by the daughter of Pharaoh—what a culture misalignment that was.

Like him, I'd been looking for the home that had haunted and eluded me. I'd been wandering ever since leaving Ethiopia for college. Or since leaving Maji for boarding school, packing up everything I owned and relocating, like the transhumant Nuers, who shift between their villages and cattle camps in the *toich*, a familiar pattern year after year.

Or maybe I needed to go back even further, to those days before conscious memory, when Mom and Dad made what she called their *covenant with chaos* and packed clothes and shoes for three girls for five years, sealed them in fifty-five-gallon shipping drums, and moved to Ethiopia. The disjoints in my life had begun so early and come so often there was no way to isolate the moment when I first began to wonder where I could find home.

By the time I became an adult, I'd learned to look around every few years, as if to say, *What? Still here?* On schedule, a creeping, undefined restlessness. A person with my history couldn't depend on how she *felt* to know where she belonged. Maybe I always belonged, just as truly as I would always feel that I didn't.

The first time the Hebrew people found themselves in the desert without water, God told Moses to strike the rock. He did, and water flowed. Years later, when they were thirsty in the desert again, God told Moses to speak to the rock. But he was fed up with the people's chronic complaining. He gave the rock a good whack. And God denied him the Promised Land.

It had always seemed a harsh punishment for justified anger. But maybe I'd read the story wrong. Maybe God saw that his long discontinuous path had left Moses tied in angry knots. He couldn't have enjoyed the Promised Land in the state he'd gotten into. God gave him grace on Mount Nebo instead.

Maybe a retired and rested Moses came out of his heavy sheepskin tent every morning. Maybe he watched the sun rise behind the mountain and shine on the camp of his successor, Joshua, and the tough new generation of Hebrews. Maybe a dust devil whirled up below him in the desert; the Jordan River sparkled; the walls of Jericho lit up like gold in the morning light. And there was nothing more for Moses to do but put down his roots at last in the place God had brought him to.

On the plane that bucked updrafts on its way to Loki, I wrenched my thoughts from the mistakes I'd made. The past couldn't be different. The future might. I thought about home. I made promises. I would manage, whatever mood Mark was in. I would hug the boys. I would have a bath, eat bread and cheese, or a mango. Maybe a mango would exorcise this spirit of regret. And then I would sleep in a real bed. When I woke up, it would be time to stop running away to South Sudan.

I wish I could go back and point out to the woman on the floor of that plane how smart she was—she'd been right in the first place, when she saw in Waat that there would be no women's development until there was peace. And no one, even God, actually expected her to figure out every complexity on the fault line between her orderly culture and a cowboy culture torn to shreds by war. She was allowed to be simply a messy human being and still be loved.

I want to tell her that a woman can't love a man out of deeply engrained habits of blame and resentment. It doesn't work that way. She couldn't actually do right enough to heal his years of childhood trauma. She couldn't do more than ask forgiveness for her own part in hurting him. Mark had to decide for himself whether to focus on harm or grace.

It was time to stand my ground with Mark and reach, like the Nuers and Dinkas, for peace beyond words on paper. And if Mark didn't want peace, it was time for me to face my fear of losing love.

Flying to Loki, it was also time to let another new batch of young idealists run through UN orientation and then give South Sudan all they could for two or three years. I'd given four years and the best I had. And I had been one of the lucky ones, who did get to have a big success. We'd made peace in Wunlit.

The plane descended. Pressure built up in my ears and popped. We landed on the big Loki tarmac. There was no freight to unload; nothing came out of South Sudan but exhausted people.

James's wife and kids gathered up their cloth bundles. I hoisted my duffle strap over my shoulder. Together we tramped down the ramp and onto the still glittering asphalt, sticky from the hot desert day. The New Sudan Council of Churches' base-camp pickup pulled up. The pilot greeted the driver and bummed a ride back to KATE Camp. He hopped into the front seat. James's family and I climbed over the wheels and into the pickup bed. I perched on the wheel-well cover and braced my feet wide for balance.

At the edge of the tarmac, James's nephew banged twice on the roof of the cab. He jumped down when the driver stopped, and no one said a thing. We all understood that they had a more circuitous path into Kenya than the rest of us. Where they would walk, who would receive them, and who would help them get their legal status, I didn't know. But thousands of people had done it, and James must have coached them. The nephew lifted down the bundles, then the babies. When James's wife got safely down, she turned and looked at me.

I held out my hand. *"Ku wa ke mal,"* I said: *Go in peace.* She bowed her head, then lifted her eyes to me again.

"Ku wa ke Kwoth," she said, using the other Nuer farewell: *Go with God.*

CHAPTER 29

Peace with Mark did come. It was grace, not of my doing.

One day, he was reading the book of Isaiah, that prophet who could shift so nimbly from railing and woe to comfort and hope. Isaiah promised that God would shine light on the darkness of people who do away with the pointing of the finger. Mark was startled.

Isaiah said God isn't pleased with people who judge others harshly. Mark's great sense of outrage was shaken.

People who stopped pointing the finger would be called *repairers of the breach*, Isaiah said, *restorers of streets and dwellings*. Repairing and restoring was what Mark did best. He became increasingly calm.

He made reservations for us one night at the Mathaiga Club, an old colonial-days restaurant near our home in Nairobi. It was frequented by round-bellied Kenyan men who ate there at business meetings or out for dinner with their portly wives. We'd come a couple of times, the rich menu and shocking bill always a bit of a stretch for my guilt-prone psyche.

I laughed, as I always did, at the plaid carpet laid out like a kilt on the dining room floor. I relaxed into the elegance of glinting silverware, the starched white napkins and tablecloths, the trickling water from a fountain in the corner, surrounded by giant tropical plants. And Mark's warmth was a balm. How could I not be pleased to be there, if this was where Mark wanted to bring me?

He surprised me over crème caramel with a diamond ring. We'd been too poor for diamonds when we were twenty-two.

He took both of our simple gold bands down to an Indian jeweler—the delicate scallops etched into the edges of mine had already worn away—and had them cast into a new, heavier gold band for himself.

We decided if the world didn't end on December 31, 1999, we would renew our vows and make a new beginning. I bought dozens of beeswax candles, in case the world didn't end, but the electric grid went down.

We promised again to love and cherish each other in better and worse, as long as we both lived. We were on the cusp of fifty, on the edge of a new millennium. And that peace covenant, sealed by our new rings, gave us back our comfortable companionship, the oldest-kid teamwork, the friendship-passion mix we'd found after the pain of the Chicago years. We had such different gifts, we enjoyed visiting each other's world, reading and talking together in evenings that were more and more left to us as the boys grew up.

But Mark wandered back into his dark valley of resentment nine years later, back in Portland, when my dad lay dying.

My sister had given Dad new running shoes for his eighty-fifth birthday. She promised to buy him another pair when he wore those out. Dad had taken *TIME* Magazine's longevity tests and crowed that he'd outlive his mom, who had made it to ninety-nine and a half. We all believed him, because he was still jogging laps around the park across the street from his home. He lifted weights at 24-Hour Fitness.

But he had a seizure one day and passed out while driving. His foot slipped off the gas pedal and he drifted into a tree off Ainsworth Avenue. Strangers called 911. I was the one he called from the hospital emergency room.

We were stunned by his diagnosis—a brain tumor. My siblings and I thanked everyone who offered help and circled the wagons, rotating the drive to his daily radiation treatments ourselves. Near the end, one of us slept every night on the couch at the foot of his hospital bed in the living room.

Mark had come to consider Dad as much his father as mine. Now,

I disappeared into a fog of shock, Mom was fading into dementia, and the best family Mark had ever known was disintegrating. His grief again showed up as a cloud of rage. The old ghost returned, the one he had concocted in Kenya—part disrespectful wife and part angry mother.

How could nine loving years pass and be gone? Could grace be given only to be taken away? Again and again?

Mark reluctantly agreed to go with me to the intake interview for another marriage counselor. He sat sullen on the other end of the couch. "You'll just gang up on me," he said. We didn't go back.

I had a US-based traveling job now, promoting partnerships between Presbyterian churches in the US and Ethiopia. It's what I knew how to do, and I was still making the larger half of our family income. Mark would hug me tight before I left for the airport, but I'd come home to that iced-in man I got to know so well in Kenya.

"How can I be making you mad?" I'd protest. "I wasn't even here!"

It was the prophet Isaiah who got through to Mark again. In a prophesy about the Messiah, Isaiah says, *He has borne our griefs and carried our sorrows....by His stripes we are healed.*

Mark burst into tears. "All this time," he said, digging in his pocket for one of his engine-oil-stained handkerchiefs. "All this time, I thought the person who hurt me had to do something to heal me. Mom. You. I didn't know *God* did it." He had assumed that if I didn't do something to make his pain go away, it meant I didn't love him.

Healing is mysterious. Something that hovers, waiting for our hearts to open and accept.

This time it saw Mark through his own death, when we were sixty-three. A nagging pain, sometimes in his chest, sometimes, confusingly, in his lower back, led to an endoscopy. The surgeon came out looking solemn. I braced myself. He drew a rough sketch of the digestive system. He scribbled a dark patch at the top of the stomach and went quickly on. *We'll operate. We'll fight it— radiation, chemo. Your husband is young. We'll win this.*

I read all about the surgery online. It was gruesome—they would remove a critical section of Mark's digestive system. He would never be robustly healthy again. I looked up the cancer survival statistics. They were even more grim. I kept them to myself.

The surgery was scheduled. But the doctor kept following the cancer as it showed up on screens like crumbs on a trail. First in Mark's near-by lymph nodes. Then in lymph nodes in his groin.

I went into the surgery orientation covering my dread for Mark's sake.

The surgeon pointed to an x-ray of Mark's upper femur. To a gray shadow on the white bone. "We won't be doing any surgery," he said, and looked away.

Mark and I drove home giddy, laughing with relief. It was only as we drove up the gradual hill to our little farm in Salem, Oregon that I sobered. "I think we may have mistaken a silver lining for the cloud."

Miriam, now a nurse practitioner, confirmed it. "Mom, what the surgeon saw was metastasis. He was saying *inoperable*."

Two months after Mark's diagnosis, no one realized that he was refusing to follow instructions, taking the Oxycodone every couple of hours, when he felt the pain, not on the prescribed four-hour schedule. It was so like Mark. We should have guessed.

It caused a crisis when the hospice nurse decided a patch would serve him better. The patch, of course, was calibrated to his prescription, not to his pain-relief usage. His pain shot so high he went into shock. The nurse called an ambulance and sent him to ER to stabilize.

I spent the day at the hospital. Miriam came to join me behind the canvas curtains shielding Mark's gurney. We visited softly as he slept, knocked out and resting at last. He was no longer the intense-looking boy I'd met forty-seven years before. After he turned forty, he'd finally thickened. A bit of a belly was nothing to pay for more heft all over, he said—he was especially happy to be rid of skinny legs. The lank black hair that once fell across his forehead, that I had cut a hundred times for him, had grayed and receded. Short hair and a bald center gave him a distinguished look, and he kept his thick beard neatly trimmed.

Before they sent him home from the ER, Mark introduced Miriam to the doctor. Mark told the doctor about our reunion plans, our kids gathering, bringing our six grandchildren. A final time. All of us together.

"We could prescribe a blood transfusion for you," the doctor said. "It might give you a little more energy for being with your family."

Mark eagerly agreed.

Back at the hospital several days later, he was wheeled away. I walked alone, out of the chilly waiting room, to Bend's sunny warmth. I sat on lush grass, with my back against a tall Douglas fir. Throughout my adult life, whether it was Chicago, Portland, Addis Ababa, or Nairobi, Mark had been there. He'd been a mish-kid too. He'd known me since I was sixteen. He'd anchored me. He'd bound me to Ethiopia. For better or worse, he'd been the home I always wandered back to.

I wrote in my journal. *What will become of me?* I closed my eyes and rested my head against the rough bark. I was losing sleep, either because my thoughts spun to the future at night, or because I lay and listened to Mark breathing restlessly beside me. There was no answer to my question, except to say, *Yes* to the shocking unknown. Except to trust.

For our reunion, we rented a big house in Sun River, Oregon over Labor Day weekend. Jesse and Kenny both had babies, so we gave them the ground floor rooms with ensuite bathrooms. But climbing to the second floor made Mark's pain worse. I felt bad I hadn't thought about him better. He had become far more fragile than the babies or their parents.

On Sunday afternoon, our kids packed up a picnic and went to the pool. I fixed sandwiches for Mark and me and put chips from someone else's food box on our plates for a treat. It was too late to care about healthy food for Mark, and I was losing weight. We ate in the quiet, a relief from the chaos of thirty-somethings and their children.

Mark put his hand on mine, looked at me straight on, and said, "You know. I'm dying."

Well, obviously. He was on hospice. But it was amazingly easy to take the idea of hospice and put it in one compartment, take the concept of his actually dying and tuck it away somewhere else.

I pulled my hand out from under his. I laid it gently on top. "I know."

"I didn't get the blood transfusion for the kids," he said. "I got it because I want to make love one more time."

Mark often fell into paranoia at the end. It may have been the morphine, which only kept his pain to a dull, but enervating, level three out of ten. Or the doctor said the cancer may have metastasized to his brain, but because Mark was on hospice, there were no more tests. It didn't really matter where the strange thoughts were coming from.

Thieves have taken the ribbons!

What should I tell the police about the murder?

I haven't been a good man. God won't want me.

At first I tried to talk him down from his panics. I learned instead to first crush the tiny Lorazepam pill, dissolve the powder in a few milliliters of water in a syringe, and flood it under his tongue. Then, waiting for it to put him to sleep, I talked. I used my most tender, my most reassuring voice.

"Your brain is shorting out," I said to my husband, who could fix anything, but loved electricity best. "Your brain is going *'bzzt, bzzt.'* This pill will turn the breaker off. When you wake up, it will be reset."

"You've been such a support," he said. "What would we have done without you?"

🐦

I laughed at the way he said it. But what would he have done without me? I was the only woman he'd ever dared love. He'd let me into his heart. Our children had followed. How could either of us regret how many times we'd had to remake our mistakes?

As he drifted off into a druggy haze, I felt the completeness of my forgiveness. Mark had done his best. I knew that in the deepest, truest place. As hard as he'd been for me to live with, he'd been even harder company for himself. Had he forgiven himself? It was too late to ask.

But that happened thirteen years after we left Kenya. We had no way in Nairobi to know how the story of our partnership was going to end.

After the Wunlit Peace Conference, I never went back into South Sudan. Flights did start going in and out of Ler again; I'm sure the woman and her daughter with the fluffy dress got on a plane sooner or later—her husband was a commander. But I was too ashamed to ask James when he came to Nairobi later that spring.

I did give him my campstool, though. On his way back to Loki with it, his Land Cruiser overturned. James and the driver got rides into the nearest town for help. When they got back, the SUV had been looted and the campstool was gone. James was remarkably free of regret when he told me about it. That's a gift thirty years of war have given the Sudanese people. They hope for the best, but they are not overly surprised or discouraged when the best is not forthcoming. They and their nation wander on in their own wilderness, trying again and again to find that promised peace.

Bill Lowrey organized two more peace conferences in other South Sudan hot spots. I stayed home, teaching at the boys' school, and Mark traveled with Bill to run the sound systems. At the third, around midnight campfires, another Sudanese with a doctorate raised a third liberation army. The first two warlord doctors blamed Bill. Friends warned him it wasn't safe for him to return. It was over, until after the war ended, between Bill and the Nuers.

The three doctors never came together. Nuer clans to the east fought each other again. But the peace between Nuers and Dinkas on the West Bank of the White Nile did hold until fighting between North and South Sudan ended, and South Sudan became what they called the world's newest baby nation.

Mark and I spent that last year in Nairobi, and then it was over between us and the Nuers.

But I still remember words I learned of their language. I can see the wide sunset sky. I smell the dust and the mud. I taste the sorghum. South Sudan is imprinted in my heart. I belonged there, once. I belonged, and I didn't belong, a paradox that was true then, and will always be true for me in Africa. It was in South Sudan that I found myself on a path for making peace with it.

When there is no good answer, there will still be grace. *Today is tomorrow, we are home.*

And somewhere in East Africa, someone is sitting on my campstool.

ACKNOWLEDGEMENTS

The project of writing a book—even a second book—is daunting, and it can't be undertaken without a team of support. I want to first acknowledge the four women who have done the most to be that team for me: my author sister Jane Kurtz, who has also been my lifetime playmate and cheerleader; and the other three women in the Fat Friday critique group: Barbara Davis Kroon, Lily Gardner Butts and Susan G. Whitcher.

Editor Jessica Powers and publicist Ashawnta Jackson, both of Catalyst Press—thank you for working hard to bring intangible creations into a form that can be shared with the world.

A special thank you to Machot A. Malou, my official fact checker. He was a delegate from Yirol to the Wunlit Peace Conference on the West Bank of the White Nile in 1999. He is now researching and recording oral histories about the years of peace that ensued. He thanked me for writing the story, and now I thank him for confirming the historic details of it. Unfortunately, we did not meet each other at the conference; God willing, someday we will again be in the same place at the same time!

Bill Lowrey has played many roles in my life: friend and advisor during those tough years working in South Sudan; mentor as I searched for direction after Mark died; early reader of my manuscript and generous giver of both encouragement and correction. Now Bill has connected me with South Sudanese and others to read and blurb my version of historic moments we shared.

Finally, I would thank my husband, my dog and my cats for keeping me company as I wrote. However, I don't have any. So to escape the quiet of revising and editing at home during these Covid years, I often walked to Café Eleven on Grand Avenue and Rosa Parks Boulevard in Portland, Oregon. I want to thank owner Ankur and his team of baristas for giving me a table, chai lattes, company, and sometimes Ethiopian jazz to write by.

GLOSSARY

Nuer and Dinka

Bor White:	Maboir, the white one
Diit Wide:	Big
Elong:	Very
Gua Good:	Beautiful, clever, wonderful in any way
Hun gora:	I want
Kel:	One
Ku wa:	Go with (as in go in peace, go with God)
Kwoth:	God
Mal:	Peace
Male:	Nuer greeting (pronounced ma-lay)
Nya:	Daughter of (used metaphorically in girl's names, e.g. Daughter of Peace)
Peu:	Water
Pwak:	Bath
Sheebak:	Dinka greeting
Toich:	Green, also used as a noun for pastures

Swahili

Cho:	Latrine, restroom
Hakuna matata:	No problem
Hakuna:	None, nothing
Sana:	Very much
Visuri:	Well (can be a question and the answer)

CPSIA information can be obtained
at www.ICGtesting.com
Printed in the USA
JSHW020837260322
24214JS00005B/6